Daily Reflections

for **Educators, Coaches, Leaders,** and **Life**

T0356430

Other Redleaf Press books by Constant Hine:

Transformational Coaching for Early Childhood Educators

Daily Reflections

for **Educators, Coaches, Leaders,** and **Life**

CONSTANT HINE

Redleaf Press

www.redleafpresss.org
800-423-8309

Published by Redleaf Press

10 Yorkton Court

St. Paul, MN 55117

www.redleafpress.org

First edition 2024

Cover design by Renee Hammes

Cover photograph by stock.adobe.com

Interior design by Renee Hammes

Typeset in Marion, Blithe, Mr Eaves Mod OT

Interior illustrations by stock.adobe.com

Printed in the United States of America

31 30 29 28 27 26 25 24   1 2 3 4 5 6 7 8

Library of Congress Cataloging-in-Publication Data

Names: Hine, Constant, author.

Title: Daily reflections for educators, coaches, leaders, and life / by Constant Hine.

Description: First edition. | St. Paul, MN : Redleaf Press, 2024. |

   Summary: "Developing a reflective mindset helps us become self-empowered, lifelong problem solvers who create meaningful and fulfilling lives both personally and professionally. Coaches, leaders, and all agents of change in early childhood education need to hone their own reflective practices not only to gain self-awareness and make mindful decisions but also to facilitate reflection with the people they support"-- Provided by publisher.

Identifiers: LCCN 2023056906 (print) | LCCN 2023056907 (ebook) | ISBN 9781605547817 (paperback) | ISBN 9781605547824 (ebook)

Subjects: LCSH: Early childhood teachers--Psychology. | Early childhood teachers--Professional relation ships. | Early childhood education--Psychological aspects. | Reflective teaching.

Classification: LCC LB1775.6 .H549 2024 (print) | LCC LB1775.6 (ebook) | DDC 372.2101/9--dc23/ eng/20240109

LC record available at https://lccn.loc.gov/2023056906

LC ebook record available at https://lccn.loc.gov/2023056907

Printed on acid-free paper

To each of those who have gone before me and whose shoulders I have stood on. For each of you who are willing to reflect and travel within and to then offer your shoulder for others to stand on in their journey of transformation.

Contents

Acknowledgments...x

Introduction xii

How to Use This Book xv

Power and Purpose of Reflection xv

Reflection as a Lifestyle xvi

Key Elements of Reflection...xvii

Methods of Reflecting xvii

CHAPTER 1   **Awareness and Mindfulness**..1

    REFLECTION..1

    FOCUS ATTENTION 17

    AWARENESS AND MINDFULNESS....................................20

    SELF-RESPONSIBILITY AND CHOICE 26

CHAPTER 2   **Attitude and Perspective: Know Thyself** 35

    ATTITUDES...35

    THE NEGATIVE VOICE INSIDE 43

    PERSPECTIVE..49

    FAILURE AND MISTAKES...53

    OPTIMISM 62

CHAPTER 3   **Change and Transformation** 67

    STICKY, SUSTAINABLE CHANGE 67

    LEARNING TO CHANGE 76

    BUSYNESS AND DISTRACTION.......................................84

    HABITS AND SMALL STEPS 91

    CHANGE IS CHOICE...98

CHAPTER 4   **Purpose and Motivation** 101

    FINDING AND FOLLOWING YOUR PURPOSE 101

    MOTIVATING SELF...109

    MOTIVATING OTHERS 114

    EXCUSES AND NOT GIVING UP 120

    FOCUSING ON WHAT YOU WANT 128

CHAPTER 5   **Hopes and Dreams into Goals** **133**

         HOPES AND DREAMS 133

         WHO DO YOU WANT TO BE? 138

         ACHIEVING GOALS 143

         OVERCOMING CHALLENGES TO SUCCESS 152

CHAPTER 6   **Mobilize: Plan and Take Action** **165**

         MAKING DECISIONS 165

         TAKING ACTION AND MAKING CHANGES 170

         FOCUS CHOICES AND TIME 178

         OVERCOMING OBSTACLES AND
         IMPROVING CONTINUOUSLY 185

         REFLECTING ON ACTION 192

CHAPTER 7   **Experiment and Practice** **199**

         GETTING BETTER AT GETTING BETTER 199

         LEARNING FROM EXPERIENCE 207

         HARNESSING YOUR HABITS 213

         TRYING WITH OPTIMISM 220

         SUCCESS AND FAILURE 224

CHAPTER 8   **Resiliency and Stress** **231**

         MANAGING STRESS 231

         BUILDING RESILIENCE 235

         WELL-BEING: MIND, BODY, HEART, SPIRIT 241

         MEDITATION AND REFLECTION 248

         INNER STRENGTH 254

CHAPTER 9   **Emotions, Feelings, and Self-Regulation** **263**

         UNDERSTANDING OUR EMOTIONS
         AND FEELINGS 263

         EMOTIONAL INTELLIGENCE 271

         FACING OUR FEARS 275

         SELF-REGULATION AND SELF-CONTROL 282

         INTERNAL BELIEFS 290

CHAPTER 10   **Efficacy and Influence** **295**

      AUTHENTICITY AND INSPIRING OTHERS 295

      MINDSETS, POWER, AND CONFLICT.. 301

      BEING SELF-AWARE 310

      SERVANT LEADERSHIP AND HUMILITY 316

      REACHING OUR FULL POTENTIAL.. 319

CHAPTER 11   **Personal and Social Identity**...**327**

      REFLECTING FOR SELF-UNDERSTANDING 327

      RESPECTING DIVERSITY AND
      UNDERSTANDING CULTURE..331

      WORKING THROUGH BIAS... 341

      EQUITY...353

      POWER 357

CHAPTER 12   **Communication and Relationships**..**363**

      THE ART OF LISTENING..363

      QUESTIONING AND INQUIRY...371

      KINDNESS AND HUMILITY 375

      CONFLICT 380

      BUILDING AUTHENTIC CONNECTIONS
      AND RELATIONSHIPS 387

      Summary.. **394**

Acknowledgments

I want to acknowledge The Lady, Kalindi, and the many spiritual leaders and fellows at the Center of the Golden One who have been my teachers and mentors on my journey over the last thirty years, as I am learning how to reflect and transform. You've helped me aim my attention to find my way within to my "inner temple," to experience deep connection, light, and love. Strengthening my inner compass has increased my ability to mindfully make positive choices about my thoughts, feelings, and behaviors. I am inspired by and deeply grateful for your example, guidance, and accompaniment.

I am grateful for my colleagues and friends who stuck by my side while I was in the middle of a messy mud puddle, unraveling my path and discovering how to trust until I could see the light on the other side. Thank you for talking me off the ledge when my mind and inner voice were unkind, harsh, and discouraging. You have been my life rafts to deepen my trust as I gathered the courage to dream boldly and not let fear stop me from taking action, especially in writing this book. Debra Larsen, my amazing coach who offers perspective, encouragement, and sage advice spiritually, professionally, and emotionally, thank you for being my "projector" and rock-solid support. To Julian Martinez and Josie Montilla, so much gratitude for being my priceless daily reflection buddies and dear friends. Michele Campbell and Ronna Evans, thanks for our endless walks and talks, witnessing my journey while I have been writing this book. Ann Marie Martin, your visionary thinking is always such an inspiration and springboard and I just delight in having you as a creative playmate.

And lastly, I want to recognize and thank Melissa York, my editor at Redleaf Press, for your gracious manner, skillful direction, and magical and collaborative editing prowess.

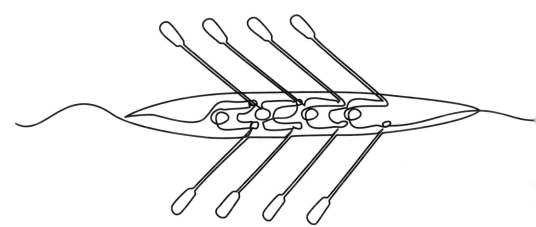

Introduction

Over the last twenty years I have spent working with coaches, leaders, and educators as a coach, consultant, and adult educator, I have discovered the most essential quality that results in people making meaningful and "sticky" sustainable change: reflection. Reflection is not a skill we are taught in our typical educational experiences. People need support to learn how to reflect as a skill and to develop a reflective mindset and approach, so they become self-empowered and lifelong problem solvers who create meaningful and fulfilling lives personally and professionally. Reflection is not an event, not just an activity, but a lifestyle. Reflection engages us in the process of continuous learning, to continue to grow and learn and become more of the person we want to be.

There are many environmental, health, social, and equity issues that impact us all no matter our industry, field, or personal scope of concern. The need to become more mindful and reflective about how we make decisions and move forward has never been more urgent. It is time for each of us individually and collectively to step up and expand our capacity to be

resilient and responsive to address the issues we face. Equally we need to slow down and embody reflective practices and habits to create intentional and caring communities, effective inclusive workplace cultures, and vibrant families that empower and support each person to thrive, become, and contribute their best selves.

Educators, coaches, and leaders (or anyone who is a change agent helping others to grow, learn, and change) need to hone their own reflective practices not only to gain self-awareness and make mindful decisions but also to facilitate reflection with the people they support, so they too make intentional choices to influence and achieve the success they desire. The impact this can have on the people you directly support in business, government, schools, or communities will strengthen us all, not only your people. In the field of education and early childhood, this support can have a profound effect not only on the people you support directly but also on the children and families they in turn serve and support. Coaches, leaders, and change agents need to be an example of someone who has routine reflective practices, changing themselves while demonstrating and inspiring others to do the same. Who you are makes a difference. What you do makes a difference.

I hope this book contributes to your understanding that the power of reflection can catapult you and the people around you into completely different outcomes to live meaningful and valuable lives. May this reflective journey be a walk of becoming your truest self and being compassionate with yourself and with others in the process of transforming to become a more *human* human being.

How to Use This Book

I offer this book as a daily guide to help change agents such as educators, coaches, leaders, and anyone who wants to deepen their reflective practices. This book offers twelve reflective themes for cultivating both personal and professional self-realization and becoming a transformational change agent who helps others do the same. These twelve themes correlate with the seven components of my *GROOMER Framework for Change*™ model for facilitating transformational change, presented in my book *Transformational Coaching for Early Childhood Educators* (Redleaf Press 2019). There are 365 entries, one for each day of the year. Each entry has a quote, a commentary, and a suggestion for reflective practice. One entry every week offers the opportunity to review the previous week or sets you up with a focus for the coming week.

Those who want a reflective practice to focus on each day can follow the entries sequentially. Others may want to choose a particularly appealing theme that addresses their current needs or interests and start there. You may want to read several entries in a set repeatedly each day for a week, to deepen a particular inquiry or nurture a specific awakening or habit. Groups may use this book as a guide for a collective experience to discuss and foster reflective practice in a workplace, or with a professional team or a Professional Learning Community (PLC).

Readers may use this book to individually deepen their own effectiveness; to offer insights in leadership, coaching, or educational training programs; or to use with teams to explore how to collectively achieve team or company goals, increase staff morale, empower employees, facilitate changes in the workplace culture, or ensure that equity practices and behaviors are implemented in the workplace by facilitating and fostering reflection at all levels of an organization.

The purpose of this reflective guide is to encourage you and to embed reflective practice into your daily life. Trust yourself as you choose how to use this guide. Take whatever reflective next step you can, however small—just don't give up. Keep going and keep practicing. Thank you for what you personally do to raise your own consciousness, in whatever ways you do so, and for then turning around to support others to do the same. My hope is that this book will help you embed into your days the regular habits of reflection that you may find meaningful and transformational in your life and work. I hope it also offers you a home base to return to as often as needed to continue to deepen your reflection on any of the themes or to hone your specific reflection practices over the years as you evolve and your circumstances change.

Power and Purpose of Reflection

Reflection is thinking seriously. It is a tool for focusing on something that puts it at the center of our attention. Reflection expands our awareness, knowledge, or perception of a situation or a fact. Awareness creates mindfulness, which is a quality or a state of being conscious or aware of something. When we're reflecting, we recognize what it is that we need to focus on and then take time to explore, contemplate, and inquire. Witnessing and being aware of how you think and behave, through different lenses, is the core of reflective practice. The purpose of reflection is to know yourself, become self-aware, become more mindful, increase in thoughtfulness, and make intentional positive choices.

It is much easier said than done to witness and have acceptance for your feelings, your thoughts, and your sensations, but if you can respectfully acknowledge them and see them, even if they're disturbing, it will help show where to focus your awareness. This opens doorways for choice to create the life you want, to achieve the outcomes you desire.

There is a big difference between knowing what to do and doing it consistently. Many people understand what they should do and don't do it. Or on the flip side, they know what they shouldn't do, but they do it anyway. Having knowledge does not change behavior. It takes intentional reflection to see how your values and beliefs create your thoughts and feelings. Examining how your foundational values, beliefs, thoughts, and feelings underpin your behaviors, actions, and habits is necessary to make changes to accomplish what you want. To get "sticky" sustainable change requires reflection on what a person wants, what's currently happening, what's in the way, and what possible actions will lead to achieving their goals. In addition, it takes practice, experimentation, learning from mistakes, and tolerating the discomfort of change. It takes reflective focus on this whole process to become aware and make mindful choices for how to act—to achieve goals, change habits, improve personal or professional practices—to live the life you want. Educators, coaches, leaders, and change agents help facilitate this reflective process for others by giving them a chance to examine what they are doing in light of their intentions.

Reflection as a Lifestyle

I have learned that expanding my awareness is a continual process, a lifestyle. It's why we call them reflective practices, not reflective perfects! Accepting that I'm not perfect is an important part of growth and change. I just have to keep becoming more aware to help me act mindfully and with intention to keep making choices that go toward what I want. I ask myself why I am doing what I'm doing. What's motivating me? It's an opportunity to dive deeply within and inquire who or what is steering the ship of my life. Am I going in the direction I want? How can I better steer my ship?

Reflection opens a window to a motivating sense of purpose and personal passion. Reflection can shift our attention away from the expectations of the external material world so we discover a deeper source of inner guidance that is more focused and connected with our purpose and passion, necessary for making mindful, life-empowering choices. Reflective practices can connect you to that place within yourself, so you find your "inner yes" and resist letting the pressures of the outside world steer your ship. It takes reflection to find your true inner rudder. I invite you to join me in this journey.

Key Elements of Reflection

Reflecting is not just a mental cognitive process. Going within to seek a guiding light, a reliable inner voice, or a sense of alignment is an act of reflection. A lot of reflection is an inward journey beyond the mind. It might be touching in with your heart, your inner sacral center, or an inner compass. For some, this True North experience might be a sense of a higher power, or God—whatever you call it, there's a place within that can be a guiding rudder for you. And sometimes reflecting feels more like awakening than actual intellectual or critical thinking.

You need to slow down to pause, to create space, to help you focus. A key to reflection is to wonder, inquire, and question. It's not so much about having a right answer or even a right question, but discerning which questions are relevant for you, given where you are and what you are focusing on. When you choose what to focus on, it can be helpful to start your reflective journey with a question . . . and follow it where it takes you, not necessarily trying to answer it. Do you find more questions? Different perspectives? Often we need to mull over the question before we even attempt to narrow in for an answer or try to "fix" or change something. We have to embrace brainstorming possibilities to expand our reflective muscle, staying open to possibilities before we commit to making intentional choices.

An aspect of reflection includes discernment, evaluation, and analysis. These new understandings and expanded awareness help us draw conclusions that inform and guide future actions and behaviors. Reflection fosters continuous quality improvement—a dedication to getting better at getting better—that is both personal and professional. Reflection is key to being a lifelong learner, gaining self-awareness, and becoming an impactful educator, transformational coach, or servant leader.

Methods of Reflecting

There is no one right way to reflect. Reflections can be formal and informal. They can be indoors or outdoors. You can reflect by yourself or with someone else. There are many reflective methods, styles, and strategies. We ideally want to use a variety of approaches to best match our needs, desires, and current circumstances. I like to say there are many flavors of reflecting, and I offer a menu of options you can choose from. I will suggest a variety of these reflective flavors throughout this book to nurture and expand your reflective experiences and stretch your comfort zone, in the hope that you will discover some that resonate with you and become part of a daily reflective routine.

The following is a list of possible reflective approaches or methods. Specific strategies will be offered as a "Reflection Practice" each day of this book. Explore these reflective approaches on your own and have fun!

QUESTIONING

Questioning is a primary key in opening the doorway to reflection, especially as you learn how to ask what I call "juicy" questions. Questions can help you clarify and aim your focus on what needs your attention or what you want. Questions can deepen your exploration of any issue or circumstance. Questions can expand your perspective and perceptions. Asking questions from different perspectives can reveal new insights. Letting one question lead you to another question is like climbing a ladder to gain a better view of the situation at hand.

I have made a list of "Forever Questions" that help me dive deeper regardless of the topic. Just one question from the list might get me started. You might want to start your own list of Forever Questions. The discovery comes from exploring and finding out what the questions are. It is the process of asking yourself questions that results in opening your thinking.

A FEW FOREVER QUESTIONS

- What's working and what's not working?
- What would be helpful to do more of/less of?
- What is it I know and don't know?
- What am I assuming?
- What do I have choice or control about given this topic?
- What am I missing?
- What can I let go of, accept, or forgive?
- What am I holding on to?
- What do I want?
- Why is this a problem or trigger for me?

- **What is my obstacle or barrier?**

- **Am I operating from fear or trust?**

- **What am I afraid of?**

- **How can I not let the fear stop me?**

- **What is holding me back?**

- **What is another perspective or way of looking at this?**

- **How might the other person be viewing this; what's their vantage point?**

- **Am I trying to do this alone?**

- **Who could I ask for help or delegate to?**

- **Am I willing to take a risk? Maybe fail in order to learn? Why or why not?**

- **What's the best or worst thing that could happen?**

- **What is the pattern?**

- **What are some options and possibilities?**

- **If I wasn't worried about being judged or making a mistake, what would I do?**

MEDITATION/PRAYER

Pause, slow down, and go within to strengthen your sense of inner connection and access the place beyond the mind. For some it comes in the form of connecting with a "higher power"—God, the divine, love, truth, peace, or whatever term works for you. For some it will be turning toward that which is greater than yourself. Being in nature does this for some.

There are many styles of meditation, prayer, and mindfulness practices, each with unique ways of helping you turn within. Explore and try a variety of approaches to find ones that align with your style and what you want.

I have been practicing the active Gourasana Meditation Practice (GMP)* for thirty years. It resonates with me because it incorporates moving the body to help me go within, so I don't have to sit still. If you have difficulty sitting still, this is an approach you could try. A wide variety of music is played, and the practice encourages you to open and release any emotions, energy, or intensity that are in the way of either being able to find calm and/or expressing authentic connection, joy, and love. You can explore moving your body, making sounds, crying, praying, or just being still. There is no right way to find your way within.

Enjoying Calm and Quiet

Slow down and ponder . . . mull things over. There is no right way, but slowing down will help. Explore stillness. This might mean sitting quietly with a cup of tea, staring out the window watching squirrels, being alone or with others. It can be indoors or in nature.

Try taking time to quiet the chatter of your mind or set the mind aside and focus on your heart. It can be taking a moment between meetings to calm and quiet yourself, or starting the day by centering yourself, preparing for and wondering about the coming day, or reviewing and debriefing at the end of the day.

Writing

Writing bears witness to your thoughts and feelings, and it can give you perspective. It can be a discovery process beyond just reporting. Write or journal on paper, on a computer, or even on your phone. Your ideas might come in paragraphs or bullet points or snatches of words or phrases. Your writing could be making a list of what you want to remember so tasks or ideas don't keep you up at night. You can be creative, using colored markers or drawing or doodling with your writing. Consider writing as recording, sharing, revealing, and documenting your journey or making your transformation visible with words as your reflection method.

READING

You may find meaning as you read wise words, daily quotes, poems, or inspirational or devotional writings. You might peruse books that foster reflection or learning on a specific topic. Read for guidance, finding the inspiration to keep going, to take a risk, to remember who you are and what you want, or to stay focused and take aim. This book is an example of reading daily reflections.

REFLECTING ON WORDS OR QUOTES

Quotes may help you focus and stay mindful of a direction you want to cultivate. I used the quote "Awareness is born of heart, not of mind" from my spiritual teacher, The Lady, for a year to aim my attention while I wrote this book. I posted it on the wall in my office and had it on my bedside. I offer a quote for each daily entry in this book. You might want to take the quotes that inspire you the most and copy and post them somewhere to help you focus. You can also find inspirational desk calendars on a topic of interest that offer a daily quote.

Post handmade signs or even just sticky notes to remind you of a focus or a positive behavior you want to practice or a thought pattern or habit you want to break. It might be as simple as putting up a sign with a single word or quality you want to aim for. You can purchase formal sign books that stand on a table for you to flip to an inspirational or helpful page.

DRAWING OR USING IMAGES

Use images, photos, or art as inspiration for your reflections. Explore drawing, doodling, painting, or graphic designs to uncover or represent your thoughts, ideas, and reflections. Use visual images or drawings to help you stay focused on the purpose of your reflection. The visual tool of mind mapping can unravel ideas or explore connections about any topic. A mind map is a diagram for representing tasks, words, concepts, or items linked to and arranged around a central concept or subject, using a nonlinear graphical layout that allows the creator to build an intuitive framework around a central concept.

TALKING

Like writing, talking bears witness to your inner values, thoughts, assumptions, and feelings. It gives you access to yourself, and you observe yourself to gain self-awareness. For some, talking is the preferred way of reflecting. It's the foundational method used in coaching, counseling, team meetings, and strategic planning sessions. Talking can help you unravel confusing experiences or jumbled feelings. It is not uncommon to talk to a friend or partner to gain clarity. Talking offers a perspective to hear what is going on inside yourself. Talking with someone is different than thinking by yourself.

Having collaborative sessions with another person or group of people to create, design, and brainstorm is a very effective reflection strategy. A debrief session to discuss how an interaction, meeting, or coaching session went offers reflective perspective and can inform future actions.

Discussion and conversations are important for collaborating, cultivating workplace cultural awareness, and exploring diverse voices to raise awareness and expand perspectives.

Moving Your Body

Many people find that to reflect, focus, and think they need to move their bodies. Walking (fast or slow), running, playing basketball, dancing, doing yoga, or cleaning house are common examples. Having fidget toys in meetings or during classes helps some people stay focused, attentive, and thoughtfully engaged.

Sometimes using body sensations or movement is more helpful in fostering self-regulation and gaining insight than approaching something cognitively with the mind. Clearing your head and releasing tension and emotions physically can help you gain perspective and become calm enough to think and deeply reflect. Many spiritual traditions use dance as an avenue for going within, praying, and finding connection.

THINKING

Thinking cognitively comes in many modes: brainstorming, reviewing, debriefing, analyzing, evaluating, pondering, and even daydreaming. For some this might be planned, linear, and sequential, while for others it can be spontaneous, organic, and nonlinear. Your focus can be on close-up details or with an overview "from the balcony" perspective. It can also be creative, visionary, out of the box, or associative thinking. It might be using inductive or deductive reasoning and logic. Strategic planning, action planning, and goal setting are ways to think reflectively, such as using a **SWOT** method—examining **S**trengths, **W**eaknesses, **O**pportunities, and **T**hreats—for reflective analysis and forward planning. Keep an open mind and experiment with a variety of ways to think.

Avoid getting stuck in a rut of reflecting in only one way. But no matter how you do it, reflection takes time, and you must make the time for it. I hope this book will support you to embrace reflection as a daily practice and embed it in your personal and professional life. May your reflective journey open new worlds of insights for growing and learning, support you in making desired changes personally, and deepen your professional practices as an educator, coach, or leader to more effectively cultivate reflection in those you serve.

*For more information see Gourasana Meditation Practice: https://centerofthegoldenone.com/meditation-us.

Chapter 1

AWARENESS AND MINDFULNESS

This chapter or month aims to build an understanding of the importance of reflection, as well as a knowledge of what routine reflective practices contribute to fostering awareness and empowering thoughtful conscious choices. Expanding awareness is the keystone for fruitful learning, growing, and changing. Information alone does not change behaviors. Becoming self-aware and helping others become aware is the underlying support needed to nurture mindfulness to make positive proactive intentional decisions.

Reflection

Reflection is our basic tool to expand awareness and cultivate mindfulness. Reflection requires purposeful effort, focused consideration, and intentional time. When you embed reflective practices into your regular routines, using a variety of reflective strategies creates a richness in your life.

"Who looks outside, dreams; who looks inside, awakes."

—Carl Jung

Going within, you will find a vast and rich territory full of information, discoveries, and treasures. Whether you encounter the bright spots of joy, love, certainty, and trust or the dark corners that harbor fear, doubt, insecurity, pain, conflict, or judgment, this inner world is the only place for you to ultimately find peace, wisdom, freedom, and guidance. It will take courage and fortitude to explore because at times it's scary to see and face our whole imperfect selves with honesty and to witness and own the remarkable strength and power within us. This inner journey is the foundation of self-growth, as we find purpose and make mindful decisions that empower ourselves and others and help us be of service in the world. This is the domain of inner guidance: finding your life compass and connection to Source (however you may define or experience that). Reflection is a form of self-listening; reflection is a way to listen to others; reflection is a way to help others to listen to themselves. Make a commitment to take this journey and help others to do the same. Take a **VOW** to find your **V**oice **O**f **W**isdom.

REFLECTIVE PRACTICE
Write about why taking the journey of reflection to go within is important to you. Think about some benefits you hope to attain. Are you willing to do what it takes to deepen your reflective practices and habits, even if this means making changes?

2

"We do not learn from experience. ... We learn from reflecting on experience."

—Often attributed to John Dewey

Putting value on experiences is important. But learning from those experiences will occur only if we take the time to reflect on what has happened. What did we learn? How did we learn it? If the experience was challenging or we made a mistake or a misstep, then reflecting on what we learned helps turn our mistakes into learning experiences. Otherwise, we're likely to repeat the same mistake. Looking back is important even if you are part of a celebration or another wonderful experience: taking time to reflect on the experience is a way of respecting its importance. It's all too easy to get complacent or dismiss a positive experience. And in that way, we don't let it soak in deeply, letting it influence our heart, mind, and soul. Reflection adds meaning and value to your life and the experiences you have. Reflection can be a quick jotting down of notes, a journaling of your reflections, or even debriefing by telling stories and sharing experiences with other people, friends, and family.

REFLECTIVE PRACTICE
Recall a recent experience you had. Take a moment to think and reflect about it. Why was it important? What did you gain from it? What did you learn? How did it affect the direction you're moving in your life now, and why? You can reflect by sitting quietly and thinking, writing, or talking with someone about the experience. Then notice the effect that taking the time to reflect had on your experience and consider how it enriched your learning.

3

"You will attract into your life whatever you focus on."

—Jack Canfield

One of the purposes of reflection is that it helps you focus. What you focus on can be anything that's necessary, important, meaningful, or relevant for you. Notice that what you focus on expands in your awareness, like when you buy a new car and you suddenly start seeing that same car everywhere. If you focus on your problems, what you're complaining about, or negative thinking, those will expand your focus on them and fill up your attention. And that of course just makes it worse. So it's important to be mindful and choose what you focus on. Focusing on what you want—and who you want to be—and holding positive perspectives will attract into your life what you want, rather than what you don't want. Reflecting regularly about who you want to be will help you build your life journey, the pathways and actions you need to take to get where you want to go. Shifting your attitude from negative thinking to possibility thinking will start to create new life experiences and opportunities. But it will take changing a thought and probably a habit to end up where you want. You do not have to hold yourself the victim of your circumstances. Many people have lived through extremely difficult life circumstances and found that freedom is more related to their mindset than their circumstances. Holocaust survivors such as Victor Frankl and Edith Eger write that the key to gaining power, creating a life you want, and becoming who you want to be has to do with your mindset and attitude, with the deliberate choice not to live with a victim mentality.

REFLECTIVE PRACTICE
Think of something you have recently been complaining about. Given that situation, what do you actually want to happen? What is within your control? Spend the next several days or even weeks reflecting and focusing on what you want. Focus on where you have control and can make choices. Will you focus on the circumstance or on how you respond to the circumstance? Make your responses as concrete and specific as you can. Write or draw about it or talk with a friend about it.

4

"You are what you think about all day long."

—Common wisdom

These words make me want to be very mindful of what I'm thinking about all day! Using curiosity without judgment is important as we practice reflection to expand our awareness. If my attention is on completing tasks and crossing things off my to-do list all day, then I am a "task doer." Is that really who I want to be? Take some time to focus with wonder on what you are thinking about. No need to try to change it or do anything about it at first. Just notice and witness your thinking. This observation skill must be strengthened before you launch into action plans to change things. Observation and collecting data (in all forms) are in themselves reflection skills to aid in creating intentional goals and action plans that will help you become who you want to be. As you allow yourself the grace to witness yourself with compassion and kindness, you will learn how to extend this sensitivity to others. Learning to witness and observe yourself is a mindfulness practice. What you focus on and think about will have the key you need for the first step on the journey to desired outcomes. Where am I now? What is my starting point?

REFLECTIVE PRACTICE
Use a small notebook and write quick notes or bullet points highlighting what you have been thinking about several times throughout the day. You can set a timer to remind you. Do it at the beginning and end of the day or at each mealtime. Practice this for a week or two and see if there are any patterns.

5

"Thinking without awareness is the main dilemma of human existence."

—Eckhart Tolle

Have you ever caught yourself saying to someone, either aloud or in your head, "What were you thinking?" I think that is the essence of this quote. How often people do something without thinking! Or their actions are so self-absorbed they are unaware of the people around them and the effect they are having. We all do this at one time or another. It's a good reminder of the importance of expanding our awareness. Awareness affords us greater perspective, a wider consideration of our needs and others'. Expanding awareness is like taking blinders off to expose a much wider world. Most people don't intend to hurt, cause pain, or show disrespect. Again, how often have we said or heard, "I didn't mean to hurt you; it wasn't intentional." Yet the impact is still hurtful. Lack of intention is a sign that the person needs awareness and reflection. Expanding our awareness is our responsibility and can have a profound effect on our communication and relationships.

REFLECTIVE PRACTICE
Take time today to contemplate the difference between thinking and reflecting.

6

"People are too quick to pass judgment and too slow to self-reflect."

—Anonymous

Putting value on experiences is important. But learning from those experiences will come only if we take the time to reflect on what has happened. What did we learn? How did we learn it? If the experience was challenging or we made a mistake or a misstep, then reflecting on what we learned helps turn our mistakes into learning experiences. Otherwise, we're likely to repeat the same mistake. Looking back is important even if you have a celebration or a wonderful experience: taking time to reflect on the experience is a way of respecting its importance. It's all too easy to get complacent or dismiss a positive experience. And in that way we don't let it soak in deeply, letting it influence our heart, mind, and soul. Reflection adds meaning and value to your life and the experiences you have. Reflection can be a quick jotting down of notes, a journaling of your reflections, or even debriefing, telling stories and sharing experiences with other people, friends, and family.

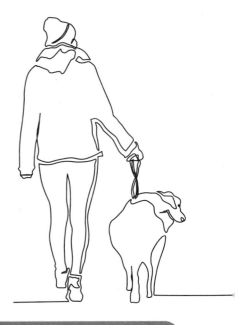

REFLECTIVE PRACTICE

On a walk or on your way to work today ask yourself what benefit you might find in doing some self-reflection about your perspective. Reflect on what you have strong opinions about or think about some judgments you frequently have. Where did these come from? Are you mistaking your perspective for facts and truth?

7

"Time spent in self-reflection is never wasted—it is an intimate date with yourself."

—Dr. Paul T.P. Wong

What quote, message, or reflective practice from this week stuck with you? Why? How was it meaningful? In what ways did that message or reflection from the past week help you better understand yourself? Meditate, journal, take a contemplative walk, or talk with someone about your discoveries.

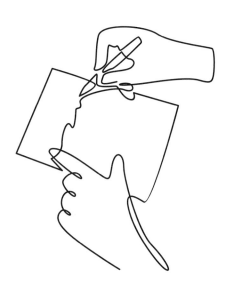

8

"Self-reflection requires that you question your assumptions and your habits and ask whether they are useful in dealing with the world around you."

—Daniel Dobrygowski

Intentional reflection expands our self-understanding and self-awareness, which are foundations for open-minded, respectful, collaborative, and inclusive relations and equitable policies. Personal reflection and shared reflective practices are essential in the programs, schools, and companies where we work, allowing us to make respectful and equitable decisions and create policies that have proactive and positive impacts on the employees and the people they serve. Building a work culture that cultivates reflection and implements mindful policies requires leaders who actively practice and model self-reflection.

REFLECTIVE PRACTICE
What is one reflective practice or habit you can begin or expand upon at work that could positively affect yourself or the individuals you work with by setting a tone that reflection is part of your workplace culture?

9

"If you do what you've always done, you'll get what you've always gotten."

—Common wisdom

Be mindful of the human tendency to rely or fall back on familiar strategies. Under pressure, we default to doing what we have always done, even if we know it doesn't work. Familiar feels safe, and familiarity can falsely lead us to believing the old way is a good idea. We often do this when we are challenged by a particular situation, when our skills are not fully developed, when we feel the need to prove what we know, or when we are trying to reassure ourselves that we are being helpful or making a difference. It is important to nurture your ability to take risks and tolerate feeling unsafe and uncomfortable in order to change habits of mind and behaviors. Studies show that short breaks of even a minute can make a difference. A short break gets you out of habitual thinking and behaviors and provides space for awareness to arise, so you see things more clearly. It's an opportunity to take a balcony view.

REFLECTIVE PRACTICE

Take regular breaks. It could be just putting your hand on your heart and taking a few breaths or standing up to stretch. Perhaps fill your water bottle or look at a cartoon. It could be taking a walk around the parking lot or playing one song that makes you dance and move your body. Set a timer or mindfulness app to go off at the top of each hour, then stop and pause. Pick something and try it!

"Reflection is defined as a future-oriented but retrospective process that involves a review of incidents and experiences, a critical analysis of their causes and effects that leads to new understandings and appreciations, and the drawing of conclusions that guide future action and behavior."

—Attributed to David Boud

Reflection happens in the present moment. It is a focused act of thinking or contemplation. It is often used to bridge "Where am I?" back to "Where have I come from?" or "What is influencing my current state of mind or perspective?" The purpose or benefit of reflecting is to proactively inform the decisions, choices, and behaviors we make for the future. Sometimes when you are reflecting, it doesn't really feel like an active review of the past. It might be more like a discovery or investigation of the present moment and your state of being or mindset. Or perhaps it might be focused on the future, considering what's needed in a specific situation or clarifying what we want. Yet we are always informed by where we have been, including our previous personal and cultural experiences that shape our values, beliefs, assumptions, and expectations.

REFLECTIVE PRACTICE
When intentionally reflecting on a specific focus or topic, ask yourself, "Is my focus on the past, present, or future?" Contemplate how they might be connected.

11

"Self-reflection entails asking yourself questions about your values, assessing your strengths and failures, thinking about your perceptions and interactions with others, and imagining where you want to take your life in the future."

—Attributed to Robert L. Rosen

Our past journey influences our current position. At some level, there is always a subconscious past lingering in the present. The knowledge and understandings we have gained over time and our personal and social identity (influenced by our family, culture and customs, sexual and gender identity, and ethnicity, as well as our socioeconomic, education, religious/spiritual, and trauma experiences) influence not only our view of the world but our assumptions and expectations. Our personal lens—an unspoken point of view or frame of reference—influences our current thinking, beliefs, feelings, and actions. As we expand our self-awareness, we become more mindful of our frame of reference and the impact this can have on our biases, or the way we mistake our perspective for facts. Humans by nature are meaning-making machines. Our frame of reference is our built-in lens for assigning and making meaning. A major aspect of becoming self-aware is being conscious of the influential elements of the frame of reference that construct our personal and social identity, our past and current experiences, and how we view the world. It's important to own where our perceptions and meaning making comes from and to examine what conditioning or assumptions may need some modification or revision to consciously affect how we move forward and think about the future. Through mindful awareness, we can make intentional choices about what we want to carry forward. Reflection is a significant doorway, an opportunity to transform our future and our destiny.

REFLECTIVE PRACTICE
Complete a ***Frame of Reference*** reflective practice. Write down anything that is part of your own frame of reference—what influences how you view the world. Write down your values and beliefs; any significant life experiences; your education and learning experiences; your gender expression, sexuality, and sexual expression; and any socioeconomic impacts. Consider social identity influences that affected your experiences of privilege and oppression, such as race, nationalism, ableism, and so on. This Frame of Reference becomes a core self-reflective tool. Consider it a living document that you add to over time as you have additional insights. Consider reviewing and adding to it annually, perhaps on your birthday. Write this in a place where you will be able to find it in the future.

https://www.redleafpress.org/dre/1-11.pdf

12

"Your soul needs time for solitude and self-reflection. In order to love, lead, heal, and create, you must nourish yourself first."

—Attributed to Louise Hay

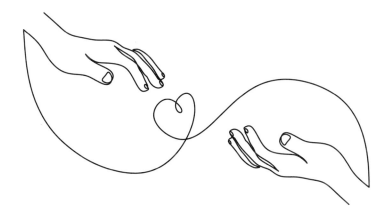

Reflection is a pathway to "knowing thyself," for learning about yourself—your strengths, your shortcomings, your habits of responding in stressful situations, crisis, or conflicts, and how you do or don't inspire or empower others. It can generate more proactive decisions and actions, defuse triggered and impulsive reactions, and offer a mindful pause in which you can choose more empowering and respectful responses in any given moment. Intentional reflective practices are essential to gaining self-awareness, which is foundational if you are to respectfully interact with people who have different viewpoints, experiences, or cultures than you.

REFLECTIVE PRACTICE
Do you feel nourished so that you can give nourishment to others in turn? In what ways do you create time for self-reflection and solitude? Is it enough?

"The elevation of your own consciousness helps the overall consciousness of the planet."

—Gourasana*

Awakening your own consciousness certainly has an impact on your own life. Philosophers, spiritual advisers, and world leaders agree and are supported by current science proving that the power of self-awareness makes a profound difference in many ways. Reflection is the key to unlocking awareness. Ultimately, reflective practices that expand awareness lead to mindful choices and more positive thoughts, emotions, and behaviors. As you make an effort to become aware and raise your own consciousness, don't underestimate how it touches the people around you and the people around them. Like dropping a pebble in the water causes a ripple effect, your consciousness influences the people and the world around you in boundless ways you might never know about or even understand. Every small step toward increasing your awareness and becoming more mindful makes a difference. Who you are and how you behave makes a difference.

REFLECTIVE PRACTICE
Choose an area of your life you know you need to think more about. It could be an area where you are experiencing challenges or feel stuck, a goal you want to achieve, or perhaps a habit you want to change or a desired attitude or quality. What is one reflective practice you can begin doing today to expand your awareness? Perhaps it's sitting quietly or meditating each morning to contemplate this area, or maybe it's writing regularly about it or discussing it with someone you trust. Perhaps all three. Choose the topic and start whatever type of reflection you want today.

* Gourasana, Founder of Center of The Golden One®, *Breaking the Cycle of Birth and Death*, #142, www.CenteroftheGoldenOne.com.

14

"Experience is not the best teacher. It sounds like heresy, but when you think about it, it's reflection on experience that makes it educational."

—Dr. George E. Forman

In this past week, what experiences affected you the most? Take some time to reflect about each experience and why it was meaningful. What or how can you learn from that experience?

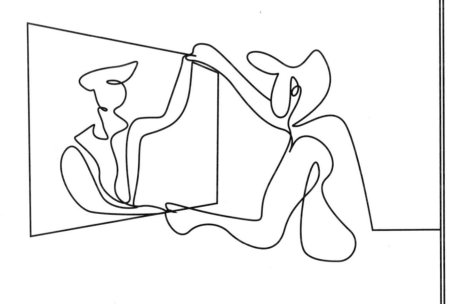

"My content is not as important as the audience's interaction with the content."

—Robert Garmston

As educators, coaches, and leaders, we often make the mistake of believing that information is what people need in order to learn and change. But information rarely changes behaviors. Information might be a starting place, if you are sharing some content, facts, or theories that could be relevant to people or help in a given situation. But determining which content or information is actually relevant and meaningful to the learner is an essential beginning. Too often we provide information we think is important or would help a person or a team. We often get attached to our content and perspective and can figuratively pummel people with information, thinking it will make a difference. But often it doesn't, because the information doesn't foster "sticky" change that lasts. What does make a difference is recognizing that learning really occurs only when you provide opportunities for learners to engage with the content. This might include time and opportunity for them to reflect about its relevance to their life or their situations. It could involve using discussions or meaningful activities or projects for individuals to explore, practice, and wonder about whatever content you are providing. Their engagement with the content matters more than the simple presentation of content. Reflection is the first tool people need to learn deeply.

REFLECTIVE PRACTICE

If you do formal teaching or training of individuals, consider providing less content and building in more reflection, asking provocative questions and allowing time for authentic and meaningful discussion with pairs and small groups. If you provide resources or information to people, consider how the resource itself may not be the help people need. Maybe you need to have a conversation about the relevance of the information and how the people you are serving might want to explore or use the information, or discuss the barriers they might face in trying to use or implement the information. Being a partner to help them to think things through may be more valuable than providing the information, whether presenting formally or informally.

Focus Attention

Focusing your attention and clarifying your contemplations will guide your reflection and hone your reflective habits, steering your decisions and actions.

"The journey of a thousand miles begins with a single step."

—Tao Te Ching

In the book *One Small Step Can Change Your Life: The Kaizen Way*, Robert Maurer shows how to apply the ancient Japanese philosophy of kaizen to modern living by using small steps to accomplish big goals. He says kaizen has two definitions: (1) using very small steps to improve a habit, process, or product and (2) using very small moments to inspire new products and inventions. Focusing your attention and reflection on small steps and small moments is a powerful way to nurture growth, drive change, and develop new habits. Starting reflective habits can feel overwhelming, but the kaizen way can provide a gentle, compassionate, and very effective approach.

REFLECTIVE PRACTICE
Choose a small step to embed as a daily reflective habit. For example, to begin meditating, start with just five minutes a day. To begin a journaling or reflective writing practice, use a small notebook or pad (3 x 5 or 4 x 6) and write only one page daily. Try starting the day by directing your attention to who you want to be each day. Or perhaps at the end of the day write a simple review of what worked and what didn't. Another small step is to write one thing you are grateful for daily.

17

"Where we put our attention our behavior goes."

—Raymond Reyes

What behaviors do you want to nurture in yourself? Ask yourself a prompting question about whatever needs your attention. Your brain is awakened and delighted by questions. If you repeat the question with constant focus over the course of several days or weeks—or for however long it takes—the hippocampus (the part of the brain that stores information) will have no choice but to address it. Make your questions small and focus on small steps you can take—use the kaizen way. Your brain will start to partner with you and begin to give you answers, in its own way and on its own timetable. Stay focused, stay tuned in, and listen. Let the questions lead your focus and then follow with gentleness, patience, and openness.

REFLECTIVE PRACTICE
Given your unique situation, what's your question? Ask it every day for at least a week and continue if you find it helpful.
- If you want to cultivate a more positive outlook or are facing negative thinking, ask yourself, "What is one thing I like about myself today?" Or "What is one small thing that is special about me (about my spouse, my colleague, my organization)?"
- If you want to achieve a goal, ask yourself, "What is one small step I could take toward my goal?"
- If you are worried about failing or doing something wrong, ask yourself, "If I were guaranteed not to fail, what would I do differently?"

"We learn best with focused attention. As we focus on what we're learning, the brain maps that information on what we already know, making new neural connections."

—Daniel Goleman

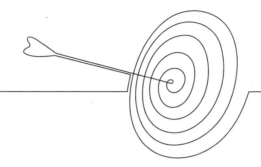

The human brain cannot entertain a positive and negative thought at the same time. It really is so important to choose what to focus on, so you can focus on what you want and aim for it with a positive outlook. Help yourself by choosing the positive thoughts that will inspire you forward. Do not focus on discouraging thoughts or negative self-talk. Make it a daily habit to aim your focus, and you can tailor your attention as needed to address whatever is currently important to you.

REFLECTIVE PRACTICE

As you are getting ready for work or your day, identify one thing you know needs your attention today. As you continue getting dressed, eating, and perhaps traveling to work, reflect on who you want to be today, given this focus of attention. Think about it from the perspective of what you want, embracing a positive, optimistic view of possibility. You do not need to figure out how today. Just focus simply on who you want to be. Try holding this perspective of who you want to be, given your chosen focus, for five minutes each morning this week.

19

"Mindful meditation should always be used in the service of enhancing, not displacing, people's rational and analytical thought processes about their careers and personal lives."

— David Brendel

Mindful meditation is a unique kind of meditation that helps people hone their ability to focus their attention on the present moment. It helps us learn how to step aside from distractions and increase our attention on bodily sensations in the moment to stay focused. Mindful meditations help expand self-awareness, so we remain calm and equipoised in moments of distress. It can be a powerful tool, and it is often an excellent entry to meditation for folks who feel they are too busy to meditate. You can find many options on YouTube, or search for mindful meditation apps or ask people you know for referrals.

REFLECTIVE PRACTICE
Select a mindful meditation practice of your choosing and practice it regularly for a month to expand your experience surrounding how this particular meditation approach might benefit you.

Awareness and Mindfulness

Reflection is how we expand our awareness. Expanding our self-awareness ushers in the possibility for being present in the moment; in turn, this helps us positively manage and direct our lives. Awareness and mindfulness are the foundations for directing intentional choices to live the life you want, be who you want to be, and reach your goals.

> "The intent of any mindfulness practice is to learn to know yourself, not to become peaceful. Knowing how your own mind works makes it possible to stay present and engaged in hyper-charged situations without losing your cool."

(20)

—Margaret Wheatley

I think people can easily confuse a personal opinion or viewpoint as truth, rather than recognizing it as just their personal perspective. When it is connected to a strong belief or value, we can often get defensive, take a posturing attitude, or attach strong emotions to the opinion we hold. It takes self-awareness to discern a difference between a personal opinion and a fact. It requires mindfulness to be aware of the emotional charge in a situation or to see that we are taking an aggressive or defensive positioning. Mindfulness helps us understand this as a symptom that we need a self-intervention, before we take a reactive action. This reactiveness can easily cause a disconnect within ourselves or separation from others that we might regret. Other common symptoms of disempowering attitudes or perspectives might be mentally building a case about a person or situation, feeling the need to prove a point, or needing to be "right" or "not wrong." These attitudes will only create separation within the mind and the heart. Using awareness and practicing mindfulness creates the space necessary to gain perspective beyond yourself and to regulate your emotions to stay present and poised in the face of differences of opinion, perspectives, and values, in order to continue to move with intention toward connection rather than causing separation from others.

REFLECTIVE PRACTICE
Think of a situation in which you had a strong opinion or viewpoint when speaking with someone. Reflect on whether or not you were taking a position that your opinion was "truth" and your viewpoint was "right." Did your position cause connection or separation? Was that your intent? What are symptoms to watch for, to become mindful of, that indicate you are becoming emotionally charged or righteously positioned? Make a list of your own emotional, physical, or mental attitude symptoms that a storm is coming. If you can become mindful of your symptoms, you have the opportunity to make less reactive and more responsive choices in the moment, choices that will help you avoid losing your cool.

21

"Self-reflection is a humbling process. It's essential to find out why you think, say, and do certain things—then better yourself."

—Sonya Teclai

Did you expand your awareness surrounding why you thought, said, or did something this week? How can that realization contribute to bettering yourself? If you didn't discover anything this week, take a moment to identify a question to ask yourself about a thought or behavior you have that is worth examining and reflecting on.

why

22

"Two skills define a mindful mind: focus and awareness. Focus is the ability to concentrate on what you're doing in the moment, while awareness is the ability to recognize and release unnecessary distractions as they arise."

—Rasmus Hougaard and Jacqueline Carter

Mindfulness is not having a full mind. It's quite the opposite! A mindfulness practice allows you to clear your mind or create more space internally, using awareness to be present and attentive in the moment. Bringing your attention and focus to the present moment is one aspect of this practice—to check in with yourself, to take the pulse of your state of being, or to pay full attention and focus on what it is you are doing.

Often people find it difficult to focus because of the numerous distractions or noise they encounter, both internally and externally. Common external distractions are surrounding sounds and images—voices, radio, social media, notification alerts on devices and phones, or even light from the TV or other devices. Consider what choices you can make to minimize unnecessary notification sounds or visual alerts. Do you really need a sound or visual notification for every new email or text you receive? Can you modify the range of hours when these notifications come? Would this alone create a calmer internal space for you, without necessarily having to create more time to be mindful? Another big distraction is multitasking—doing more than one task at the same time or switching back and forth between one thing and another. Research suggests that multitasking can actually hamper your productivity by reducing your comprehension, attention, and overall performance. It interferes with your attempts to focus on doing one thing at a time, a basic mindfulness skill.

REFLECTIVE PRACTICE

During your day today, write a list of the external noises that distract you . . . things that interrupt your focus or interfere with your awareness of your current state of being. This exercise in itself is a reflective practice that will expand your awareness of external distractions. Become aware of which external distractions you have control over and make note of those. Don't worry or force yourself to change anything right now. Give yourself space to practice mindfulness—witnessing and observing yourself.

23

"You don't have to be an expert in a particular field of endeavor to be an effective coach. I don't teach people anything about golf. All I do is help create awareness and self-responsibility in the person being coached. Their own high awareness is their teacher."

—John Whitmore

No one can expand the awareness of another person. We can only facilitate reflection that hopefully results in more awareness and mindfulness. Think about a coach as a change agent rather than a content expert. This way of thinking transfers the power to the person being coached by trusting in their ability and by facilitating their reflections to expand their own awareness and foster learning. Shifting away from our own desire to be an expert, we find that having answers or knowledge can actually get in the way of truly supporting someone to learn and become self-responsible. Information alone does not change behavior; change requires reflection and practice. We all know things we "should" do but don't do them. The information isn't the catalyst for change. Helping people change their thoughts, feelings, or behaviors requires cultivating a person's ability to clarify what they want and developing a plan or pathway for how to achieve their goal. But perhaps the most important role of a coach is to facilitate the other's ability to identify obstacles and challenges, and to encourage them to keep practicing and tolerating the discomfort and vulnerability they will encounter on their journey of changing, learning, and growing. As coaches, we also need to accept the discomfort and vulnerability of changing our own behaviors to reframe our mindset as a change agent, not a content expert. We too have to practice and "walk the talk."

REFLECTIVE PRACTICE
As content experts, coaches tend to talk a lot, "teaching" and offering suggestions. To become a change agent, practice pausing, listening, inquiring, and asking questions more than telling and talking. Practice biting your tongue when you are tempted to talk. Pay attention if you have an impulse or habit of talking first. Watch yourself. As you expand your awareness, begin to be more mindful of your choices and actions and shift to listening and inquiring. Aim for the coaching 80/20 guideline to speak only 20 percent of the time while letting the other person speak 80 percent of the time as they direct the conversation. Be compassionate with yourself as you explore this.

24

"Usually our awareness is so completely taken up with our inner talk that we do not experience ourselves as separate from it. With more awareness, however, we are able to step back from our imaginary conversation and observe it."

—Don Richard Riso and Russ Hudson

It can be beneficial to identify whether our distractions are external or internal. In Reflection 22, the focus was on external distractions and noise. Today we will focus on internal noise. We have more control over our internal noise and distraction than over external distractions. This is not the same as saying they are easier to deal with, but that internal distractions are 100 percent in our zone of responsibility and choice. Common internal distractions are overly busy minds, constant mental commentary (about just about everything), disempowering attitudes or perceptions, expectations and judgments of ourselves and others, and emotional reactions (fear, anxiety, overwhelm, and so forth), often created by our mental mindset more than external circumstances. A common internal distraction is FOMO (fear of missing out) that has arisen due to our constant use of technology and social media. Allow your focus today to be just observing the sources of internal noise in your world. This is an important first step toward deciding what to do about it. You can't change what you cannot see. Practice the art of witnessing without judgment and resist the need to take action right now.

REFLECTIVE PRACTICE

During your day today, write a list of the internal noises that distract you, things that interrupt your focus on what you are doing or your awareness of your current state of being. What internal beliefs cause you to multitask? What feelings or assumptions influence your choices for the notification settings for alerts on your devices? Don't underestimate the power of self-observation as a self-awareness practice. Continue this practice for several days to continue to expand your awareness. Begin to differentiate between which noises are external and which are internal distractions. Make notes so you can remember.

25

"The world as we have created it is a process of our thinking. It cannot be changed without changing our thinking."

—Albert Einstein

The power of our thoughts can't be underestimated. Our thoughts are the foundation for our world view, how we experience our life and all the challenges and successes we face. Our values, beliefs, and thoughts create the lens through which we experience everything. If we are not having the experience in life, work, or family that we want, the place to first focus is not on our external circumstances and other people, but rather within ourselves. Focus on what you think, on your perspectives, and on your attitudes that set the stage for how you interpret and experience the world and yourself. Changing our thinking, which is within our choice and control, can ultimately change our lives. It is amazing how frequently it seems as if other people and situations changed, when actually our perspective and how we interpret challenge and success shifted within us.

REFLECTIVE PRACTICE

Today notice the correlation between your thoughts, your outlook, and how you interpret your experiences as either challenging or successful. For example, I woke up the other day feeling stressed and overwhelmed about my workload. I took time to reflect on what was really underneath the overwhelm. I discovered I had a self-expectation that I had to complete all the tasks. I then assigned a meaning that if I didn't, I was failing or I wasn't good enough. But in reality, I had choice about the project time frames. I saw that I was pressuring myself with a deadline. I also had to really challenge the old belief or assumption I was making that completing tasks was the measure of a successful and productive day. It was an internal belief that didn't really match my current values. Shifting my perspective allowed me to make some choices about my workload and, more importantly, about aligning my unexamined beliefs with my current values.

Self-Responsibility and Choice

Having the ability to intentionally respond—rather than react—to circumstances, people, and even your own thoughts and emotions is the essence of being self-responsible for your choices. Your choices in your external circumstances may be very limited. The place to focus, where you do have control, is on your internal perspectives and attitudes and how these influence your choices. How you choose to respond to circumstances is where freedom lies.

26

"The foundation of freedom is the power to choose"

—Edith Eger

Reflection expands our awareness, which in turn fosters mindfulness. Being mindful and fully present and intentional in the moment offers clarity and an expansive perspective, as if you are standing on a balcony with a wider viewpoint. With reflection, a higher perspective is possible—where you get above personal emotional reactions and disempowering thoughts. Keeping your focus on where you have choice opens options and counters the pull of victim thinking, believing you have no power or control. But in truth, we do have control over our beliefs, thoughts, and feelings and how we choose to respond. Our perspective—our attitude or how we view things—is the key to discovering where we have choice, even in the face of extremely challenging circumstances that we have little or no control over. Control comes from staying focused on where we do have choice, on ourselves and our reactions, and investing our energy and time there. This power of focus is life altering and opens the door to possibilities through our intentional choices. This power of choice in your perspective and outlook is the source of true freedom, regardless of external circumstances. Think of someone with terminal cancer who chooses to focus on living a quality life, given the limited options they can control. How you respond to any circumstance is always in your power to choose, and experiencing this choice creates freedom in life.

REFLECTIVE PRACTICE
Identify a challenging situation in your life. Consider where you have choice and where you don't. What choices do you have about your beliefs, thoughts, and feelings about the situation? What options and choices do you have, or not, about the external circumstance? What shift in perspective might alter how you think or feel about this situation or the meaning you give it? Would gaining a broader perspective help, or perhaps a more detailed, specific vantage point could make a difference? As you clarify where you do have choice, focus your continued reflection and thinking there. Share your insights and wonderings with another person.

27

"The power of choice is just a matter of changing your mind. You have to put your whole self behind it and just say, 'I am just going to change my mind.' That is the power of choice."

—Kalindi*

You can shift your negative attitude away from dwelling on difficulty or troubles by choosing to change your mind. It will take intention and focus. It will require your desire to do this. Allow yourself to feel your desire and to focus on what you want. Desire is everything! Consider the benefits you will gain from changing your mind and attitude. Your desire for this, to have a more empowering and positive perspective, is possible, and it is your choice. It is actually a simple action, but it requires consistent practice and mindfulness to keep choosing moment by moment what you are thinking. Keep choosing the thoughts you want to live in and be guided by.

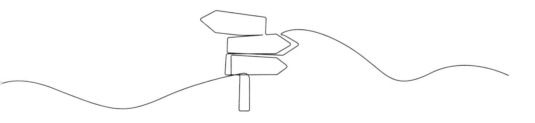

REFLECTIVE PRACTICE
Identify an attitude or thought you want to change. Write it down. Then clarify what replacement thought you want to have instead. Creatively express the reason you want this change. For example, draw a picture that represents what this new choice offers you. Put your representation somewhere you will see it every day, like on your bathroom mirror or at your desk; choose a song or make a playlist of music that inspires you to stay focused on making this change and listen to it each morning; or make a vision board—a collage with images and words cut out from magazines or photos.

* Kalindi, *The Break-Free Message*, pg. 229, www.CenteroftheGoldenOne.com.

28

"What good is self-awareness if we aren't using it to take external action and be better people in the world?"

—Elizabeth Solomon

What have you become aware of this past week that will lead you to take action? What is a possible next step?

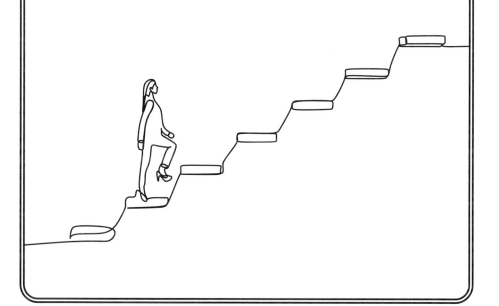

29

"Our emotions are so central to any action we take that a lack of understanding how we feel is tantamount to deciding to build a bridge without any awareness of the materials that will be used."

—James Bradford Terrell and Marcia Hughes

An emotionally intelligent person is aware of and responsible for their thoughts, emotions, and behaviors. They are able to respond intentionally (response-able) rather than react impulsively. Build emotional awareness through reflection by acknowledging your emotions, attitudes, thoughts, and actions in writing or conversations. Emotions don't fall out of the sky but are usually connected to a perception, thought, or social context. For example, when we are reactively triggered, we have a heightened and quick response caused by an interpretive thought, strong opinion, or strong feelings to something that happened. For example, when someone cuts you off in traffic, when your partner is complaining or blaming you for something, or when a child is whining, we immediately assign a meaning to it, and we have a thought or judgment about the situation, person, or behavior. Perhaps we think they are bad, rude, selfish, arrogant, or similar. Strong feelings then quickly flood in: anger, shame, defense, or fear. This rush of emotions is actually triggered based on our evaluation of the situation and what we make it mean. (Someone else in the exact same situation might respond entirely differently.) Taking time to slow down and become aware of our quick evaluative meaning and why this results in our specific emotional reaction can open up new self-understanding, letting us learn to catch when we are triggered and instead consider possible alternative responses. This will likely start with reflection after the situation and your triggered reaction and take time and practice. Expanding one's emotional vocabulary expands our ability to understand ourselves—what's meaningful to us as well as what's motivating our actions. Reflecting on our emotions and the why of our feelings yields vital information to help you respond rather than react.

REFLECTIVE PRACTICE

Think of a time when you were quickly reactive and triggered or stuck in bad or negative feelings. Answer the following questions sequentially:

PART 1: CURRENT STORY

https://www.
redleafpress.org/
dre/1-29.pdf

1. What happened (the triggering situation)? Be specific and concrete.
2. What thoughts and perspectives did you have about this situation/the person/yourself? What story did you create about what happened and what you made it mean?
3. How did you react emotionally? Clarify what specific feelings it triggered—anger, fear, anxiety, sadness, pain?
4. With what behavior(s) did you react? For example, did you cry, argue, or yell in anger, shut down and go silent, or defend, protect, and close your heart? Make a list of your typical emotions and reactions.
5. What was the outcome based on your response?

"Self-control is strength. Right thought is mastery. Calmness is power."

—James Allen

Self-control is the ability to regulate, choose, and alter your responses to avoid undesirable behaviors, increase desirable ones, and achieve what we want in life and at work. To exercise self-control takes awareness of what you are thinking, so it undergirds your responses and behaviors. It takes self-control to regulate your thoughts, feelings, and behaviors. Mindful attention to your thoughts, as well as awareness of situations or circumstances that tend to trigger you emotionally, will be part of the process of making conscious choices to achieve what you want and behave how you want. Mindfulness is like creating a center of calm in the eye of a storm. Inserting some pause and space between a circumstance and how you think about the situation and how you then respond is the zone of mindfulness and where choice dwells.

REFLECTIVE PRACTICE · PART 2: REVIEW YOUR CURRENT STORY

Use the same situation as yesterday, or another triggering situation you have faced.

1. Clarify what you mentally thought in those moments. What were the attitudes of your thoughts and perspectives? How did you interpret the significance of the trigger? What meaning did you construct about that triggering situation? Write examples of your thoughts.

2. How do you typically react in your head? For example, do you have negative thinking, discouragement, or judgments (of yourself or others)? Do you build a case against someone, collecting evidence or proving a point? Do you justify your behaviors because of how you feel or what you believe?

3. Once you have clarified each part of this, which might take several days, ask yourself whether these reactions are how you want to feel, think, and behave. Are these reactions what you want to choose in the future? You don't need to know right now how to change them. Allow yourself to reflect on, contemplate, and feel your desire. Start to reflect on how you do want to respond instead, given the same challenging situation. Trust that your desire and reflection will lead you to what's next without having to push yourself. Trust your timing and pacing.

31

"What happens is of little significance compared with the stories we tell ourselves about what happens. Events matter little, only stories of events affect us."

—Rabih Alameddine

You are probably familiar with the image of an adult standing between two fighting children with a hand on each of their foreheads holding them apart. This is a good image for the role mindfulness plays between our thoughts and feelings and our behaviors and responses. Not all your thoughts are true, and blindly believing them can be trouble. Reflective practices that help you notice and become aware of your thoughts and the interpretation or meaning your thoughts make (the story we tell ourselves) when facing a challenge is one side. The other side is becoming aware of what kinds of emotions and emotional responses you have, connected to those thoughts and interpretations (our story) about the challenge or triggering situation. Feelings aren't random. They are connected to past experiences, connected to how we think and how we interpret our experiences—our inner story. Becoming mindful of the thoughts and feelings we are having—the story we are telling ourselves—is where we can insert that pause, space, and calm so we can make intentional choices. We can choose whether to believe our own thoughts or at least to begin to question our perspective. The opportunity to rewrite our story can help us build self-regulation, honoring that moment of pause, like the adult holding squabbling children apart, to slow down our emotional reactions and behaviors to intentionally choose how to respond rather than unconsciously reacting in ways we may regret later.

Chapter 2

ATTITUDE AND PERSPECTIVE: KNOW THYSELF

The meaning and significance we attribute to our life experiences, both challenging and rewarding, is directly correlated to the perspective or lens through which we view and interpret our experiences. Building on ideas introduced last month, this month explores how turning within to reflect and focus on beliefs, attitudes, and perspective is where we have the power to make proactive choices, despite external life challenges or extreme circumstances such as systemic racism, serious illness, or disasters. Taking time to reflect and getting to know yourself expands your vantage point, your ability to purposefully engage and live an empowered life.

Attitudes

Developing reflective practices to expand awareness and to better get to know thyself is essential. Both positive and disempowering internal attitudes are an area for lifelong focused reflection. Our internal mental and emotional landscape has a tremendous impact on the choices we make and the direction of our lives.

"There can be no happiness if the things we believe in are different from the things we do."

—Attributed to Freya Madeline Stark

Your values and beliefs are the guiding principles that indicate the direction to travel and the criteria for your choice of actions. When our choices and actions are not aligned with our values, it creates inner conflict, struggle, and dissatisfaction. When you are experiencing discord or dissatisfaction, examine your actions in light of your beliefs and values and ask yourself if they are aligned. If they are not, examine whether your values need updating or you need to modify your actions. This might require making some hard choices and doing some soul-searching, but it's worth it to live a life that is fulfilling. It might take courage while tolerating the discomfort of change, not letting your fear stop you. But being aligned on the inside is worth that investment in yourself.

REFLECTIVE PRACTICE
In your role as leader or coach, or in life in general, are you experiencing any dissatisfaction, inner struggle, or conflict between what you are doing, how you are behaving, and what you believe or value? Journal about this or talk with a trusted friend or colleague to unravel the real source of your discomfort, clarify your values, and get honest about your actions and behaviors that are not aligned.

2

"Remember—80% of success is mindset, attitudes and beliefs. 20% is implementation. Consequently, having the tools to change what is going on in your head can have immense positive impact on your life and in your work. Today's thoughts, attitudes and beliefs create tomorrow's outcomes."

—Jonathan Manske

Circumstances don't determine or create our experience of success or failure. The ways we respond to our circumstances are determined by our attitudes, perspectives, and beliefs, as well as how we define success or failure, all of which underpins the choices and decisions we make. Becoming aware of and learning to positively shift our mindset has more to do with what we deem as successful outcomes. When people lack self-awareness, they are not very tuned in to their own thoughts, feelings, and motivations. You can't change what you can't see. Coaches and leaders focus on helping people become aware of, focus on, and manage their perceptions, which in turn impacts their decisions, choices, and outcomes. For several years in my employment with a particular company, I was very happy with my work and my colleagues. But as a few years passed, I became more aware of confusing and conflicting workplace practices—what they stated as their values and standards did not match my experience. At first, I dismissed what I was experiencing and overlooked inappropriate interpersonal behaviors and unrealistic and inconsistent demands from leadership. But in time, I realized I was unhappy and not feeling aligned with what I was experiencing. I wasn't sure how to handle my situation, letting my fear of leaving the position or not having a job inhibit me. Shortly after that, I was unexpectedly fired. I was shocked and upset. But within a few weeks, I discovered I was actually relieved and grateful that I had been fired because I realized I had not been making choices that were aligned with my own values when working there. I was able to refocus myself, and my next professional steps unfolded in a way that was exactly what I wanted. The shift in my perception of getting fired changed my whole attitude, and rather than feeling wronged, angry, and betrayed, I felt freedom and gratitude and discovered new creativity.

REFLECTIVE PRACTICE
Have you experienced a success or something you considered a failure that when examined and viewed through a different attitude or perspective shifted your evaluation of the experience, outcome, or results? What helped you make that mindset shift? How can your experience help you to encourage and promote similar changes in the people you support?

"Learn from the past, live in the now, and be optimistic about the future."

—Anonymous

The skill and habit of reflection is key to gaining access to the past and becoming mindful in the present so you can make intentional choices for the future. Through awareness and examination of your attitudes, mindset, or world view, you have a choice. You can learn to monitor and guide what you think, how you feel, and how you behave, which in turn affects your future, despite your circumstances. Using reflection to expand awareness to shift our perspectives and nurture empowering attitudes increases our ability to make mindful choices that offer both hope and freedom.

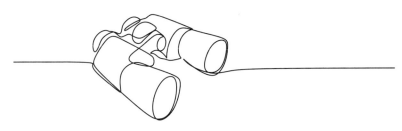

REFLECTIVE PRACTICE

Create a quiet moment while going to work. Do not listen to anything—no music, radio, news, podcasts, or talking on the phone. If you work at home, create a similar quiet moment. In this quiet space, clarify any areas where you feel you don't have choices or control. Reflect on any links between your past and your current life that cause you to conclude that you do not have a choice about how you think, feel, or behave. Refocus on areas where you actually do have choice and control. Observe how this can reframe your attitudes and behaviors. Build this focus as a habit of quiet reflective contemplation.

4

"An excuse is worse and more terrible than a lie, for an excuse is a lie guarded."

—Alexander Pope

It takes self-awareness and honesty to really acknowledge when we are making excuses. An excuse can be blaming others. Or it might be a habit of always having a reason for what you do or don't do, which seems so rational or obvious. We typically believe our excuses are true. Excuses can be a form of fooling ourselves, which is why they can be worse than a lie—they are slippery and tricky to catch. That's why it takes humility and really being honest with ourselves to pay attention and identify what our excuses look like, sound like, and feel like. Making excuses can be very connected with core disempowering fears like wanting to avoid getting in trouble, making mistakes, or doing things wrong, which trigger a need to have or give excuses. Until we start to observe what's underneath the behavior, it is not likely to change. Sometimes we don't even believe our own excuses, but the need to get off the "hot spot" overpowers our own integrity. It takes self-compassion coupled with a desire to grow and become more of who you know yourself to truly be. Be willing to focus on when you make excuses, why you make excuses, and what habitual excuses you use. It takes courage to tolerate some discomfort in order to grow.

REFLECTIVE PRACTICE
List your five most common excuses.

5

"When we . . . allow awareness to expand . . . we will gain objectivity and perspective about what we are doing. As a result, we will suffer less."

—Riso and Russ Hudson

The power of reflection helps us gain perspective about what we are thinking—our inner talk—and how this influences our feelings and causes or motivates the actions we do or don't take and the habits we develop. Awareness promotes mindfulness and the ability to witness ourselves in the moment, allowing an opportunity to intentionally choose how we respond to our own thoughts, other people, or external circumstances. It takes repeated practice to keep reflecting to expand our self-awareness so we can clarify and focus on where we do have a choice: either a shift in perspective or a willingness to take an action even in the face of being vulnerable or uncomfortable or while dealing with really difficult situations. We can unlock our internal attitude prisons and become unburdened so we can take actions and choose to be who we want to be without giving up, even though the journey may be long, with highs and lows.

REFLECTIVE PRACTICE
Choose an area of your life where you feel held back or uncomfortable taking a risk, or just want to feel more freed up. Or consider something else you really want but that feels out of reach right now. Practice reflecting about this area, keeping in mind both your internal landscape and perspective as well as the external circumstances. Reflect using any way or method that suits you—writing, talking, drawing, listening to or making music, or moving your body—just do this reflective practice repeatedly to keep your focus on this area. Start a daily reflective practice and help yourself become more aware of what's really going on—your thoughts, specific inner voices, feelings, passions, perspectives, and responses or reactions to external situations. Use this reflective practice with intention so you can make more deliberate choices to become all you want to be.

6 "Cultivate the habit of being grateful for every good thing that comes to you, and to give thanks continuously. And because all things have contributed to your advancement, you should include all things in your gratitude."

—Widely attributed to Ralph Waldo Emerson

To cultivate the habit of gratitude, begin to focus on the good things that have come your way, big or small, or the advantages you experience daily, such as shelter, food, and clothing. As you strengthen your habit of gratitude, begin to reflect on things that at one point felt challenging but that, with time, you discovered had an unseen silver lining or helped you learn a valuable lesson. Identify the life threads of your history of experiences and people and uncover how they have positively contributed to who you are or qualities you have today.

REFLECTIVE PRACTICE
Start and end the day with an expression of gratitude. Think it, speak it, or write it.

"To discard a negative thought, write it down on a piece of paper. Honor its message by thinking about it. Take a key lesson from it. Ask how it can contribute to your growth by being a learning opportunity. Then dispose of the paper (shred it, burn it, bury it), and the thought will disappear along with it. You've learned from the bad thought—keep the lesson but discard the self-criticism."

—Kondo and Scott Sonenshein

What negative thought was dominant this week? Follow the directions offered above—write it on a piece of paper, think about it, and identify a key lesson from it. Consider how it can contribute to your growth. Then dispose of the paper.

8 "You have two choices, to control your mind or to let your mind control you."

—Attributed to Paulo Coelho

Choosing what you think gives you freedom from within as well as freedom to direct the course of your life as you want. Many people who don't realize their thoughts are actually creating their reactions to life circumstances are unconsciously stuck in a victim perspective, falsely feeling powerless and assuming they have no choice. This results in anxious feelings and stressful reactions to life's challenges. The power to choose your thinking and control your mind has a huge impact on your feelings. You can choose to intentionally respond to the challenges that life brings each of us, rather than reacting emotionally from fear, doubt, and anxiety. The choice is yours.

> **REFLECTIVE PRACTICE**
> Identify one area of your life in which your mind, thoughts, or attitudes control how you feel and make you react negatively or in a disempowering way to challenging circumstances or experiences. Ask yourself if you want to change your mind and shift this. Just contemplate this, being as honest with yourself as you can. Resist any temptation to worry about not knowing how to change; don't try to take action at this time. Allow yourself a calm, nonjudgmental state of mind to witness and notice your thoughts and your desire to make a different choice. That is the action for right now. Keep it simple and be kind to yourself in this inquiry.

The Negative Voice Inside

One of the most disempowering influences we have is our inner critic, the voice in our heads that persistently causes doubt, fear, comparison, judgment, and discouragement that undermines us and keeps us reluctant to pursue what we really want. When we take focused attention to identify these voices, how they uniquely present for each of us, we can stop believing them and make powerful alternative pathways.

9

"Women often deplete their own energy by conducting an inner dialogue more unkind than any that would be tolerated in the outside world."

—Imetai M. Henderson, D.O.M.

The voices in our minds can be quite negative as we carry on an ongoing internal commentary about other people and about ourselves. We might not even recognize this happening because these voices are so familiar. Becoming aware of our inner dialogue is essential before we can change it. You can't change what you can't see. The unkind and negative self-talk plays the role of an inner bully—we bully ourselves and pay a price for that. Without awareness, we suffer as a victim to that voice because we believe what it tells us, and that in turn undermines our self-esteem, confidence, and hope. It takes courage to become conscious of that negative voice, to witness the unkindness and its impact. But taking the time, with gentleness and patience, to observe and identify the negative self-talk is the first step and opens the opportunity to shift and replace it. Only when you can witness and hear the voice and know it's not worth listening to can you choose not to listen to it, to replace it with an empowering message in the moment. It is possible to delete that unkind inner dialogue, like deleting a playlist. Treat yourself as kindly as you would a young child when a bully speaks to them, encouraging them and helping them see that what the bully says is not true.

REFLECTIVE PRACTICE

Take a small notebook and, throughout the day or at the end of the day, write down all the things the negative, unkind inner voice said to you. Write them down so you can identify and recognize that voice. Write every day for a month and you will become very aware when the voice is speaking in its many tones with its variety of messages. Practice witnessing and observing the voice without judging yourself for having that voice—that would just be more self-bullying dialogue. Let your awareness grow, without any expectations that you will do anything to change it, and after a month you will likely find the awareness you have gained is what you needed to delete the voice.

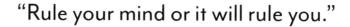

"Rule your mind or it will rule you."

10

—Horace

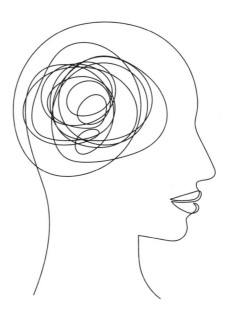

Not all your thoughts are true, empowering, or worth listening to. It takes intentional reflection to pay attention to your thoughts so that you become mindful of who is doing the thinking. Pay attention to your thoughts and what the specific messages are. Are you directing your thoughts, or are they directing you? When you pay attention and listen to the voice of your mind, you can choose what you will listen to and what you won't. It can help to write down the messages you do not want to continue thinking; this way you can identify that voice and not listen. You have 100 percent agency in what you think, and this choice opens the door to freedom from doubt, negative thinking, and judgment. Your thoughts and attitudes are the main lever to use to create the life you want to live. Invest in yourself by choosing the thoughts you will listen to, and delete the rest.

REFLECTIVE PRACTICE
List five ways you are more free because you can control your thoughts and actions.

"It's all in the mind, you know?"

—George Harrison

Over the years I have discovered that my mind often dominates and can actually disempower and bully me or cause internal pressure and unwanted expectations. I have learned to identify the symptoms so I recognize when this is happening. For me, it often results in feelings of constriction, or a constant mental barrage of "should be" self-talk that creates judgments and expectations of myself and others. I end up feeling anger, blame, guilt, or shame. None of which I want! I have had to pay closer attention to the symptoms that show my mind is dominating. As I have expanded my awareness around this, I am better at identifying these symptoms earlier, so I can be preventative and intervene when it is happening in order to make a shift in the moment. Being watchful of the mind, including our beliefs, attitudes, and thoughts, helps us become mindful, make intentional decisions, and act in alignment with who we really want to be—not be a victim of our mind or our circumstances.

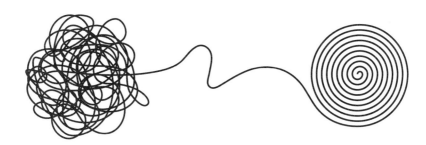

REFLECTIVE PRACTICE
What are your indicators or symptoms that your mind is dominating or bullying you or others?

"The next time you have any disempowering thoughts, quickly expel them."

—Christopher Dines

The first step is becoming aware of when you are having a disempowering thought. Labeling the types of disempowering thoughts can help you more easily identify them and catch them in the act. The fifteen most common disempowering thoughts I've identified are these: Negative Filter, Black-and-White Thinking, Universalization, Assumptions, Catastrophizing, Personalization, Shoulds (expectations and judgments), Labeling (stereotyping), Blaming, Victim Thinking, Being Right, Not Being Wrong, Fear of Failure, Emotional Reasoning (believing your thoughts are truth), and Fallacy of Change (assuming you can convince or cajole other people to change to suit you).* Once you can identify the most prevalent disempowering perspectives, then you can heighten your awareness to detect when they are the active playlist in your mind. You can't change what you can't see. Then you can become the DJ of your mind and cut off the disempowering thoughts as they start to play. See them, say "Not that!"—then delete them!

REFLECTIVE PRACTICE
Review the list of the fifteen most common disempowering perspectives above. Check which ones play in your mind. Don't be surprised if there are many; that's the typical response. Then choose and circle the top one or two that plague you the most. Write a list of the various ways that disempowering thought or voice sounds in your head. The more you can write down and clarify, the better you will be at catching it in action and stopping it.

* Constant Hine, *Transformational Coaching for Early Childhood Educators* (St. Paul, MN: Redleaf Press, 2019), 137–38.

"Thoughts aren't facts, so don't take them seriously."

13

—Widely attributed to Ruby Wax

Making time to pause and reflect can change not only our relationship to other people but also our relationship to ourselves. It's important to meet people where they are at, not how we want them to be. We also need to accept ourselves where we are at, including how we currently think, feel, and behave, inclusive of our character foibles and the illusory ways we think. To do otherwise would mean operating from judgment and expectations and assuming they are truth rather than engaging our perspective and opinions. When we tend to believe that our thoughts and feelings are factual and permanent—that this is just the way it is—we are falling into a dangerous trap that builds on unexamined assumptions, erodes self-esteem and confidence, generates bias, undermines trust, and disempowers relationships. This is not a productive direction! It is our responsibility to choose our thoughts and practice self-regulation of our attitudes.

REFLECTIVE PRACTICE

Take some time at the beginning of each day to ask yourself if you are starting the day with any negative or disempowering thoughts or attitudes, perhaps before getting out of bed. Remind yourself that thoughts aren't facts and you have a choice in what you think. Aim your thoughts toward a positive and empowering perspective. If you are unclear what that empowering thought or perspective could be, start with acknowledging something you are grateful for. Gratitude changes attitude. Build this as a daily practice, even if it starts with only five minutes a day.

"What does your attitude proclaim to the world about you today? It is never too late to change your story—start by changing your thoughts and pay attention to your attitude."

—Attributed to Bob Proctor

Are you stuck in an attitude or with a thought that does not let you move forward? Ask yourself, "Who is doing the thinking in my mind?" Is the thought disempowering or empowering? If it's disempowering, say, "Not that!" Delete the disempowering thought(s) like a bad playlist. Replace a disempowering thought with an empowering one. Use a reminder sign with the empowering thought and post it somewhere you will see it every day to help you focus on it.

Perspective

The key to being self-empowered, rather than a victim of your circumstances, is being aware of and responsible for your perspectives. Incorporate ongoing reflective practices to examine your perspective and viewpoints.

15

"What is difficult to solve with one paradigm becomes easy to solve with another."

—Attributed to Joel Barker

Perspective is the lens through which we view our world and ourselves. It determines how we interpret our experiences and circumstances—how we give meaning. Shifting our perspective can have a profound effect on our experiences and what they mean to us. Imagine perspective as a camera through which we observe, witness, and record what we experience through our senses, our body, and our mind. The angle of the camera can make a difference. For example, is your camera lens a wide lens (a balcony view) or a magnifying zoom lens (a close-up of details)? Is your camera lens facing outward, witnessing and focusing on what is happening around you, or is the camera lens facing inward on what is happening inside you—in your mind, in your body, with your emotions? All these perspectives are valuable and important. Timing and being able to switch between these camera views or perspective lenses can greatly shift your overall paradigm of how you view the world, yourself, and problems that might need a new viewpoint to find solutions.

REFLECTIVE PRACTICE
Work on becoming intentionally aware of the lens and angle of your perspective camera. Explore different lenses and practice selecting and shifting between them—take a balcony view and then close in on the details; look outward and look inward. With practice, you can be mindful of your perspective in any moment and even shift the lens to influence desired experiences, solutions, and outcomes.

16

"It is a narrow mind which can look at a subject from various points of view."

—George Eliot

Since my mind can be so dominant, I have learned to intentionally ask for the perspective and voice of my heart and my spirit through reflective practices, especially with meditation or taking moments of quiet to check in. I also have learned to listen to my body's perspective, giving this voice equal time to the mind voice. My body's voice is simple and clear and very informative, but I have had to stop, create space, and listen carefully. Sometimes it speaks softly. When I am lost in my mind's perspective, my body often has to scream to get my attention. I can end up with a pulled muscle or becoming sick or exhausted. I have to pay close attention to any symptoms that my mind is dominating. I am learning to be more proactive—to listen to the quieter voice of my spirit, heart, or body more often. As I expand my awareness and my ability to listen, my body doesn't need to scream as often. I am learning to rest when my body speaks. I used to just override that voice and push through it. This is really self-bullying. If I treat myself this way, I am more likely to treat others in a similar dominating way, without taking heed or even inquiring about their perspective or hearing their voice. Do you have an inner bully or a dominating perspective? It might be your emotions dominating your mind or your body. Or like me, the mind is dominating the body and emotions. It can be very different for each of us. How can you create inner equality and equity within yourself and advocate for yourself with yourself?

REFLECTIVE PRACTICE

Explore your inner points of view or voices—look at the mind's view, the body's view, the emotional view, and the spiritual or soul view. Differentiate these viewpoints. Can you hear all the voices? Does one dominate the others? How can you make more space to hear all the voices and the potentially important messages they have for you about any given situation or experience? Create a habit of intentionally asking for feedback from all your inner perspectives before making big decisions or taking action.

"There are things known and there are things unknown, and in between are the doors of perception."

17

—Unknown

Margaret Wheatley's view of leadership is grounded in the basic principle of self-awareness. She states that "critical leadership is to actively deal with perceptions."* Being able to examine and explore perception requires clarity about what is known and unknown, especially when dealing with other people, not to mention one's self. A leader requires listening and problem-solving skills, an attitude of inquiry, and a capacity to tolerate and resolve conflicts. To build and hone these skills requires making time to think, to be calm and still, and to listen quietly within, resisting impatience and distractions like phones. This builds the ability to not react instantly but to proceed mindfully and to awaken our powers of perception. Leaders establish learning as the priority and start with the tool of reflection to expand self-awareness.

REFLECTIVE PRACTICE
Learn today by doing three things—listen, think, and act.

* Margaret J. Wheatley, *Who Do We Choose To Be? Facing Reality, Claiming Leadership, Restoring Sanity* (Oakland, CA: Berrett-Koehler, 2017), 198.

18

"What assumption am I making, that I am not aware I'm making, that gives me what I see? And when you have an answer to that question, ask yourself this one: What might I now invent, that I haven't yet invented, that would give me other choices?"

—Rosamund Stone Zander and Benjamin Zander

How we invent our viewpoints dictates what we actually see. And often our sight is limited. Recognize that our perceptions are created and spring from our past experiences, our frame of reference, and our personal and social identities, then consider how the amount of creativity, choice, and freedom you experience are directly connected to your perceptions. Exploring the origins of your perceptions and the assumptions on which they are based lets you consider and choose which beliefs, thoughts, and feelings are taking you in the direction you want, and which are not. That's a powerful awareness with the key to choosing your freedom.

> **REFLECTIVE PRACTICE**
> Identify one assumption you are making that may be holding you back by limiting your perception of what's possible. Identify one assumption you make that contributes to your creativity, willingness to take risks, and bold dreaming. What are your insights about inventing viewpoints that give you new choices?

Failure and Mistakes

We all received early messages about the dangers of failure or making mistakes from family or society. This specific kind of fear can be quite derailing, and it discourages you from taking the kind of bold, courageous actions that are necessary to grow, step up, and bloom in your life. Risk intolerance does not need to set the tone for your life. Reflection can help redesign these obstacles and barriers.

19

"Resilient people don't see failure as the end, but the beginning—and they don't let failing affect how they view their own abilities or self-worth. Working through failures helps us recognize our strengths and development areas, and see where we can improve and grow. If we let it, it can show us which path we need to take to succeed, helping to create a better plan of action for the future."

—Gemma Leigh Roberts

How we think and feel about what constitutes a failure stems from the conditioning we received through family, our schooling, society, and media in our early formative life. Unless we intentionally examine this area, we can react unconsciously or be triggered by the idea of making a mistake or experiencing failure about anything, when any mistake can actually be a transformative opportunity. We can intentionally choose to think more positively about mistakes and failures. Not living a fear-based life is a game changer. When faced with challenges and the possibility of failure, it is our inner perspective and beliefs, not our external circumstances, from which true freedom comes. It's not conditional to how small or big a mistake or failure is; it's more about having the courage to take action and, if necessary, learn from failures and mistakes. It's your choice. Never fear failure as it could lead to your greatest success.

REFLECTIVE PRACTICE
Create two columns on a piece of paper. On the left side, write down negative messages you have received in your life, from any source, about mistakes or failures. In the right column, write down empowering messages you have received in your life about mistakes or failures. Recall a recent time when you were faced with a challenge or the fear of failure and identify which column the voice in your head is from. You and only you have the power to choose which messages you play repeatedly within yourself. You can change the message. Identify your most common negative message in the left column, then reframe it or replace it with an empowering message. Practice replacing the negative message(s) with the new reframed message each time the negative message pops up in your head. It takes practice and repetition, so repeat it over and over until it becomes a habit. Be kind to yourself while practicing this reflection. Beware of any negative inner messages that you should be doing this perfectly or any judgment of yourself as you become more aware of how many negative messages you've received.

20

"Do the best you can until you know better. Then when you know better, do better."

—Widely attributed to Maya Angelou

We are perpetually in some stage of learning and growing. The key is learning both from your successful experiences and from our missteps or failures, without judging either, to change an attitude, belief, reaction, behavior, or habit and become more of who you want to be. You can only do what you know until something wakes you up or you learn alternatives. It's essential to be compassionate and kind with yourself as you get better at getting better. Life is not about perfecting, it's about practicing, and that's the only way growth and development happens—for children and adults both. We are all becoming . . . so be kind to yourself and others as we journey.

REFLECTIVE PRACTICE

Identify an area of your life where you have been hard on yourself, been judgmental, or disempowered yourself. How can you reframe this area by looking at your continuum of growth over time? How might you be harshly judging your previous self? Transformation is accumulative, developmental, and very individual. Having more yet to improve doesn't invalidate the steps you've taken. When you know better, do better, and be kind to yourself along the way.

"Wishing you a heart open
enough to stay curious,
strong enough to face pain,
and brave enough to feel joy."

—Brené Brown

Have you been curious this week? About what? How have
you been strong or brave?

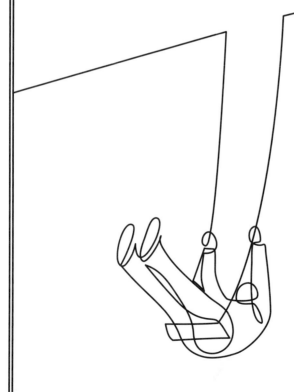

22

"It is not unusual for all people to revert to familiar habits when stressed and challenged, even if those habits do not work effectively and are not what is really needed or intended."

—Constant Hine and Robin Levy

To change habits we have to change the brain. Our brain is biologically wired to seek rewards, joy, and accomplishments, which cause it to release the hormone dopamine. When you experience the opposite and feel disappointment with little or no rewards, your brain's "kill switch" flips. This is the habenula in the brain, which integrates complex brain functions and is often called the antireward center or the kill switch. In the face of repeated failure, the habenula can shut down motivation and stop the release of dopamine. This happens quickly and often, especially when we focus too much on goals and performance. A performance mindset is fueled by outcome and performance goals, performance tracking, competitions, and extrinsic rewards. This is often why when we set goals and don't have a lot of success, we give up when we are not able to change our habits. The brain prefers and defaults to familiar and automatic neural pathways—which can include avoiding anything new or uncomfortable. Tolerating the discomfort of the unfamiliar while trying to learn new habits needs an impetus. Certainly, goals are not a bad thing, but they often aren't what people need to start or focus. For many people, starting with a focus on inquiry and a discovery approach is more motivational and successful. These approaches allow discovering and clarifying goals to naturally come later, after experimentation and learning. Supporting a motivational learning approach rather than using a pressured external compliance approach can be a more successful approach to changing habits.

REFLECTIVE PRACTICE
Do you make the assumption that change has to start with a clarified goal? Consider starting by focusing on your desire. Be creative and take time to discover and clarify what you want and what motivates you to grow and risk change. Consider the possible benefits of new habits. Something that positively pulls you forward, like a magnet, is going to create stronger chances of successfully changing habits.

23

"Coaches do not work to change overt behaviors. These behaviors change as a result of refined perception and cognitive processes."

—Arthur Costa and Robert Garmston

Change is often uncomfortable. Coaches must help people reframe their perspective that facing challenges is bad and should be avoided, and instead to see them as a normal part of the change process. Coaches help people tolerate the discomfort of uncertainty, reframing this discomfort as a way of learning from mistakes and trying new practices. As people being coached practice reflection and develop critical-thinking skills, they become more mindful and proficient at the process of learning, growing, and changing. If you are coaching others, focus your attention on helping people examine and reflect on their perceptions and attitudes and how these affect their behaviors and practices. Through the power of reflection, people will change themselves in deep sustainable ways we cannot manage from the outside. Trying to adjust their overt behaviors, like trying to fix them or adjust their dials, usually just causes resistance and defensiveness on their part.

REFLECTIVE PRACTICE
Are you experiencing resistance or defensiveness from the people you are working with or trying to support? Take some time to ask yourself honestly whether you are trying to change people and their behaviors. It may be that the resistance is less about the other person and more an indicator that your approach is not working—that they are reacting to you, not necessarily to the change itself. Examine the relationship between your intent and the actual effect you are having, without blaming the other person or yourself. When there is an intent-impact gap, it's time to explore your attitudes and the unexamined behaviors underlying your approach of helping to see if it's actually "fixing." How might you shift your approach to fostering inquiry, reflection, and critical thinking rather than giving advice, suggestions, and fixes?

24

"Success is going from failure to failure without losing your enthusiasm."

—Unknown

You can choose the mindset that failures are part of life, and they are often what offers our best learning. Then our perception of making mistakes or having what would commonly be called a failure takes on a new lens. Rather than becoming discouraged and self-judgmental, reframing failures as a way of getting better at what you are doing gives you an optimistic perspective as you encounter mistakes, missteps, or failures.

REFLECTIVE PRACTICE
Recall a time you think you failed or made a mistake and judged yourself for it. Name the failure or mistake—what specifically do you want to do differently or avoid repeating? Consider any lessons you learned from this experience—a need for a skill, blame you must let go of, alternative small steps you could take, or how slowing down might have made a difference. Write a list of anything you learned from that failure or mistake. Did you actually change anything due to these lessons learned? How can you avoid losing your enthusiasm when you have your next failure or make a mistake, since every human makes mistakes throughout their lifetime? How you are going to use your mistakes becomes the wiser question to pose.

25

"A brain that doesn't expect good results lacks a signal telling it, 'Take notice— wrong answer!' These brains will fail to learn from their mistakes and are less likely to improve over time."

—Tali Sharot

Catastrophic thinking is when you believe something is a lot worse than it actually is. When this happens, it leaves you feeling negatively about the situation or hopeless about the future. It also creates worry and builds stress, reinforcing negative thinking and causing a vicious cycle. Poor sleep can contribute to the tendency to catastrophize, so get some rest to help shift your perspective. Learn to focus on facts, not assumptions or fears, and avoid exaggerating so you can preserve a proportionate perspective. Remember, you are not your thoughts or your feelings. The difference between the thoughts that get stuck in your mind and the ones that float by is what you choose to focus on. Your behaviors and feelings will follow what you focus on. The choice is yours. Choose your thoughts purposefully, and learn to send yourself the signal to focus on what you want, not what you worry about.

REFLECTIVE PRACTICE
Are there any situations in which you are expecting the worst possible outcomes or you have convinced yourself that things will turn out negatively? Journal about your thinking to help you witness and gain perspective around what's actually going on in your mind. Analyze your thoughts, rather than believing in them, to make more empowering choices about which thoughts to feed and which ones to cut off and starve.

"Successful people maintain a positive focus in life no matter what is going on around them. They stay focused on their past successes rather than their past failures, and on the next action steps they need to take to get them closer to the fulfillment of their goals rather than all the other distractions that life presents to them."

—Jack Canfield

Successful people look forward toward the horizon, not in the rearview mirror. The power of having a positive and optimistic attitude cannot be underestimated; it fuels motivation. Being tenacious and focusing on the steps you must take to arrive at the destination you want are the nuts and bolts of success, beyond having vision. If you want to end up at your destination, you have to be specific about where you are going and clarify how you will know when you got there. I have an ongoing goal of getting at least eight hours of sleep each night. I know why getting enough sleep is important to me, for many reasons. But I need to frequently adapt my strategies to match what's currently happening in my life. I have a lot of energy, so I need to help myself wind down my energy to even get sleepy. I set an alarm to give me an hour warning to start winding down. For a while, I took a bath or drank calming tea to calm me down. But I noticed I was checking emails while I drank tea, so that didn't work. I had to change my strategy to include no device time an hour before sleep. It was a harder habit to practice, but it really helped me get to bed on time. Then at times I simply ignore the alarm. This means I need to revisit my motivation and devise new strategies. It seems to be an ever-evolving process.

REFLECTIVE PRACTICE
Review a goal you have been working on accomplishing and remind yourself why this goal is important to you. Make a list of the specific milestones and actions you will need to achieve in order to reach this goal. Identify and refine any next steps you need to take, given your current state of affairs or unanticipated challenges you have run into.

> ## "We must accept finite disappointment, but never lose infinite hope."
> —Martin Luther King Jr.

When you keep the perspective that life has a predictable rhythm, a dance that includes joy and success sprinkled with disappointments and setbacks, it helps prevent you from interpreting challenges and difficulties as something wrong and then feeling hopeless and giving up. Becoming more resilient includes strengthening your flexibility and adaptability, learning from mistakes and obstacles, and believing you have the capacity to overcome, even if you don't know how in the moment. Tolerating the discomfort of feeling disappointed respects and honors our human feelings, giving us time to regroup and turn to the source of what feeds the hope within us to get back out there.

REFLECTIVE PRACTICE
What gives you hope? What keeps your engine running even in the face of a setback?

Optimism

Explore what optimism is and embrace that it is a learned quality and perspective that opens doorways of hope, possibility, and empowering endeavors. Optimism is not only a mindset but a quality or character trait, nurturing adaptability, assuming positive intent, and believing that effort can make a difference that fosters positive successful outcomes.

28

"Gratitude comes not in spite of our problems, but rather because of them"

—Mary Pipher

What themes do you notice in your gratitude?

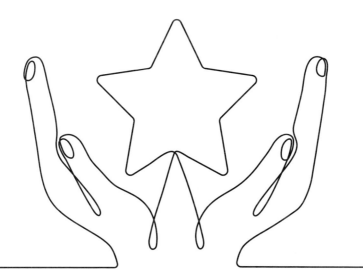

29

"Maintaining hope in the face of adversity is a skill that takes regular practice. . . . The ability to sustain a positive outlook means tending to it constantly."

—Attributed to William James

Given the demands, changes, and uncertainty of our current world, now is exactly when we most need to gather our inner grit, heart, compassion, and flexibility in order to respond to situations with intention and possibility, rather than reacting from fear in a familiar and habitual manner. Perhaps you have become numb to the status quo of life and need to wake up—kind of like when your foot falls asleep. It is important to be aware that, as circulation returns to the sleeping appendage, and as we notice the need to shift perspective and change awareness, the subsequent awakening is often uncomfortable—a sense of emotional pins and needles. Now is the time to witness our current disempowering thoughts and behavior. How do we let go of emotional reactions, such as giving in to overwhelm and fear, to instead cultivate the inner qualities needed to push forward with possibility? How do we facilitate change and meaningful learning in ourselves and others? These are big questions for which there are no quick fixes. As whole human beings with overlapping personal and professional identities, how we situate ourselves in our hearts and attitudes makes a profound difference in our ability to positively impact the growth and development of ourselves and other professionals we work with.*

REFLECTIVE PRACTICE
What inner qualities do you need to cultivate so you do not give up and so you expand your awareness of what is limiting you in order to ultimately make any necessary changes?

* Excerpted from Robin Levy and Constant Hine, "When the Cure Begins: Individual Choices Lead to Lasting Change," *Exchange* 257 (January/February 2021).

"Optimism is like a muscle—you just have to train it."

—Tchiki Davis

Optimism is a choice; it doesn't just happen to you. You have to willingly turn your mind toward being positive. At times this takes effort, so the more you practice this as a daily habit—like brushing your teeth—even when you are tired or down, the more you will maintain the habit. Being grateful is an excellent way to strengthen optimism. Intentionally looking for things to be grateful for is a way of turning your mind toward the positive, and it tends to take your heart along for the ride. Learn to savor the good.

REFLECTIVE PRACTICE
When you are going through a hard time, ponder what you could potentially gain from the experience. Reframe the situation and intentionally look for opportunity instead of ruminating on the loss.

31

> "Do not get lost in a sea of despair. Be hopeful, be optimistic. Our struggle is not the struggle of a day, a week, a month, a year, it is the struggle of a lifetime"
>
> —James Allen

Today's reality can feel bleak and overwhelming if we choose to look through a hazy, discouraging lens. Complex social justice issues require each of us to focus our attention and become more self-aware. Some of us have been aware for a long time and are frustrated. Many others are just beginning to see the systemic inequity and injustice in the treatment of people, especially people of color, causing us as a society to reexamine what it means to care for the people in our families, organizations, and communities. These concurrent issues require us to adapt responsively and make intentional choices about who we want to be as individuals and what we will do moving forward. For each individual, lasting change happens one small choice, one tiny step, one little stretch at a time. Small changes require patience and compassion for one another, and for ourselves, because to really look inside our hearts—to honestly see which feelings and thoughts need examination and possible modification—requires fortitude, courage, and self-compassion. Now is the time to leverage individual choices to make authentic personal and lasting social change. The choices we make matter. Imagine what the next generation, today's young children, might accomplish if each one of us could model moving forward with awareness and grit, in the face of discomfort, to generate future possibilities.*

REFLECTIVE PRACTICE · PART 2: REVIEW YOUR CURRENT STORY
When you reexamine what it means to care for and be inclusive of all people, what beliefs, feelings, and thoughts do you have that need more consideration and possible modification to make authentic personal change? How can you approach this with optimism and hope?

* Excerpted from Robin Levy and Constant Hine, "When the Cure Begins: Individual Choices Lead to Lasting Change," *Exchange* 257 (January/February 2021): 3–4.

Chapter 3

CHANGE AND TRANSFORMATION

"Sticky" change is the result of transformative change that sustains over time and through obstacles. Change really occurs only in the present moment, with each choice we make, and it requires being mindful and intentional. We have no choice over the future. Change happens as an individual shifts a perspective, a behavior, or an action. One choice, one action at a time. Those choices, repeated over time, become habits and result in sustainable transformation.

Sticky, Sustainable Change

Not all change is sticky, sustainable change. It's not uncommon for people to start with good intentions to change but, after a few months or after encountering some challenges, to then revert to old familiar behaviors, even if they are ineffective or don't support the desired outcomes. It takes awareness, concentrated focus, and perseverance to make lasting change.

1

"Things do not change; we change."

—Henry David Thoreau

Sustainable, lasting change requires us to reflect on how our values, beliefs, thoughts, and emotions influence our behaviors. It requires our attention and intention to go beyond thinking that setting a goal or outcome or creating an action plan is enough. A plan is only a map of a journey to get to a desired destination or goal; making a map is not the same thing as actually taking the trip. A goal and a plan are not a guarantee that any lasting change will happen. Unanticipated bumps, curves, and dead ends will always come our way. Reflecting and focusing on the journey while it's happening adds perspective and offers opportunities for refinement, modifications, and intentional choices in the moment. This may reveal assumptions or deepen questions or even reroute the plan or modify the original goal. The process of learning and achieving sticky change requires reflection before, during, and after the experience or the journey. Mindfully witnessing how we travel on any journey can reveal useful patterns and processes that we can intentionally use in the future to ease the mind and increase emotional trust, nurturing our stamina for persistence and our skills for the next journey.

REFLECTIVE PRACTICE
Review a recent time you had a desired goal or recognized that you needed to change and were successful. Map the journey you took by drawing or writing to reveal the patterns and processes you used. Ask yourself the following questions: Were you intentionally focused on something you wanted? Or did life circumstances bring about the situation? Did you have a plan? What known or unexpected challenges or obstacles did you encounter? What inner qualities did you call upon or need to strengthen to succeed? Did you have to modify or refine the plan? How? Did the original goal become more refined or change because of your journey?

2

"People do not resist change, they resist being changed."

—Common wisdom

To make progress supporting or coaching people, you will need to diagnose why the coachee is resisting you. Perhaps they are reluctant to accept any coaching from anyone, or they may just be reluctant to work with you as a coach at the current time. A person must have motivation to be open to and interested in change. It may be that the person is unclear about why they would want to change and grow, or perhaps they have conflicting feelings. They may also have preexisting negative ideas or previous experiences of coaching that are worth discussing. Look deeper and diagnose what's underneath their resistance.

REFLECTIVE PRACTICE
Identify your most reluctant coachee or person you support as a leader or educator. Clarify what you know (not what you assume) and what you don't know about their motivation and readiness to change. Create a plan that leads with your curiosity, considering how you might learn more about them and what really motivates them, including questions you could ask.

"A key to successful change is in knowing what stage you are in for the problem at hand. People who try to accomplish changes they are not ready for set themselves up for failure. . . . You can't skip stages. Most successful self-changers follow the same road for every problem."

—James Prochaska, John Norcross, and Carlo DiClemente

Change readiness is developmental and individual. Change readiness is also related to risk tolerance. Those who have experienced trauma in their background or have had negative experiences that cause a fear of change will embrace change uniquely and likely more slowly than others. Don't assume everyone has or should have the same approach as yourself (whether this manifests as resistance or willingness). Much of the work of leadership is dealing with people's perceptions, not just accomplishing outcomes. In the book *Changing for Good*, James Prochaska, John Norcross, and Carlo DiClemente identify six stages of change: 1) Precontemplation—resisting change, 2) Contemplation—change on the horizon, 3) Preparation—getting ready, 4) Action—time to move, 5) Maintenance—staying there, 6) Relapse—lapse or setback. It is important as a leader or coach to be mindful of where people are in their readiness for change in a particular situation. Insisting or trying to persuade someone who is not ready will only slow down the process and create more resistance. A more effective stance to take is one of inquiry and curiosity. Have authentic conversations about where someone is. Creating a nonjudgmental culture, neutral tone, and accepting manner will help identify what kind of individualized support, strengthening, encouragement, coaching, and pacing will promote change through each of the stages. Remember that one person can be very open and embrace change in one area and be hesitant about another situation. Change readiness is situation specific.

REFLECTIVE PRACTICE
Identify a habit of thinking, feeling, or behaving you have had difficulty changing or keeping consistent. Review the six stages of change and assess which stage matches how you authentically feel about that situation, not what you think you should be doing. Reflect on your concerns and fears, and then respect your own pacing in your readiness for change. Consider why (or whether) you really want to change that habit. Clarifying what you really want might be the key to unraveling the pacing and accuracy of your next steps. Learning to trust this process for yourself can be crucial for understanding, having compassion, and being able to respectfully support others to change.

4

"You will either step forward into growth, or you will step back into safety."

—Abraham Maslow

When we frame our lives around needing to feel safe at all times, it inhibits the learning that fosters growth because learning so often requires us to tolerate discomfort. Discomfort usually doesn't feel safe or easy. It is necessary that people feel a basic level of physical and emotional safety to feel respected, heard, and cared for so they can take a risk to learn and grow. Yet the need for safety can hold us back. We must become able to tolerate the fear of taking a risk. It is not that you are unafraid, but that you don't let the fear stop you.

REFLECTIVE PRACTICE
When issues of safety press in on you, consider shifting your perspective from how to be safe to asking yourself, "What will it take for me to be courageous in this situation and take action in the face of my fear?"

5

"The great courageous act that we must all do is to have the courage to step out of our history and past so that we can live our dreams."

—Attributed to Oprah Winfrey

It takes grit to muster the internal stamina to achieve goals that take time and intention to accomplish, and it takes passion to reach for new outcomes. Grit does not require a high IQ or good grades because it is not about intelligence or cognition. Instead, it is about heart and a desire to move forward. It takes courage and inner strength to be flexible and to adapt to changing demands and circumstances, not letting fear stop us, and staying open so we can change and adapt as needed. Open-minded vulnerability helps us trust internal nudges from within. It takes grit to be open and vulnerable, a true sign of inner strength. Rekindle your heart's desire by exploring what will inspire you to change, stretch, and examine values, attitudes, and biases you may not have seen before—to tolerate the pins and needles of your awakening consciousness.*

REFLECTIVE PRACTICE
Ponder a mindset, disempowering feeling, habit, or behavior from your past that is no longer helpful to you now. What do you need to step out of so you can live your dreams?

* Excerpted from Robin Levy and Constant Hine, "When the Cure Begins: Individual Choices Lead to Lasting Change," *Exchange* 257 (January/February 2021).

6

> "As a . . . leader, . . . I am a creator of paths filled with curiosity, wonder, and exploration, figuring out how to create space for connection where each individual is honored and embraced for who they are and who they want to become. I hold a vision of creating a legacy of hope and bravery (professional), of authenticity (home, personal, professional), and of love for family and community. Journaling helps me bring that into being."

—Kelly Ramsey

Educator and leader Kelly Ramsey shares insights about the power of journaling as a reflective tool for unfolding your questions, wonderings, and discoveries. Over time, journaling can reveal your story of becoming—who you want to be and who you are becoming as a leader, educator, coach or in any other venture in your life. As you write about your journey for yourself, journaling offers a perspective for making meaning of your experiences. You can witness whether you are weaving in your values and beliefs with your practices and actions and check if they are aligned with your hopes and vision. Essentially, journaling supplies the information and opportunities to make thoughtful choices either to sail forward or to change course if needed.

REFLECTIVE PRACTICE
Explore using journaling as a personal space and method for unfolding your questions, wonderings, bumps, and discoveries about your journey. Let go of any self-expectations surrounding how you should write and be open to creative or just ordinary writing. Engage with yourself as you would with a young child learning to write or talk—be kind, encouraging, and respectful.

7

"Often it isn't the mountains ahead that wear you out, it's the little pebble in your shoe."

—Attributed to Muhammad Ali

Review your past week. What has been a pebble in your shoe that has distracted you, tired you out, or made you walk more slowly?

8

"For me, becoming isn't about arriving somewhere or achieving a certain aim. I see it instead as forward motion, a means of evolving, a way to reach continuously toward a better self. The journey doesn't end."

—Michelle Obama

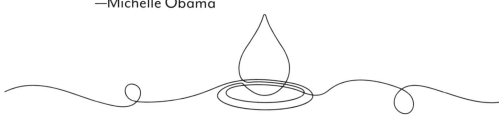

Focusing your intent on expanding your awareness is a significant avenue for transformation and change. Each small intentional step you take to expand your awareness is change in action. Focusing your attention and efforts to enhance your positive inner qualities, increase your flexibility, and practice mindful decision-making will strengthen your personal journey, changing your course forward. Striving to become better, to solve problems, to have control of your mind and emotions, to find inner freedom, to live wisely, and to have love, care, and respect for all people is possible only with more awareness and self-knowledge. Being transparent and sharing your own personal journey and the changes you had to make can influence others as they travel their own paths, inspiring them to make their own mindful actions and course corrections. The journey of bettering yourself, learning, and evolving doesn't really end; it just deepens and spreads. Expanding and changing your own consciousness is like dropping a pebble in the water, and the ripples of impact are boundless.

REFLECTIVE PRACTICE
In what ways do you want to know yourself better? Why? Write or draw a picture of how becoming more self-aware and conscious is a journey you want to travel to support your own transformation.

"We cannot change anything until we accept it."

9

—Widely attributed to Carl Jung

Meeting people where they are at, just the way they are right now, without expectations or feeling that they should be different, is respectful—and it is the only way to have an authentic relationship or connection with anyone. To truly witness someone as they are, without judgment, is a remarkable gift to offer. This is equally true for yourself. Accepting yourself, just the way you are—flaws and all—is the only way you can respectfully and kindly interact with yourself. If you want to qualitatively change, you must accept yourself and others as is. If not, you will fall prey to approaching yourself and others from a position of trying to fix things, which is disempowering. Acceptance holds a treasured key to making transformational sticky change that launches from an honest reckoning with the current reality, the authentic starting place. Expecting something else, refusing the current situation, or disapproving of it just slows down, distracts, or detours the whole change process. Creating a goal or desired outcome based on a disappointing judgment or a false starting place will never fare well for a successful journey. With honest acceptance of what is, real growth, change, and achievement of a true vision and goal are possible.

> **REFLECTIVE PRACTICE**
> In yourself, what do you want to change? Do you authentically accept yourself as you are right now? What does acceptance mean to you? What might you have to accept? How might this offer you a better starting place to become who you want to be? Do you coach or support someone for whom you need to reflect on these same questions to serve them more successfully and respectfully?

Learning to Change

When you learn how to change it becomes a valuable skill that is transferable to any kind of change that needs to happen. To become successful at change requires more than solving a specific problem; it's more about embracing a mindset and developing routine reflective habits to navigate change as a lifestyle.

10

"Learning how to change is learning to change."

—Attributed to George Leonard

As a coach or leader, you need to be a change agent, not just a content expert. Change is often uncomfortable. Help people reframe challenges and see them as a normal part of the change process. Help people tolerate the discomfort of uncertainty, learning from mistakes and trying new practices. As they practice reflection and develop critical-thinking skills, they will become more mindful and proficient at the process of learning, growing, and changing. This nurtures sticky change.

REFLECTIVE PRACTICE
How did you learn how to change? Consider if it was from book learning or knowledge of specific content, from someone giving you advice or telling you what to do, or from something else. Reflect on the difference between having knowledge and actually implementing a change of habit, thought, or feeling. Who or what has helped you be successful at changing? What happened or how did the person help you through the change process? Take a walk and contemplate this, and then journal or talk with someone about it.

11

"Critically reflective teaching happens when we identify and scrutinize assumptions that undergird how we work. . . . Seeing how we think and work through different lenses is the core process of reflective practice. The most effective way to become aware of these assumptions is to view our practice from different perspectives. Seeing how we think and work through different lenses is the core process of reflective practice."

—Dr. Stephen D. Brookfield

Critical thinking is one aspect of reflective practice. For educators, as well as those in any other work or career, taking time to identify and examine the assumptions we operate from is how we can continue to grow, learn, and refine our professional practices. Ask more questions and seek to understand rather than to be understood. Explore different perspectives to widen your world view. Listening to diverse voices will make us better informed and will expand our ability to meet the needs and goals of those we work with and serve.

REFLECTIVE PRACTICE
Shift your focus from using your own perspective as the starting point. Be curious about the perspective or journey from another person's path and experiences. Pick a person who might have a different perspective from you; then begin to wonder about their perspective and witness how they behave. Ask that person questions about how they experience or interpret situations, listen with curiosity and without judgment, and observe how they respond differently than you would.

12

"The illiterate of the 21st century will not be those who cannot read and write, but those who cannot learn, unlearn, and relearn."

—Alvin Toffler

A coach's role is empowering people to learn how to reflect and how to thoughtfully make data-driven decisions to improve their professional practices, solve their own problems, and be responsible for their own learning, by learning how to change. The ability to unlearn and to continue learning is foundational to being successful in this age. To learn is to change, and by changing we learn. The purpose of transformational coaching and leadership is to facilitate meaningful change.

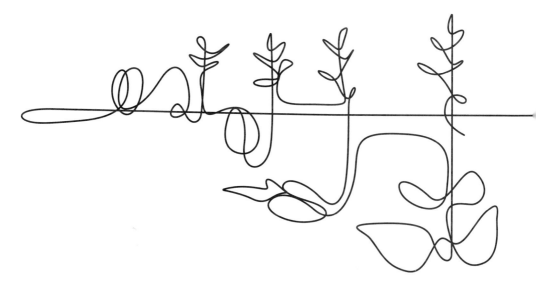

REFLECTIVE PRACTICE
Is there something you realize you need to learn, unlearn, or relearn, given your experiences and reflections from this last week or month?

13 "One of the hardest lessons in life is letting go. Change is never easy. We fight to hold on and we fight to let go."

—Anonymous

Letting go is an art, a skill, and a lifestyle. Our beliefs about change can make the process of changing smoother or more difficult. Change may not be easy, but it doesn't have to be approached as if it should be avoided—this just causes unnecessary suffering. To grow and mature, we need to cultivate the ability to tolerate discomfort—being bored, having strong feelings, knowing that someone disagrees with you or has a different perspective, not having the right answers, or knowing that sometimes there are no right answers. Expanding our capacity to tolerate discomfort is an important component of normalizing change. To shift from an emotional interpretation that change is dangerous or unsafe to viewing it as an opportunity for possibility can be life changing. If you can sprinkle a little curiosity in with the ability to tolerate change, you can greatly ease the process of transformation.

REFLECTIVE PRACTICE
What attitudes, feelings, or behaviors do you hang on to that tempt you into short-term gain but have a long-term cost? Write a list of questions to ponder and wonder why you hold on to these, but don't answer the questions. Just let curiosity lead by letting one question uncover another question.

14

"To change ourselves effectively, we first had to change our perceptions."

—Stephen R. Covey

Recall a time when you shifted a perspective, and the change you desired happened or finally stuck. How does this reflection help you think about a current change you are hoping for yourself? What perspective might need to be reframed?

15

"Take the attitude of a student, never be too big to ask questions, never know too much to learn something new."

—Attributed to Og Mandino

The wonder of a child is a marvelous model for how to best learn. Wonder leads to curiosity, questioning, and experimenting. Thinking you are supposed to know the answers or being afraid to make mistakes inhibits transformation, growth, and change. Engineers practice "ideation" and experimentation before any solid solutions are discovered. Ideation is entertaining ideas and making up possible solutions. It's not about already knowing; it's in the spirit of exploration, and it's OK that not all ideas will be viable. Many people not only have never been educated in strong, creative critical-thinking skills but also have great discomfort in considering possibilities and exploring options. Their need for answers or to not make a mistake becomes an inability to learn. Wonder, ideation, and possibility thinking is expansive and opening. Choosing actions or solutions is a narrowing or reducing direction. Both are needed, but the best action plans will come after brainstorming and considering all kinds of possibilities. Including and embracing outlandish or "unicorn" ideas can foster creative and diverse thinking, which is often needed for transformational learning and growth. Helping people to practice ideation, to consider a variety of options, and to brainstorm before choosing an action plan or assuming a solution is an important role for coaches to cultivate in people and for leaders to model and demonstrate.

REFLECTIVE PRACTICE

When coaching someone in developing an action plan, coming up with a solution, or supporting group planning meetings, use the Rule of Three to encourage people to identify at least three options before narrowing down choices and making any decisions. This eliminates the perception that there is one right answer; if only two are considered, then there is a right and a wrong answer. Having three options requires analysis and mindful choice and usually opens up thinking.

16

"Being your best is not so much about overcoming the barriers other people place in front of you as it is about overcoming the barriers we place in front of ourselves."

—Attributed to Kieren Perkins

Our most common internal barriers and obstacles where we have control are issues of attitude—limiting, disempowering, or negative perspectives. This is the territory where individual change is most needed to transform our lives and to impact how we respond to difficult life circumstances. These internal barriers are often unseen or hidden from our view. It takes reflective intention to find them, name them, and identify their symptoms so you can recognize them when they show up. If we don't do this, our disempowering perspectives and thoughts run our lives. It takes a conscious decision to shift and reframe them if you want to be free. It doesn't guarantee a quick or easy journey, but if you make a pre-commitment to yourself to flip and reframe a specific perspective, it is possible to change, and it will be worth it even if it takes effort and focused attention.

REFLECTIVE PRACTICE

Consider the ways to flip disempowering or limiting perspectives by focusing on what you want to replace them.

Name your disempowering perspective. How would you flip it? For example:

Disempowering Perspective Focus	Empowering Perspective Focus
Need for safety	A focus on courage
Fear	Trust
Afraid of making mistakes or doing it wrong	Learning opportunities
Victim consciousness and no control	Find where you do have a choice

Busyness and Distraction

Expanding our awareness of the common distractions that deter us from building supportive and reflective personal and professional habits helps to clarify where we may need to focus our attention. Identifying the unique ways each of us may use busyness or fall prey to a counterproductive, hurried life pace will help us focus and be mindful to make more positive choices.

"Too many choices can overwhelm us and cause us to not choose at all. For businesses, this means that if they offer us too many choices, we may not buy anything."

—Sheena Iyengar

We can create our own overwhelm by allowing ourselves too many choices in a day. Do you find yourself feeling either overwhelmed with how much you need to do or discouraged by what you haven't accomplished? Trying to remember all the details, to do's, actions, and thoughts can cause disturbance, stress, and worry. In addition, many people create unrealistic to-do lists with too many items to accomplish in a day. This running to-do list creates stress and is a common source of overwhelm—an emotional response to feeling like there is too much to do. Overwhelm is an internal demand related to self-expectations. Overload, on the other hand, is when we have a lot to get done in a certain time frame—it's a type of external demand. This state is usually temporary and is related to an upcoming deadline or project. This is an important distinction to make: are you experiencing overload or overwhelm, or both? You deal with each of them differently. With overload, you prioritize what's important and practice time management. It requires a change of your habits to assign activities only to the actual available hours you have in each day, not just putting things on a daily list. It will likely require slowing down, thinking critically, and analyzing your schedule. For overwhelm, shift your perspective and consider your emotional response to not getting something done. This change requires an awareness of when you are triggered emotionally. You will need to reflect and identify what the underlying belief, expectation, or assumption is. Are you afraid of doing things wrong or getting in trouble, do you feel the need to be perfect, or do you feel that your self-worth comes from being productive? To successfully change habits requires focus and attention on the simple choices we do have and exercising our control to make adjustments.

REFLECTIVE PRACTICE

If you are feeling stressed by what you have to do, take a moment to first discern what is actually causing the stress—external or internal demands. If you are dealing with external demands, you may not have much control over them, but you might be able to practice AND: Ask for help, Negotiate, or Delegate. Also focus your attention on prioritizing and creating realistic schedules for tasks. If the things on your list that cause pressure and stress are things you are expecting of yourself, then you are dealing with internal demands. You have a great deal of choice and control over what you think. Examine your thoughts and expectations, as you likely will find relief by shifting to more empowering thoughts. Try adjusting what you expect of yourself—I often have to examine the source of the demands and discern if they are self-imposed or demands from others. If they come from others, I may need to ask for help, negotiate, or delegate. Sometimes reframing your perspective can help you reprioritize. Sometimes you just need to reduce the items on your list. Maybe you can explore other creative solutions.

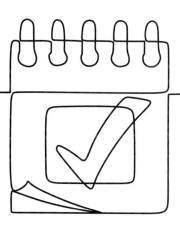

"The key is in not spending time, but in investing it."

—Stephen R. Covey

What does it mean to invest time? To invest can mean to devote time and to prioritize what's most important to you. Making time to reflect and become aware of what is most important to you can positively influence the quality of your life and revolutionize where you invest your time. An excellent investment of time is to examine your values and consider whether your actions and choices are aligned with them. Discern what is most meaningful for you so that you can make intentional choices about how to empower yourself through your use of time. When your core values create criteria for prioritizing your time, you are more likely to make time or invest time with the things that will motivate, inspire, and shape your life. If lack of time is a common barrier or obstacle for you, then it is probably important to make the time to stop and clarify what your values are. Examine where you might be unwisely investing your time, or find areas where it would be better to spend your time and attention.

REFLECTIVE PRACTICE
Make a list of what's most important to you in your life. Focus on the top five things. Assess the time you currently devote to those things each day or each week. Are you prioritizing your time to invest in the life you want to live? If it's out of balance, then decide one important action you want to make more time for and actually make time for it, so it becomes a routine habit.

19

"You must see if the activities that you are performing are what you should be doing. Are you performing unnecessary activities that are distracting you? And you need to alleviate, wherever possible, the distracting influences."

—Gourasana*

During the course of my day, I often realize I am not really doing what I intended or attending to my highest priorities. It seems I somehow get caught up in administrative tasks that are not really very important or necessary in the moment, or I go down a rabbit hole on the internet researching something, or after reading an email that bothers me, I want to deal with it because I am disturbed, even when it doesn't require my immediate attention. I distract myself. Sometimes I catch myself and refocus. Sometimes I end the day feeling frustrated or unproductive or judging myself for wasting time. If I examine what the distracting influences are, it's not really the email or the research project or the administrative tasks but rather my emotional reaction that derailed me. The distraction is the busyness in my mind, plus having an unconscious lack of focus. I can find myself distracted because I am procrastinating or avoiding what really needs my attention. I need to look and reflect a little deeper. It's only when I shift my focus from my external setting to focusing within that I can alleviate these distractions. Turning within can happen quickly, like taking a breath or a quiet moment, or it might require a longer, more mindful calming practice. In any case, it is my responsibility to increase my awareness and consider whether I am actually paying attention to where I am and what's going on within myself, and to discern whether I am working on what is actually important. Turning my attention within is to become aware. Then it's about making a choice in the moment to shift my focus and my energy.

REFLECTIVE PRACTICE
Are you aware when you are distracted? What are your symptoms or typical behaviors or thoughts when distracted—that is, your habits? What can you do to shift your focus and choose other options?

* Gourasana, *The Radical Path*, p. 132, www.CenteroftheGoldenOne.com.

"Technology has far outpaced our ability to develop norms and expectations."

20

—Coye Cheshire

The rise of rapid-fire communication technology has created the expectation that people will always be online and available. Some of these expectations are external, but they also come from expectations we have of ourselves, which might be unconscious and unexamined. Social expectations that people should immediately reply to calls, texts, emails, or social media messaging cause a great deal of stress for many people. The pressure people feel from undefined boundaries or agreements with their workplace, friends, or family can be the cause, of stress and distraction, especially with the rise of remote work. Data from a 2021 Pew Research Center survey revealed that 30 percent of Americans were almost always "constantly online," especially during the COVID-19 pandemic.* The advanced technologies, especially in handheld devices like smart-phones, have outpaced the formulation of new mutually agreed-upon communication standards, and people are not responding according to the same rules. Establishing clear understandings and agreements (in your workplace, as well as with friends and family) about response times can contribute greatly to reducing stress. Consider implementing clear expectations or requests by being specific when you text, email, or leave a voicemail, explaining when you hope to hear back from someone. Consider reflecting more on your communication etiquette. Practice kindness by alleviating unnecessary stress, by saying things like, "I don't need an immediate response, by next week is fine." If you need a timely response, indicate what you hope that time frame is, and ask if it's possible rather than just assuming and demanding that it will work for the other person. Intentionally communicating and giving specific time frames is a way to share kindness and care for others and for yourself.

> **REFLECTIVE PRACTICE**
> When communicating with others, be mindful and gracious with your time frame for an expected reply; consider how their perspective and situations might be very different from yours. How might you begin having conversations with friends and family and in your workplace about establishing and clarifying clear understandings and mutually agreed-upon response times and expectations?

* Bryan Lufkin, "The Crippling Expectation of 24/7 Digital Availability," BBC Worklife, February 8, 2022, www.bbc.com/worklife/article/20220207-the-crippling-expectation -of-247-digital-availability.

21

"Slow down to the speed of wisdom."

—Unknown

When we slow down, we can become more curious and we can see more, especially details and subtle cues. A slower pace allows you to be more kind to both yourself and others, to notice the small pleasures around you. When we give up speed, we open up time to breathe, to notice the present moment. Your mind can't follow you into depth when you are going too fast. Wisdom comes from depth. Adjust your pacing to access your wisdom. How can you slow down to tap into your wisdom this week?

22

"Yesterday is gone. Tomorrow has not yet come. We have only today. Let us begin."

—Often attributed to Mother Teresa

Keeping our focus on just today and keeping our attention in the present moment is a skill of mindfulness. One way we can add more conscious mindfulness to our daily practice is to create accurate and realistic To-Do Today Lists. A simple mindfulness practice I learned at Center of the Golden One in their Spiritual Advancement Course (SAC) is to clarify and separate what you want or need to do today, your To-Do Today List, versus a list of things you need to remember to do or attend to at some point. They call that your REmember List or "RE List." Your To-Do Today list has to correspond to the actual hours you have available to do things in each day. If you are in a meeting from nine to eleven in the morning, you are not available to handle other tasks and actions during those hours. So if you work eight hours a day, now you have only six work hours available. What's on your To-Do Today List has to be able to be accomplished in those remaining hours. It might be one big project or several smaller tasks. A RE List is a list of all the things that need your attention or that you need to remember to do at some point, but not necessarily today. This is usually a much longer list. It's recommended to record and save your cumulative RE List. It could be on paper, in a notebook, in a document on your computer, or even in an app on your phone. The intention is to keep your RE List list handy during the day so you can continue to add items. As you are planning each day, you can review your RE List to see if there are any items that need to happen on that specific day. Many daily planners offer you the option of identifying the top three, must-do-today items to help you focus your attention, prioritize, and make intentional choices in your day.

REFLECTIVE PRACTICE

Create an ongoing RE List and start using a separate To-Do Today List, listing only the items you will focus on for just one day that correlates with the actual hours available to you in your schedule that day. Consider whether this practice decreases your stress and overwhelm. Continue trying out this approach, as it takes some practice to refine and modify it.

Habits and Small Steps

Sticky change is the result of the choices we make in each moment. With mindfulness, we can stay in the present moment, and this is where we exercise conscious choice. Each small step makes a difference. Change is an accumulation of many small actions repeated over time.

23

"All big things come from small beginnings. The seed of every habit is a single, tiny decision. But as that decision is repeated, a habit sprouts and grows stronger."

—Unknown

Change happens in small steps. Creating habits of reflection happens by taking small steps. Taking ten minutes each day is a small step that can have a huge outcome. You can start to see patterns, recognize victories and celebrate them, and also identify mistakes or shortcomings and learn from them.

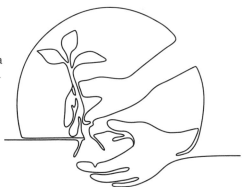

REFLECTIVE PRACTICE
Set an alarm on your phone for the end of your workday. Take ten minutes to reflect on your daily progress. Include your top wins for the day, what you learned from any missteps/mistakes/failures, what needs rethinking or change, and what you did to make a difference. Do this every day for at least a week. To make it a habit that sticks, try it for ninety days.

"The elevator to success is out of order. You'll have to use the stairs, one step at a time."

24

—Common saying

Change rarely occurs as a single event but rather as an accumulating progression of small steps. Often when people want to change something about themselves or make changes to achieve a goal, they have the notion, hope, or expectation that it can and should happen quickly, like a big aha moment. That kind of life-altering break-through can happen, but it's rare. Typically as a person starts to endeavor toward what they want, they encounter challenges or hardships, and this can cause them to lose steam. They lose motivation because change is so often hard and requires not only initiative but ongoing perseverance, grit, and heartfelt desire. Sometimes people become negative about their lack of quick progress or judge themselves and lean toward discouragement, thinking they are failing. Falling into this attitude or motivational trough is a common barrier we face when we are attempting to achieve goals or gain success. Remembering that we are taking small steps, not a quick ride in an elevator, is really the fundamental key to sustainable change. Changing atti-tudes, examining expectations, and breaking big projects into bite-size pieces are all very practical change methods, and often all three are needed in any transformational journey. A coach can be extremely helpful in assisting someone in breaking down an action plan into many small steps. Coaches also help bust the barriers people face—but not by giving solutions or advice or trying to fix the problem. Rather, by facilitating critical thinking, they help examine and reframe negative attitudes or adverse perspectives. Whether working with a coach or making a go by yourself, the path requires accepting that real change happens one step at a time, maintaining a supportive attitude, never giving up, and making many modifications along the way.

REFLECTIVE PRACTICE

Identify a change you want to make or a goal you want to achieve. Assess your true motivation to stick it out when uncomfortable difficulties arise. Write an encouraging letter to yourself now about why it's worth it. Include mention of the strengths, skills, and personal qualities you can count on in hard times. Remind yourself of a past ex-perience when you made a big change and how you got there. What were the little steps that really paid off? Tell your own story to coach yourself.

25 "Courage is only the accumulation of small steps."

—Jack Canfield

We are all beginners, each day, each step. Not knowing what's going to happen, staring into the future as if it's an abyss, can be daunting and can sometimes cause paralyzing fear. Courage is not about waiting for fear to go away—it will likely always present itself. It is about not letting the fear stop you. Sometimes all we can do is take a baby step and keep our eyes on the goal. Each tiny step matters, and they do add up. A tiny step can become a stride, and with time, one step at a time, you can do it. Overcoming fear is often about batting away the negative self-talk and fear-based thinking in our heads and seeing them for what they are . . . the voice of fear and negative thoughts, not truth! We can choose what to believe, and not all our thoughts are worth listening to!

REFLECTIVE PRACTICE
Take a moment to look back at where you were last week, last month, last year, five years ago. Those steps weren't in vain, and they do really add up. Create two signs that say, "Don't Let the Fear Stop You!" and "Never Give Up!" Post them where you will see them daily when you need encouragement to take a difficult next step.

26

"You will never change your life until you change something you do daily. The secret of your success is found in your daily routine."

—John C. Maxwell

Habits are our repeated actions. Habits can be mental patterns, emotional reactions, or behaviors and actions. Taking time to witness and examine what our habitual patterns are, we can discover entry points for opportunities for change to achieve what we really want. Use reflection to highlight habits that are not helping you achieve the outcomes you want. To change a habit often requires substituting a replacement behavior. So if you have a disempowering mental habit, identify a positive replacement thought and start to use that as often as possible. For example, I once was routinely five minutes late as a habit. I examined why, and I discovered I was often late because I distracted myself by wanting to get one more thing done. To change the habit, I had to notice the urge to do one more thing and say to myself, "No, not now." This awareness helped me make an intentional change in my habit of being late by not falling prey to my own thinking. Now I am not always perfectly on time, but I am much better. You can't change what you can't see. Look underneath an unwanted habit and see what holds it in place. Just keep at it and don't give up. Resist the expectation that you will do it perfectly. Allow yourself to learn from mistakes and missteps to get better at getting better.

REFLECTIVE PRACTICE
What is one routine or daily habit you would like to change? Examine the actual actions, thoughts, and emotions connected with that habit. Focus on which thought might need to be replaced first or consider what a replacement action, thought, or feeling might be. Try it out and experiment. Modify if necessary.

27

"There are no good habits or bad habits. There are only effective habits. . . . Does this behavior help me become the type of person I wish to be? Does this habit cast a vote for or against my desired identity?"

—James Clear

Are your current habits effective in developing yourself as a leader? Effective leaders pay attention to how people behave in their presence. Do we want to be leaders surrounded only by people who agree with us (or pretend to agree with us), even if they have different ways of thinking than we do? Leaders who value and speak to collaboration and inclusivity need to have habits of reflection to discern whether their actions are aligned with their values and what they say. Do we create a safe space for discussion, opposing perspectives, and differing voices? Making time to routinely reflect on whether our habits and actions are living expressions of who we want to be is indispensable in leading with integrity and inspiration.

REFLECTIVE PRACTICE

Do you value people with divergent thinking and opposing perspectives? Do you take note if the people around you are usually agreeing with you or if they are comfortable disagreeing or challenging your perspective? What behaviors or actions can you implement that will help you to notice and be more aware of how people interact with you? What routines or habits can you develop to strengthen your awareness and actions as a leader who walks their talk?

28

"First forget inspiration. Habit is more dependable. Habit will sustain you whether you're inspired or not."

—Octavia Butler

What habit do you want to strengthen? Do you need to revisit a decision you made about a desired action? Do you need to increase your focus on repeating the action? What is your hope or goal about this habit? How can you track and measure your success to ensure it becomes embedded as an effective habit that is part of your regular routine?

29

"Habit saved time: it's easier to do the same thing or think the same thing. Changing our minds takes attention and work."

—Margaret Wheatley

Some habits keep us stuck in place, while some habits free us up to become who we want to be. Review if your habits are opening up your opportunities or if they are fear-based and designed to protect you from experiencing risk and discomfort. Creative productive habits need to connect to your current life goals, circumstances, and lifestyle. To change a habit of mind or behavior takes effort. Habits that might have once been useful can now be constraining, inhibiting growth in areas you want. It takes desire and motivation to change. Changing habits and routine ways of thinking, feeling, and behaving is nearly always necessary for transformation and growth.

REFLECTIVE PRACTICE

Do a Habit Inventory of your personal, spiritual, and professional habits. Identify which ones are cultivating your forward growth. Which are helping you maintain and manage desired results? Which are holding you back? Which are based in fear or being used to create a false sense of safety? Maybe you don't really know why you follow certain habits anymore. Determine whether it's time for an update of your habits so you can truly become who you want to be.

https://www.redleafpress.org/dre/3-29.pdf

Change Is Choice

Freedom is born when we clarify where we have the ability, choice, and power to determine our actions without restraint. Even in the face of challenging external restrictions, we can exercise choice and make decisions without constraints from within to transform our mindset and skills, making big and small choices about how to move forward to experience freedom to change.

30

"Guilt is in the past. Worries are in the future. The only thing you can change is right here in the present."

—Edith Eger

Be aware of your feelings and thoughts and explore whether they are limiting you, inhibiting you, or trapping you in the past or future. Feelings are magnified by thoughts. If guilt has you stuck in the past, turn your attention to what you can forgive, accept, or let go of in the present moment. The present is the only place where choice exists and the only time you can control to make a change. The time is now. If you are experiencing anxiety or worry, then your focus is on the future in some way, whether it is something specific or more generally the unknown. Shift your attention to the present moment and again clarify whether you are making assumptions about the future or feeling disempowering attitudes, like catastrophizing, perfectionism, or fear of making mistakes or not doing things right. You have the power and choice to change your thinking in the present moment, and in the present moment only. Build mindful practices to help yourself stay focused on the present moment, making conscious choices about what you think at any given moment, as this impacts your emotional responses. Shift your thinking, tap into your inner wisdom, and amplify trust and faith. If there is a decision or action you can take to address your concerns, then act now.

> **REFLECTIVE PRACTICE**
> Is there a mindful practice, action, or decision you can make in the present moment that will address your perceptions or feelings of guilt or worry so you can stop focusing on the past or the future?

"Life is like a game of cards. The hand you are dealt is determinism; the way you play it is free will."

—Often attributed to Jawaharlal Nehru

The family you are born into, who you are raised by, your social identity characteristics, falling in love or having your heart broken, and getting or losing a job are all examples of the "hand you were dealt" in life's game of cards. There are many human experiences that we don't have a lot of control over or choice about. The way you play your hand is related to how you respond to the circumstances, situations, or experiences you encounter. Freedom comes from recognizing your choice—you have free will in how you respond. There may be consequences; sometimes the choice will be difficult. A lack of response is also a type of choice. Will you play it safe or take a risk? How we interpret, explain, or assign meaning to difficult situations is where our choices exist, not in the situation itself. For example, a single parent who gets fired is in an extremely challenging situation and will understandably have feelings about this experience. Yet they must choose to respond; looking for an even better job, complaining and blaming others, or choosing to sue the company are all options. Free will means choice. Having the right attitude and choosing your narrative can transform obstacles into opportunities. Discerning where and when we have choice is one of the most astonishing insights as we recognize that we are not defined by our circumstances but by how we respond to them.

REFLECTIVE PRACTICE
How much happier would you be if you focused your energy solely on what you can control? Where would you start today?

Chapter 4

PURPOSE AND MOTIVATION

To achieve what you want or to support someone else in being successful involves clarifying your purpose and cultivating the motivation to change, overcoming obstacles, and perseverance. Reaching toward what we want—rather than avoiding or trying to change what we don't want—is always more effective and empowering. Explore how to positively inspire yourself and how to facilitate others to be willing to change, and you will pave the way for learning and sustained behavioral change.

Finding and Following Your Purpose

For some, purpose feels like a calling, a fulfilment of a soul desire, or a reason for being, while for others it might be a pragmatic responsibility that has personal or social significance and meaning. Clarifying your purpose is a launchpad for understanding, amplifying, and nurturing the engine of motivation to get where you want to go.

"Shifts in how we perceive the world occur because what we experience changes the questions we ask."

—David Rock and Linda J. Page

Our willingness to dream big and act boldly is inspired by what we perceive is possible. When we are moved beyond ourselves and our daily limitations, anything is possible. To tap into possibility, we must alter, stretch, and courageously dismantle limitations within our own minds and free ourselves from the shackles of fear. What motivates each person to do that is unique. Having a sense of purpose or a willingness to dream and want more for yourself and others can propel us forward. Being open to wonder and a sense of childlike awe encourages inquiry and raises questions. Taking a risk to ask big questions without necessarily having any answers is essential. Sometimes it's having the courage to ask a small, persistent question that has been lingering in the shadows. Cultivate a reflective practice of intentionally asking more and different kinds of questions of yourself and others. Explore how this can shift perceptions and how shifting your perceptions changes the nature of your questions.

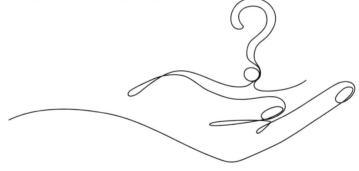

REFLECTIVE PRACTICE
Keep a journal or list of questions—without answering them. Just cultivate the art of questioning. Each day or each week, write questions that come up for you. As you collect your questions, start to notice whether there is a pattern. If you shift your vantage point or perspective, how do the questions change? You can choose specific questions to explore and write more about at another time. But begin the practice of cultivating a garden of questions.

2

"Understanding purpose is one thing, but recognizing the importance of having purpose is another. Everybody has a unique purpose in their life, whether it be to help others, provide for family, or be free."

—Attributed to Ben Gothard

Believing every person has a purpose, including yourself, is like discovering your own hero(ine)'s journey. Having clarity surrounding your purpose directs your choices and acts as a compass to lead your way toward what you want. Just having the desire to feel, know, discover, and clarify your purpose does the same thing, helping you focus your inquiry, even if it hasn't distinctly come into view yet.

REFLECTIVE PRACTICE
Do you believe every person has a unique purpose? Have you had an experience of feeling called or pulled toward a vision, an aspiration, or a desire? Was there something that supported you to experience this feeling in the past? Reflect on whether supportive people, reflective practices, or environmental influences helped nurture this feeling. Do you have desire to discover or continue unfolding this for yourself, or to explore any current inklings of purpose? Is there anything blocking you?

3

"I believe we're all put on this planet for a purpose, and we all have a different purpose."

—Ellen DeGeneres

Each individual's path is completely different, and the pathway to discovering one's purpose is also unlike any other's path. Some feel a calling or purpose to follow quite young, and this directs many of their choices and how they pursue the fulfillment of their purpose. Others might bloom in this way later in life as the journey of trial and error helps them narrow their focus over many years. The timing of discovery of one's purpose is not as important as the belief that you have a purpose and feel the desire to pursue it.

REFLECTIVE PRACTICE
Do you have a sense or understanding of your purpose? Could you name or describe the direction it pulls you? Do you know what your purpose is not, such as something you pursued at some point and discarded? Sometimes talking about or trying to describe your purpose might be more of a feeling than a specific thing. Take time to wonder about your purpose and consider whether your actions are supporting the unfolding of your purpose.

"When you find your WHY, you don't hit snooze no more! You find a way to make it happen!"

—Widely attributed to Eric Thomas

When you tap into your purpose, your calling, your internal WHY, it generates a magnetic pull for fulfillment. Trusting this pull, even if you can't name it, will lead you wisely, even if not perfectly. Sometimes it's like playing the hot-and-cold game: as you move in one direction, the pull decreases or intensifies, telling you which direction to follow. For some it might be clear. I knew I wanted to teach young children at the age of ten. My choices after high school led me in that direction but by an unconventional path. After finally fulfilling my goal and becoming an early childhood educator, my career path and life experiences caused my purpose to morph and refine, growing with me as I matured. I have been very blessed in that I had a strong inner compass to follow, and that I trusted in it, but each juncture in my life required more trust and courage so I could allow my sense of purpose to expand, deepen, and grow. And even as I pursued some directions that ultimately weren't very fulfilling, the pull within remained strong, informing my choices and course corrections when needed. My sense of purpose isn't a stagnant "I've arrived" experience—it seems to stretch with me as I grow. I am still not giving up, and this purposeful calling is helping me turn yet another life corner at the age of nearly seventy. Trust and discovery have been essential on my purpose journey.

REFLECTIVE PRACTICE
How would you tell the story of the pathway your purpose has led you on? What have been important elements in clarifying or refining your journey? If you were able to give your younger self guidance about following your purpose, what would you say? How might this be important for you to hear today?

5

"The meaning of life is to find your gift. The work of life is to develop it. The purpose of life is to give it away."

—David Viscott

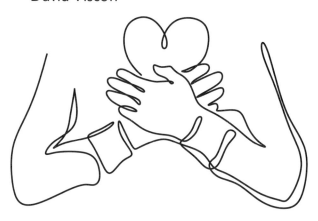

For some of us, finding our gift doesn't come easy. It can take living through trials and errors, experimenting until you realize your sweet spot. It might be a talent, a skill, something you love doing, or even a particular way of looking at things. Your gift is an important component of your purpose, like a doorway to your calling, connected to the meaning of your life, your sense of purpose, and what you find fulfilling. Some recognize and resonate with their gift and passion at an early age and hopefully trust it, follow it, and feed it. Sometimes your gift finds you and pulls you, asking you to trust. It may or may not have anything to do with your work or vocation; that is not the measure or validation of your gift. It takes courage to trust this conviction and to follow it, to overcome self-doubt and believe you have a gift. Once we acknowledge, hone, and cultivate our gift, the only true fulfillment in life comes from sharing it, giving it away.

REFLECTIVE PRACTICE

Do you know what your gift is or have any inkling of what it might be? How can you describe it with words? How would you represent it with color, shape, and imagery? Where do you feel it in your body?

6

"Trust yourself. Create the kind of self that you'll be happy to live with all your life. Make the most of yourself by fanning the tiny, inner sparks of possibility into flames of achievement."

—Attributed to Golda Meir

Trusting yourself can be easier to say than to do. You will likely feel lost and be ungrounded until self-trust is a point of reflective focus. Then you will know how to listen to your inner voice to find your "True North" to guide you to your heart's desire. We cultivate self-trust; we nurture it like a garden. It's something we invest in routinely so that when challenges and doubts show up we don't stray off course, because we have a well-worn path to find our way home to trust. Trusting yourself can't happen in the field of fear. If you are afraid of making mistakes or doing

things wrong, it will override your conviction that you have the capacity to learn from mistakes. The courage to take risks and trust yourself is connected to having faith in that which is bigger than yourself. Self-trust is not so much about believing anything your ego and self-serving mind might be saying, but rather about being able to discern the difference between mind chatter and a trustworthy inner or higher guiding voice. Purposeful self-reflection will nourish and cultivate the garden of self-trust, and the daily routine of reflective habits is the tool to weed and water this garden.

REFLECTIVE PRACTICE

In what ways do you trust yourself? How do you nurture and invest in self-trust? In what ways do you not trust yourself? What blocks you from trusting yourself?

"Surround yourself with people who believe in you more than you do in yourself."

—Attributed to Gaby Natale

Who are the people who believe in you more than you do? Have you spent enough time around them lately? Are there people you spend time with who don't believe in you? Why are you spending time with them, and how can you make different choices or modify that? What self-care practices might you have to put in place to empower yourself, so you seek the company of people who empower you?

"Doubt kills more dreams than failure ever will."

—Attributed to Gaby Natale

It takes strength and courage to dream. Pursuing your purpose and fulfilling big dreams is often intertwined with doubt, and it requires courage to not back down. Courage is being able to act even in the face of fear. Don't let fear stop you. Doubt is the opposite of trust—it is mistrust and not believing in yourself. Fear feeds on itself and causes doubt to grow. Mistakes are actually doorways for opportunity, but it takes trust to take action and open those doors. It takes a mindset that failure isn't dangerous or scary. Doubt will drain the life-force out of you and stop you from taking even small steps, much less those needed to follow your purpose. You won't even get to make a misstep. If you nurture your trust and belief in yourself and you don't feed your doubt, your doubt will shrink.

> **REFLECTIVE PRACTICE**
> What does nurturing your trust and belief in yourself look and feel like? Explore how to do this with an open mind. Mistakes are part of the journey of discovery and growing. Acknowledge your mistakes and failures by stating what they are and what you learned from them. Let these learnings shrink your fear and doubt to pave a pathway to trust.

Motivating Self

Becoming self-aware of your sense of purpose and knowing what motivates you to take action—to achieve what you want or become who you want to be—is essential to growth, perseverance, and resilience in the face of challenges. Align your pathway of choice with your beliefs and what you find intrinsically motivating, rather than designing an "ought to," compliance-oriented course of action, which rarely results in favorable outcomes.

9

"People often say that motivation doesn't last. Well, neither does bathing—that's why we recommend it daily."

—Attributed to Zig Ziglar

Looking at motivation as a daily or regular practice rather than a one-time event creates sustainable change and growth. It's easy to feel motivated when things are going easily and smoothly. It's harder to muster motivation when facing challenges and long-term difficulties that don't have easy answers. It's important to cultivate and sustain our motivation regularly, not just in times of need. People are most motivated by what matters to us, focusing on what we really want and what deeply touches our heart's desire. Having daily and regular practices that touch those deeper places of desire and longing keeps our course clear for our journey, rain or shine.

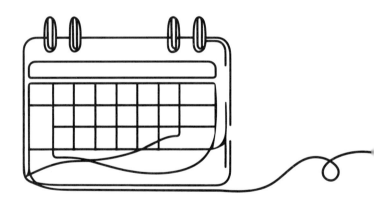

REFLECTIVE PRACTICE
Create a daily practice to cultivate and nurture your motivation. Journal about or draw a picture of what matters most to you and why it motivates you. Review your words or drawing before going to sleep every night. Each morning, write at least one thing you are grateful for.

10 "Optimism means that you remain motivated to seek a solution to whatever problems arise. Optimism does not mean being blind to the actual reality of a situation. It means maintaining a positive spirit to continue to seek a solution to any given problem. And it means recognizing that any given situation has many different aspects— positive as well as problematic."

—Dalai Lama [Tenzin Gyatso]

Being optimistic does not mean being blindly positive, wearing rose-colored glasses. Optimism is a mindset you develop; it doesn't happen to you. Optimism is a choice to frame your attitude with a lens of possibility. Having hope and an optimistic attitude in the face of challenges and obstacles creates its own motivation. It is the antidote to the discouragement that leads to giving up.

REFLECTIVE PRACTICE
Gratitude is an excellent way to lean into optimism. Write at least one thing you are grateful for every morning. To accelerate your practice, think of a problem or challenge you faced each day, and at the end of the day write about your gratitude for the experience and what you are learning.

11

"Nobody can impose your beliefs on you. It's always you who in the last instance can permit a belief to be true for you or not."

—Attributed to Marc Reklau

Becoming aware of what we believe takes intentional focus. We inherit values and beliefs from our families and our culture and adopt attitudes or perspectives from peers or our workplace. We must intentionally do an internal scan of the beliefs we are operating from. Are they aligned with your current life and what you want? Some old beliefs are deeply embedded and are the source of disempowering perspectives or undermining self-talk that does not support us. Yet we are responsible for what beliefs we let go of and which ones we choose to keep. No thought or belief can exist in you unless you permit it to. It's your responsibility to do a little housekeeping surrounding your internal beliefs to stay current with yourself and aim for what you want. The question is, are you motivated to honestly look within and examine whether your beliefs are aligned with your desires, hopes, and dreams or your sense of purpose? It will be easier and more comfortable to not look too closely.

A FEW FOREVER QUESTIONS

Consider what it would cost you or what benefits you might gain if you made an honest assessment of your beliefs. If you are motivated to take a look, here is a good place to start:

- **What age were you when you first became aware that you did not believe or no longer shared certain values and beliefs of your family of origin?**

- **Did you adopt new beliefs out of rebellion, or were they aimed at what you really wanted?**

- **Are there any beliefs you have outgrown or matured beyond? Do you recognize any that are stopping you from your goals, hopes, and visions?**

- **What alternative beliefs or values would be more supportive and aligned with your current self?**

12

"Practice doesn't just make perfect: it gives you proof. You must be fearless enough to do the work every day, and you must do it without fail, and you must do it with a clear and excited heart. You must keep showing up. You must trust that if you drive the car one mile every day, eventually you will get to California."

—Ash Ambirge

It might not feel or look glamorous or glorious, but you can accomplish whatever you want by putting one foot in front of the other, over and over again. Practice is such an underrated and unappreciated key to success. But it certainly does the job! It's important that when you invest your time in practice, repetition, and habit-making, you are doing something you really care about and want, and you "do it with a clear and excited heart." It's motivation and desire that will keep your practice engine going until you get where you want to go. Think of this as a formula: motivation + repeated practice = mastery.

REFLECTIVE PRACTICE
What is your heart's deepest desire? What do you really want and why? Speak it and bring it to life. Share your desire and why you want it with someone you trust. Are you taking action to get there, practicing the actions, and making them a lifestyle habit? List two actions you will practice repeatedly, and start today.

Motivating Others

Learning to coach and lead others to become who they want to be or to accomplish desired outcomes requires an empowering mindset. You need facilitation skills that motivate with positive incentives that are intrinsically aligned with the person you are coaching, not just what you think they need.

13

"Before you are a leader, success is all about growing yourself. When you become a leader, success is all about growing others."

—Jack Welch

In this current world with so much change and social and cultural challenges, leaders need to shift their focus from trying to change the world to investing in and honoring people and evoking their best human qualities—for that is what will make the biggest difference in true changes and improvements. Leaders must invest in developing their own personal best human qualities through reflective practices and self-awareness, demonstrating the courage to be vulnerable while sharing the learning they've gained from their own mistakes and missteps. Showing these qualities is how we inspire others to work hard and take risks, to awaken their passion to persevere in the face of inevitable challenges, and to cultivate efficacy—knowing that what they do matters and has meaning. Sharing our authentic journey openly and being seen walking our talk makes a difference and is what really motivates others to take those same risks to act with courage.

> **REFLECTIVE PRACTICE**
> How can you recognize and routinely express how much you value the contributions of each person you work with? Positive acknowledgment about specific qualities, interactions, or ideas helps people know what to repeat and develop. What routines or practices can you instill that cultivate a workplace culture that evokes and acknowledges the best human qualities of each person?

14

"I wish I could show you when you are lonely or in darkness the astonishing light of your own being."

—Hafiz

To stay connected to your inner light, build routines and practices that help you see, believe, and shine brightly. Spend time with people who see your light and reflect it back to you. How can you strengthen your own practices and habits to stay connected to your inner light? Cultivate a habit of looking for and seeing the light in the people around you. How can you refine your attention and focus on finding and acknowledging the inner light shining in those around you—while also becoming one of those people whom others benefit from being around?

"Motivation comes from working on things we care about. It also comes from working with people we care about."

15

—Sheryl Sandberg

As leaders and coaches, how we motivate and help people to create intentional professional practices is like cultivating and investing in a garden we care deeply about. We must be enthusiastic in order to care about and invest in the people we work with, as if they are our beloved garden. We must prepare, plant, water, weed, and harvest. Cocreating a trusting, respectful relationship represents the soil preparation essential to future outcomes for the people you serve and the people they serve. Adopting an attitude of curiosity, nurturing growth, honing specific practices, and facilitating their desire and motivation to change are part of planting the seeds. Each person's professional practice is an individual seed to grow. As with gardening, one cannot force a plant to grow any faster than its own development process allows. Respecting an individual's pacing is both respectful and culturally responsive. A workplace culture lacking diversity and equity, with unconscious pressuring demands or unnecessary regulations, can create obstacles and unnecessary barriers to steady growth and successful achievements. So consistently weeding unnecessary workplace barriers and nurturing and fertilizing individuals to bust personal barriers are necessary habits we cultivate to support people to succeed collectively and individually. The tools of reflection, including watering the soil with encouragement, tending the soil of relationship, and weeding out ineffective workplace and individual behaviors and negative thinking through transformational coaching and leadership are foundational for the cultivation process. Cultivating embraces action research and happens over time, ensuring that lasting, sticky change will grow from the efforts devoted to the cultivation process.*

REFLECTIVE PRACTICE
Are you tending to your garden of empowerment by investing your time and attention with care? How are you addressing workplace barriers and challenges? How do you get familiar with the goals and desires of the people you support, as well as the barriers and obstacles facing them, in order to facilitate and cultivate their individual reflective learning process and orchestrate collective reflection about workplace barriers?

* Excerpts modified from Constant Hine and Robin Levy, "Transformational Coaching: Moving Beyond Goals and Action Plans to Foster Continuous Quality Improvement," *Exchange* (November/December 2019).

16

"As we look ahead into the next century, leaders will be those who empower others."

—Attributed to Bill Gates

A key component of the transformational coaching approach is to explore and shift a person's motivational incentive from an external expectation for compliance to an internal desire for professional growth and change. By empowering the learner, transformational coaching emphasizes how the coachee can increase reflection skills, learn through trial and error, and experiment and refine their practices. Additionally, transformational coaching goes deeper than traditional transactional coaching by emphasizing and examining the underlying values and beliefs that hold both fruitful and ineffective practices and stagnant results in place. This unraveling empowers people to learn how to learn about themselves and to continue gaining self-awareness, which is the heart of transferring power to each learner. This cultivates intrinsic motivation and sets a foundation and mindset for a workplace culture of continuous quality improvement. This helps shift the mindset of both coach and coachee from one of compliance to one of continual change and improvement—embracing an attitude of lifelong learning.*

REFLECTIVE PRACTICE
How are you currently empowering others to learn how to learn, to change and grow, and to embed critical reflective practices into their professional habits? Is it working? Are there steps you want to take to deepen your empowerment skills and practices?

* Excerpts modified from Constant Hine and Robin Levy, "Transformational Coaching: Moving Beyond Goals and Action Plans to Foster Continuous Quality Improvement," *Exchange* (November/December 2019).

"Leadership is practiced not so much in words as in attitude and in actions."

17

—Widely attributed to Harold S. Geneen

Leaders inspire followers by demonstrating their values in action through their demeanor and behaviors. Leaders who talk a good game but don't feel authentic in their manner or actions lose credibility. Motivational leaders cultivate a workplace where values, encouragement, and attitudes about failure and success are nurtured through relationship and policies. Authenticity speaks louder than words.

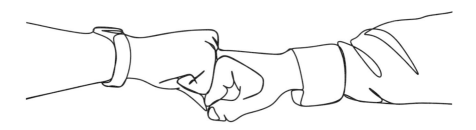

REFLECTIVE PRACTICE
What are your most foundational values? Do you demonstrate and communicate those values through your actions and your demeanor? Would the people you engage with be able to articulate what's important to you and your values if they were interviewed?

18

"Become the kind of leader that people would follow voluntarily, even if you had no title or position."

—Widely attributed to Brian Tracy

Think back to your early school years, perhaps playing a team sport, singing in a choir, or engaging in another group activity. Did the people you followed then have qualities that you respect and admire still to this day? Did you learn something about leadership through mistakes in your earlier life that is important to remember today? As you have become an adult, who are the people, in any circles of your life, you willingly follow and why? What behaviors and characteristics do leaders you admire display that inspire and motivate you? What made you want to voluntarily follow them?

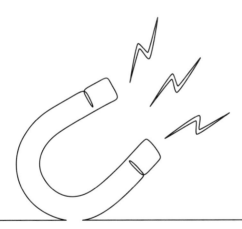

REFLECTIVE PRACTICE
List the qualities, attitudes, and behaviors of leaders you voluntarily follow and admire.

19

> "Generally, people are internally motivated when they believe in what they're doing. We are naturally creative when we want to contribute."

—Margaret Wheatley

Motivating other people is not really something we do to them. It's more about asking what matters to them and supporting them as they fan their own internal fire, helping them stay focused on the difference they are making. Asking people why they work in their industry or why they picked their career track can reveal what matters to them. It's an excellent job interview question and a great conversation to have in a first coaching meeting. When they lose steam, as we all do occasionally, you can remind them of their own story as told to you. Perhaps they are at a juncture in their work where they need a change or need to find new ways to creatively contribute. Support them in exploring this and clarifying what's really in their hearts, even if it's not a job description in your workplace. Help them reflect so they can deepen their own experience of believing in what they do, what they are proud of accomplishing, and what they hope for themselves.

REFLECTIVE PRACTICE
What are you personally proud of in your work? How do you experience meaning and feel you are contributing? Ask three other people these same questions this week.

Excuses and Not Giving Up

There are a lot of obstacles in the way of getting where we want to go. Become mindful of the mental and emotional excuses that get in your way. To help you get past your excuses, create empowering habits to keep yourself going rather than giving up.

"Ninety-nine percent of the failures come from people who have the habit of making excuses."

—Widely attributed to George Washington Carver

If you are honest with yourself about what you can do better, you can free yourself of the blame and denial that holds you back. Excuses can slip in through many cracks—blame, denial, justifications, negativity, discouragement, resignation, futility. What do your excuses sound like? In what areas of your life do you make excuses, under what circumstances? It takes effort rather than excuses to accomplish what you want. It's easy to make excuses when you are not clear about what you want or when you lack internal motivation. If you find yourself making excuses to not do something or to continue doing something that you want to change, clarify your motivation and make sure it's aimed at something you really want.

REFLECTIVE PRACTICE
What are you making excuses about? Why? What do you really want? Clarify a meaningful "so what" motivation for making the change you are facing. Be specific about what a small, simple next action could be to start the ball rolling.

21

"Leadership is about making others better as a result of your presence and making sure that impact lasts in your absence."

—Harvard Business School

As servant-leaders, we focus first on the well-being of the people we support and serve. From this focus on people, organizational or project success will flourish, as empowered people are more successful. People matter more than tasks. Is your attention on your people more than tasks? How can you personally invest in the people around you so that they thrive when you are not present and so that your investment actually multiplies and spreads to others?

22

"Every vice has its excuse ready."

—Publius Syrus

Excuses often don't sound like excuses in my head; they sound so rational! In the areas where my vices or bad habits are especially strong, my excuses are well-worn, as I have used them many times. They have nearly become second nature. I actually don't register them as excuses. It has taken a lot to get very honest with myself about what I do and don't do and why. For example, I have self-care goals and habits I want to develop. But too frequently, I have found myself using excuses: I was too tired, or something else was more important, or I just didn't have the time. I had to get very honest with myself. First, I had to investigate what was motivating my goals and consider whether I really wanted to perform those actions of self-care. I had to give myself permission to not pursue those goals. Doing that revealed my deeper desire, as I understood better why those goals were indeed important to me. Then I had to find a deeper, more honest level of commitment so my usual excuses wouldn't sound as reasonable anymore. I had to clearly identify my favorite excuses so I would be aware when they showed up and prepare myself to address them and take action anyway. I started to take action even if I didn't feel like it. I'm not perfect, but I am well along my journey of practicing habits like walking at least three times a week, doing yoga twice a week, meditating daily, and getting at least seven hours of sleep daily. And when I find my habits are falling off, I reexamine my motivation. Perhaps I need to refine the accuracy of my actions due to a change in circumstances, such as a health issue or traveling. Staying current with myself, realigning with my motivations and just starting again, or refining my habits are all important acts in self-care. It's important to avoid any self-judgment, from which typically just slows me down getting back to practicing the habits I want.

REFLECTIVE PRACTICE
What are the most common excuses you use to not take action toward something you want to do?

23

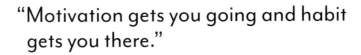

"Motivation gets you going and habit gets you there."

—Widely attributed to Zig Ziglar

Accomplishing something starts as either an idea or a heartfelt desire. If this small light at the beginning is not nurtured and cultivated, it can fade. Putting in effort, reflecting with intention, and taking action, no matter how small a step, is what will grow that light. It's not uncommon for us to bump into big barriers or small interferences in our attempts to create habits to successfully manifest our desired outcomes. Making excuses or justifying our behaviors as we give up or get distracted are common internal hurdles. It takes repeated efforts to give life to our desires—efforts that turn into mindful, consistent habits we can modify to match growing or waning motivation, to adjust our pacing, and to refine our choice of behaviors.

REFLECTIVE PRACTICE

Is there something you have been wanting to do or accomplish that you need to give more attentive thought to? How can you cultivate your desire to take the beginning steps? If you have already started taking action, what habits need refining or strengthening to fan the flames of your desire? What excuses do you need to mindfully avoid and tackle?

24

"Be yourself; everyone else is already taken."

—Commonly attributed to Oscar Wilde

Many of us suffer from imposter syndrome, a collection of feelings of inadequacy that persists despite evident success, as well as chronic self-doubt and a sense of being a fraud. Having big dreams, wanting to take bold action, to speak up, to be the leader you know you are—these are common situations that can make us doubt ourselves, pull back, and not take action. Self-doubt often creates an army of excuses for why we shouldn't pursue what we want. Discouragement and resignation make it feel reasonable to back off. Having expectations in your mind about how you should or shouldn't be feeds this self-doubt and discouragement and causes much suffering. Comparing yourself to others does the same thing. Self-acceptance for all of who you are, imperfections and talents together, takes self-honesty and self-compassion. In my own journey, it has taken trusting myself and my inner strength to be able to see what doesn't work without collapsing into self-judgment. I have to trust in myself to be able to learn, adapt, and change as needed. I try to stay focused on doing my best with what I have in the moment, without believing I need to be perfect. Cultivating my trust in my ability to repeatedly turn within to find insight, light, and guidance is important. And it does take repetition! I am finding deeper self-compassion and self-acceptance for who I am, as I am. It's not about doing everything right; it's about trusting myself. I am discovering more inner peace in being who I am, as well as freedom from the burdens of disempowering thoughts. The freedom doesn't come from not having the thoughts at all, but rather from catching them when they show up. That's when I turn to the tools I have and trust that I know how to turn away, not listen, and go within to find grace and a truer perspective.

REFLECTIVE PRACTICE
What are your typical patterns of self-doubt? What beliefs, thoughts, or excuses thwart you? What triggers these thoughts? Do you have a strategy or an inner connection or guiding voice that you can turn to in order to discern what's true and what's false? How might you strengthen this inner voice for yourself?

25

"I can accept failure, everyone fails at something. But I cannot accept not trying."

—Attributed to Michael Jordan

The fear of failure can be so paralyzing that it undermines people's willingness to try or to take risky next steps. It takes an awareness of what you want, deep motivation to take a risk and possibly face failure, and the guidance and support of a mentor, coach, or leader to keep going. Normalizing the challenges of the change process is one way to support people who are having difficulty taking risks or who feel afraid of failing. People need to be reminded that change is a process, not a destination, and change takes time and practice. Practice inherently means making mistakes, because practice is not doing it perfectly every time. Many people need reinforcement so they can tolerate the discomfort that naturally accompanies change and growth—like how having physical growing pains can be uncomfortable. But discomfort does not mean anything is wrong. Help people reevaluate their long-held beliefs, assumptions, and expectations and shift their perspective to see challenges and mistakes as a normal part of learning, growing, and changing. Implementing change-management strategies is a key part of the coach and leader's role as an agent of change.

REFLECTIVE PRACTICE
How can you strengthen or shift your own perspective to embrace change as a process and not become overly focused on outcomes for yourself? Are there facilitation skills you want to hone to help people overcome the fear of making mistakes or help them take a risk and try something new? How can you encourage others to keep trying when they want to give up?

26

"Run when you can, walk if you have to, crawl if you must; just never give up."

—Dean Karnazes

Success in achieving our goals is not so much about intelligence or even talent but about persistence and continuous effort. Successful people are action-oriented and they keep trying. Sometimes you need to let go, but don't make the mistake of giving up too soon. Some of the most successful people faced repeated obstacles and setbacks but persevered. Walt Disney's first animation company went bankrupt and he was turned down for financing Disneyland 302 times. J. K. Rowling received public assistance before she found her success with *Harry Potter*, but only after twelve publishers turned down her manuscript. Pacing your journey makes a big difference in gaining success. Due to a variety of factors, you may need to slow down, alter your speed, or modify your approach—but keep moving forward. Let go of expectations surrounding how you think you "should" do something. Stay flexible, explore your options, and stay connected to your desire and motivation. It happens only one step at a time, but it's all progress.

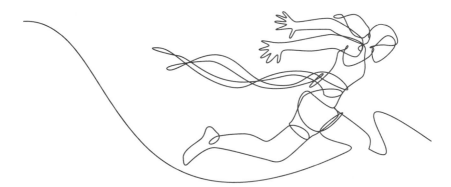

REFLECTIVE PRACTICE
What is something you have achieved by not giving up? What did you learn from this experience? Right now, are you facing something you are feeling discouraged about? Remembering past times you succeeded because you did not give up, what advice can you give yourself in this situation?

Focusing on What You Want

Aiming forward, driven by passion and letting ourselves be pulled toward something we want, is much more inspiring and motivating than just setting compliance goals or trying to fix or avoid an unwanted habit or perspective. Develop reflective practices to keep your motivation compass aimed at what you want—your True North.

27

"In my experience, there is only one motivation, and that is desire. No reasons or principle contain it or stand against it."

—Jane Smiley

The influence of desire should not be underestimated; it can override fear, not knowing how to do something, repeated challenges and barriers, resistance, and laziness. Turn within to tap into your desire and find the courage to feel and express your passion for whatever it is you truly want. If you are not experiencing a satisfying life, reflect on what you want and build your desire. Desire fuels motivation. Desire is everything! You do not need to understand your desire with your mind. Trust your desire. Your heart and actions will follow.

REFLECTIVE PRACTICE
Take a walk and focus on what you want. Use every step to intentionally build and feel your desire. If you encounter inner voices or fears, use this walk to increase your desire to have a breakthrough and let go of anything stopping you. Walk yourself into the depth of your own desire.

28

"First forget inspiration.
Habit is more dependable.
Habit will sustain you
whether you're inspired
or not."

—Sharon Salzberg

What insights and ahas are you having about the power of reflection? Why is it important to you to control where you focus your attention and to filter the thoughts you choose to listen to?

29

"Don't ask yourself what the world needs. Ask yourself what makes you come alive, and go, do that, because what the world needs is people who have come alive."

—Dr. Howard Thurman

Desire and passion are the source of your life-force. To come alive is not a mental endeavor; we can get quite trapped in our minds. Coming alive is like sparking a flame that generates from your heart and soul's longing. It's beyond words and thoughts. It can be felt or tapped into during a moment of quiet, while you are doing something you love, while praying, or even while daydreaming. Focusing on what makes you feel alive can clarify what really matters to you.

REFLECTIVE PRACTICE

Pick a song that inspires you and makes you come alive—maybe even one that makes you want to dance wildly. Use the song to set your inner compass and listen with your heart, reminding you of who you truly are and who you want to become (even if you don't know how right now). Perhaps even make an inspirational playlist. For the next week, play that song or playlist every morning to set your attitude tone and ignite your desire for the day.

Some songs that inspire me include the following: "Joy" by King & Country; "This Is Me" by Kesha; "Soul On Fire" by Third Day; "What Do You Love" by Seeb featuring Jacob Banks; "Freedom"—Pharrell Williams; "Overcomer" by Mandisa; "Just Say Yes" by Snow Patrol.

30

"Simply put, the Law of Attraction says that you will attract into your life whatever you focus on. Whatever you give your energy and attention to will come back to you. So, if you stay focused on the good and positive things in your life, you will automatically attract more good and positive things into your life. If you are focused upon lack and negativity, then that is what will be attracted into your life. . . . The Law of Attraction never stops working."

—Jack Canfield

The Law of Attraction is working in your life at this very moment. With every thought, you are creating your future, consciously or unconsciously. If you want to create a fulfilling and satisfying life, it's important to understand this fundamental key and your role in it. By intentionally choosing to respond differently to situations every day, you can consciously create a better life. It's not about the circumstances. It's about having a perspective that how you think and what you think about is what makes the difference. You can choose to think differently and more positively so you stay focused on what you want. Focusing on what you want—what's connected with your meaningful purpose—is foundational to staying motivated. By intentionally managing your thoughts and feelings, you can choose how you experience your life. You can choose to focus and think about what you want, aim your actions toward it, and experience more of the things that empower you and make you feel good. You receive what you put out there. Be intentional and choose!

REFLECTIVE PRACTICE
Be clear about what you want to experience so that when you're in doubt or facing challenges, you can stay focused in that direction, choosing a positive perspective and thoughts that will attract what you want closer to you. Become an observer of yourself, an eyewitness who sees how you think and respond to your world. Watch for any negative or disempowering thoughts and choose in the moment to reframe them as quickly as possible.

Chapter 5

HOPES AND DREAMS INTO GOALS

Nurturing significant hopes and dreams is crucial so that we create purposeful goals and achieve desired outcomes. Goals guide our focus, telling us what to pay attention to, so we get where we are going. Goals and plans guide us in the choices we make at each step along the way.

Hopes and Dreams

Embracing vulnerability to dream big without being certain of outcomes requires encouragement from yourself and from others. For some, it takes courage to become aware of one's hopes and dreams and to nurture them; for others, being concrete and specific are key.

"The significance of a man is not in what he attains, but rather in what he longs to attain."

—Commonly attributed to Khalil Gibran

It is important to have goals, whether we reach all of them or not. The longing to want more, to reach beyond our current situation or state of being, pulls us forward. Ask yourself, "Who do I want to be?" The desire to learn, grow, and become more is the engine of transformation, the motivation to tolerate the discomfort of change, to face fears, and to have the courage to take the steps to become that new person. The real transformation is in the journey of becoming.

REFLECTIVE PRACTICE
Make a list of what you want to attain, including qualities you want to demonstrate and things you really want to do. Make this list without worrying about how you might achieve any of it. Don't let your rational mind get in the way or edit anything from your list. Allow yourself to feel your longing and your passion for these things. Review your list and star the items that bring up very strong feelings of desire and appeal. Allow yourself to just observe and acknowledge these things you long to attain. Trust and let your longing lead you.

2

"Every great dream begins with a dreamer. Always remember, you have within you the strength, the patience, and the passion to reach for the stars to change the world."

—Anonymous

It takes courage to dream, to be a dreamer. When you believe in yourself, miracles can happen. Your passion will always keep you moving forward. Your strength to endure in the face of fear and doubt is like a life raft. Trust and patience will come from being connected to that which is greater than you, and to your inner guiding compass. Remember who you are and what you want.

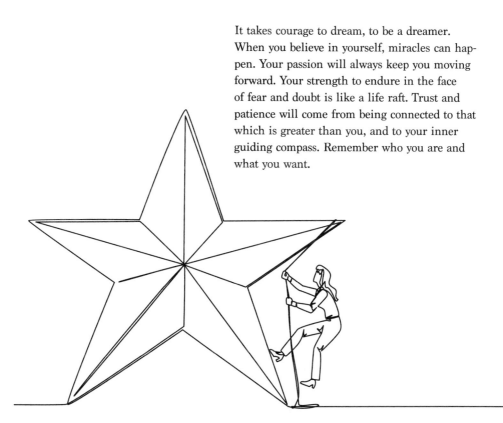

REFLECTIVE PRACTICE
What advice would you give your sixteen-year-old self about dreams, careers, and what's important?

3

"Successful people never forget what they love to do and are passionate about it. They quickly learn to follow their own path and to make the right choices, no matter how crazy or unpopular they might appear to others."

—Nigel Cumberland

Remembering what you love to do is one of the first steps to crafting meaningful goals. Many of us have set aside what we love to do for many reasons, the most common being fear, which has many faces. Fear may manifest as thinking that we can't make a living doing what we love, so therefore we can't pursue it; lacking confidence and worrying that we might fail; feeling resigned that our goal is not realistic or possible; feeling foolish or worrying about what others might say or think; or fearing that it will be too uncomfortable to change. All these voices of fear are probably familiar to you and at one time or another have stopped you. It takes courage to hold on to dreams and passions and to not let the fear stop you. There will always be reasons not to do something. Often they are excuses born from the voice of fear and justified by the mind as "being realistic." It takes courage to be honest with yourself. Think about your current or past dream(s) and recall if you have any long-forgotten goals or desires.

REFLECTIVE PRACTICE
What is your dream? What do you really want to achieve? What dreams have you set aside due to fear, resignation, lack of confidence, or other fears? Use a combination of words, pictures, or doodles to recall your dreams. First create space to clarify what you love to do or want to do.

Recognize where you are now, and where you want to be, then clarify the gap between them and explore how to close the gap. Observe if you start feeling fearful and or if your attitude becomes negative. Watch for any patterns in your reasons or excuses. This can clarify what barriers are stopping you. You can make choices about which voices you will feed and which you might want to starve to create space for your dreams and goals.

4

"If something you're engaged in doesn't bring you joy, remember that where you are now is the path that you chose in the past. Based on that understanding, ask yourself what you want to do next. If you choose to let something go, do it with gratitude. If you choose to continue, do it with conviction. Whatever your decision, if it is made deliberately and with confidence, it will surely contribute to a joyful life."

—Marie Kondo and Scott Sonenshein

Focusing on what brings joy is not some self-indulgent consideration—it's the heart of designing the direction toward a life worth living. What makes your life worth living may or may not be your work, but ensuring joy is part of your life will inspire you to move forward, to endure during challenging times, and to find meaning. Investing in a fulfilling life is not something you want to hope happens; it is something to mindfully focus on, carefully design for, and intentionally choose actions to get you there. Use joy as a guiding influence. Making deliberate choices increases your satisfaction, instills a sense of freedom, fuels joy, and helps you attain victory.

REFLECTIVE PRACTICE
Visualize how you can cultivate and nurture the joy that can motivate you to follow your dreams. In the next weeks, investigate your passion. Take note of what winds you up and energizes you—what lights you up? Write your observations down, journal about them, and make a list of questions the experiences create for you. Don't worry about having to answer any of the questions; just use the questions to cultivate your wondering about joy and purpose.

5

"If you are working on something that you really care about, you don't have to be pushed. The vision pulls you."

—Widely attributed to Steve Jobs

Following what you care about, where your passion and gift lead you, brings you the motivation and inspiration to trust your vision and heartfelt inspiration. Letting go of the reins and trusting the flow might require shifting out of your mind and trusting your heart or your gut. Often we need to give ourselves permission to follow our desires and to be led by that visionary pull.

REFLECTIVE PRACTICE

Is there something you really care about and want to pursue that you need to give yourself permission to follow? Do you have an inner pull or dream you want to pay more attention to, or do you need to nurture more trust to better clarify what your dream is? Giving yourself permission might mean listening with attention to an inner voice or pull without dismissing, criticizing, or judging what you hear. What will help you to further explore, listen to, and trust this vision or pull? Notice and observe what is blocking your trust.

Who Do You Want to Be?

Some goals are external, measurable, and quantitative. Some goals are qualitative, more about fostering personal qualities, attitudes, and behaviors that align our goals and actions with our values and hopes.

6

"Be who you are and say what you feel, because those who mind don't matter and those who matter don't mind."

—Anonymous

It might sound simple to just be yourself, but it can be harder than one would think. It takes awareness to know who we are authentically and to uncover what we really want. Most of us grew up trying to please others for approval to get the love we needed, and we developed ways of being that would accomplish this. We develop many accommodating behaviors to survive and can mistake this for success, but this isn't necessarily who we are, who we want to be, or what we really want to accomplish. It takes some attention to unravel what we really want, to understand what we honestly feel, and to find the courage to be vulnerable enough to say what's important or authentic and then take action to pursue it. Yet this is an essential part of the process of becoming who you want to be, to be able to truly care for people, to have the vision and character to share your gift, and to give life to your purpose. Becoming your authentic self, knowing what you want, and transforming as necessary is what offers a fulfilling life and inspires others.

REFLECTIVE PRACTICE
Make a list of what's most important to you from your heart, not just your worldly mind. Practice keeping your attention on these things; speak to yourself about what you really want and how you feel about it. Ask yourself what's getting in your way. As you strengthen this inner conversation, start to practice sharing with your trusted inner circle. You may discover that those who matter will rejoice in who you are. Explore how sharing with others may influence your goals, dreams, and desired outcomes.

7

"What you get by achieving your goals is not as important as what you become by achieving your goals."

—Zig Ziglar

Reflect on some recent goals you have accomplished. Who did you become by achieving your goals? Did your goal and the person you became align with your values? How can you take stock of this in the future with each success you achieve?

8

"Self-awareness means you have to start understanding yourself, what it is you need now—not what society says you need, nor what your parents, your friends, your schools or even your own mind may say you need. You need to start paying attention to how you feel about everything and develop this intuitive power."

—Gourasana*

There will never be a shortage of well-meaning people and loved ones who will advise you and create expectations surrounding how you should be, act, and do. Even your own mind can do this if it's unconnected from your inner light and desire. At those times it's important to discern your mind's "should" from your gut or intuition's pull or greater desire. Giving oneself the space to dream, have vision, and set meaningful goals requires touching within and giving yourself permission to discover or become aware of what you really want or who you want to be. What is true for you may not comply with common pathways or others' expectations. It takes attentive listening to your deeper true voice to find your own truth. It takes time and slowing down to listen to the whispers and sometimes loud shouting from the heart. Being true and authentic to yourself is your guiding light, even though it will likely disappoint somebody else out there.

REFLECTIVE PRACTICE
What does nurturing your trust and belief in yourself look and feel like? Explore how to do this with an open mind. Mistakes are part of the journey of discovery and growing. Acknowledge your mistakes and failures by stating what they are and what you learned from them. Let these learnings shrink your fear and doubt to pave a pathway to trust.

* Gourasana, *Breaking the Cycle of Birth and Death*, #307, www.CenteroftheGoldenOne.com.

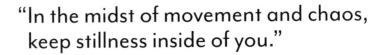

"In the midst of movement and chaos, keep stillness inside of you."

9

—Widely attributed to Deepak Chopra

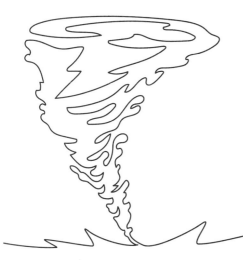

For the most part, the material world is a place of chaos, busyness, and disturbance—not a peaceful place. This is why it's so important that we each forge our ability to go within to establish a center of calm and connectedness. This center will offer us stability and balance and keep us focused on what matters. Use your awareness to discern when you are becoming disturbed so that in the moment you can turn your attention within to change your energy and perspective. This will prevent you from acting out, following bad habits, or getting distracted from your desired outcomes. You can radically change your life by practicing going within and tapping into your place of stillness, calm, and connection—even if it's only to stop, breathe, and shift your perspective. A routine meditation practice creates a familiar pathway to go to within, and it will strengthen your ability to return as needed.

REFLECTIVE PRACTICE

Start each day with some kind of calming practice—calm your mind, emotions, and body to center yourself within. Establish this place as an inner sanctuary with a well-worn path so that you can easily turn to it anytime, even in the midst of chaos. This sets the tone for your day, helps you refocus on what you want or who you want to be, and can help you to not become caught up in the first disturbance that hits you.

"What you're thinking is what you're becoming."

—Widely attributed to Muhammad Ali

Our thoughts are like lights in the night showing the direction of the path we are walking. What we think is where we go. We need reflective practices that keep our thoughts focused on what we want, including the qualities and habits we desire, to get where we want to go. If you are not going in the direction you want, check in and clarify what you are thinking and discern whether any changes in thinking are needed. If you are pleased with your direction, keep going. Become aware of what you are thinking, and be sure to capitalize on and repeat those thoughts. If you have a desire to bloom into a more positive, hopeful, caring, loving, and inspiring person, get clear on what kinds of thoughts you need to cultivate, and plant those thought seeds today!

REFLECTIVE PRACTICE
Identify a quality or way of being you would like to develop further or set as a goal. Write down a few examples of thoughts that would embody and cultivate those behaviors. Keep it simple, and be bold!

Achieving Goals

There are many skills, qualities, mindsets, and behaviors needed to achieve any goal. Explore a variety of reflective practices to develop these qualities, to obtain your goals and support others to do the same.

"People with goals succeed because they know where they are going."

11

—Earl Nightingale

Be specific about setting goals and articulating what you want to accomplish. Include criteria for success; that is, how will you know whether you have succeeded? If you want to go to New York City, does that mean just landing at the airport, or does it mean you want to attend a Broadway show? Goals without plans are just dreams. You have to be specific about how you are going to get there, which involves creating an action plan, but you must also be willing to adapt your plan when you encounter obstacles along the journey. When clarifying your goals, be concrete, specific, and adaptable. If you make a plan to fly to New York City and then find out the plane tickets are sold out or too expensive, you may need to drive instead or save money and go at a later date. Perhaps you want to visit historical landmarks along the road, not just drive through on a lengthy road trip. Remember that the journey and how we get to our destination are also important parts of the experience.

A FEW FOREVER QUESTIONS

Consider what it would cost you or what benefits you might gain if you made an honest assessment of your beliefs. If you are motivated to take a look, here is a good place to start:

- Identify a goal you want to achieve. Write down the specifics of your goal and the criteria for knowing you have accomplished it.
- Develop an action plan with detailed steps, broken into small sequential stepping stones. Visualize the details of the journey as best you can. Determine what qualities or experiences during the journey are important to you.
- Review your goal and action plan weekly to determine whether any refinements or modifications are necessary.

12

"If you don't know where you are going, you will probably end up somewhere else."

—Laurence J. Peter

Having a vision or a goal is stating where you want to go, where you want to end up. This creates the guide rails for your choices and actions and helps you stay focused. Many options will present themselves in a day, a month, a year, or a lifetime, and if you don't have a good connection with what you want and where you want to go, you can easily be distracted and blown by the winds of life. It's important to review your goals and keep them current with your desires and life circumstances. Refining goals and visions is an active engagement process that requires reflection and consideration. Goals and visions inform how we spend our time, the kinds of activities we choose to do, and how we prioritize our choices. Allotting time to visualize your goals, for all aspects of your life, is part of planning for a meaningful, fulfilling life. Then once you know what or where you want to end up, being concrete and specific about your activities and how you spend your time will map your path to get there.

REFLECTIVE PRACTICE
Visualize your month or week in light of your goals. Look at your schedule and review the categories of your life that need attention so that you end up where you want to be. Take time each month and week to make specific choices and build habits that support your goal.

13

"Whenever you want to achieve something, keep your eyes open, concentrate and make sure you know exactly what it is you want. No one can hit their target with their eyes closed."

—Paulo Coelho

There is a difference between living your life with focused intention and just waking up each day and moving forward. Many of us have set a goal but, with time, have fallen back into familiar routines, just plodding along. We lost sight of our vision and became disconnected from what we wanted, stopped making intentional aims to achieve it, or gave up in discouragement. It takes a certain amount of single-minded focus to aim our thoughts and actions to get where we want to go. Many success stories come down to a person having a focused aim. You cannot spread yourself too thin or get caught up in multitasking. Consider your vision and goals as a committed relationship that you need to invest in, spend time with, and give care and attention to. Don't take your desire for granted or it will fade.

REFLECTIVE PRACTICE
Do you know what you want? What does it mean to you to keep your eyes open and focus on and invest in your goal?

"With consistency and reps and routine you're going to achieve your goals and get where you want to be."

—Mandy Rose

Where do you need to be more consistent to achieve your goals? What routines do you need to establish or refine to get where you want to be?

15

"Setting goals is the first step in turning the invisible into the visible."

—Tony Robbins

Goals are simply stating what you want to happen. A goal can be a feeling, an image, a concrete accomplishment, or a finish line. Each of us relates to goals differently. Some are put off just by the word *goal*, which can feel intimidating or formal. As a coach, I have found that simply asking people what they want to happen is a more natural, conversational way to help someone clarify a goal. Ask them to describe their desire using adjectives and to provide descriptions of how they will know they have gotten there—these details make their desired outcomes concrete and specific, making their goals visible.

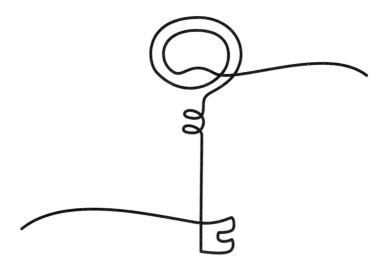

REFLECTIVE PRACTICE
Contemplate something you want to happen. How will you know when you get there or accomplish it? Be concrete and specific. If you coach others, practice avoiding the word *goal*; instead encourage people to specifically and concretely describe what they want to happen.

"It is not usually our ideas that make us optimistic or pessimistic, but it is our optimism or our pessimism . . . that makes our ideas."

—Miguel de Unamuno

Achieving goals and being optimistic is a dynamic relationship worth deepening and nurturing. Optimism is defined as hopefulness and confidence about the future or the success of something, and for some people, looking on the bright side comes naturally. In the book *Learned Optimism*, American psychologist Dr. Martin Seligman found optimism to be a predictor of success. Having an attitude of optimism can be more influential for developing one's career than having a specific talent or skill. A recent study showed that optimistic people tend to make more money, are promoted more often, and make better financial decisions. Studies show that about 25 percent of optimism is hereditary,* but a good deal of optimism is a learned mindset, which we can all acquire. Here are a few strategies:

REFLECTIVE PRACTICE
Choose at least one of the five strategies suggested below to practice cultivating a more optimistic perspective.
1. Become aware of pessimistic thoughts, for example, by doing a daily reflective observation of the quality of your thoughts.
2. Challenge your pessimistic thoughts by asking yourself whether they are true and questioning what faulty evidence is influencing you or your assumptions.
3. Be the DJ of your mind and reframe pessimistic thoughts by considering other ways to view a situation.
4. Focus on the positive by writing daily what you are grateful for.
5. Spend time with other people who are optimistic—optimism and pessimism are "catchy."
6. Be mindful of the content and perspective you consume through the news and social media—create content balance.
Choose at least one of the six strategies suggested above to practice cultivating a more optimistic perspective.

* Robert Plomin et al., "Optimism, Pessimism and Mental Health: A Twin/Adoption Analysis," *Personality and Individual Differences* 13, issue 8 (August 1992): 921–930, www.sciencedirect.com/science/article/abs/pii/019188699290009E?via%3Dihub.

17

"Remember to celebrate milestones as you prepare for the road ahead."

—Commonly attributed to Nelson Mandela

Learn to celebrate your successes along your journey as well as goals you achieve. It is not boasting; it's recognizing how your endeavors made a difference and reenergizing yourself to keep going. Slow down to specifically acknowledge and register what your successes are. Don't just move on to the next thing. This is a form of dismissing yourself, minimizing your choices and what you have accomplished. In order to be glad and celebrate the successes of others, start with yourself. Explore a variety of ways to celebrate. Certainly many people include things like a special meal or favorite treat. Those typical things are just fine, but get creative and expand your list. Try giving yourself more time and space to do things that inspire and nurture you. It could be time to daydream, play with a pet, take a long walk in nature, have a picnic, go to a movie or an art museum, go on a vacation, or just spend time by yourself.

REFLECTIVE PRACTICE
Make a list of at least ten ways to celebrate, like a menu of options. Don't forget to include items that do not cost money. It can be very motivational to clarify what reward you will gain by accomplishing a goal in the established time frame. Next time you set a goal, build in the celebration!

18

"I never cease to be amazed at the power of the coaching process to draw out the skills or talent that was previously hidden within an individual, and which invariably finds a way to solve a problem previously thought unsolvable."

—John Russell

Coaches who have the mindset that their role is to be a change agent, rather than a content expert, engage in distinctive behaviors and coaching practices. As a change agent, the coach's purpose is to facilitate the individual through their own learning and discovery, not to give advice or answers or tell them where to aim. Helping people clarify goals that are meaningful to them rather than imposing compliance-based expectations has a profound effect on whether a person will achieve sustainable change. The role and behaviors of a coach are not the same as those of a teacher or consultant. It's not about giving information as if to fill someone up, or advising a coachee as if to direct them, but rather facilitating reflection so the coachee discovers how to turn within and pull forth their own inner creative approach to finding the attitudes, behaviors, and actions to achieve their goals. Even if there are mandated goals, helping people unravel the personal relevance of such goals will be critical to activating their motivation. Certainly people will, at times, need information, suggestions, and supervision—but that is really the role of a teacher, consultant, or supervisor, not the primary role of a coach. Your role as a coach is to follow their lead by listening, paraphrasing, inquiring, and reframing, rather than thinking you need to lead or manage them. The coach is not in front of their coachee, laying the path; rather, they journey as a partner side by side, shoulder to shoulder with their coachee, empowering them to become aware, to trust themselves through trial and error to find new possibilities and develop the habits of a lifelong learner.

REFLECTIVE PRACTICE
Are you leading by using teaching, suggesting, advising, and controlling strategies, thinking a coach needs to be in front of or above the coachee? Do you trust the intrinsic process that coaching opens through facilitating reflection to expand awareness, or are you trying to convince or lead the individual toward what you think they need? In what ways are you drawing out skills, talents, or goals rather than trying to fill up your coachee with knowledge or direct them to comply? Are you investing in and practicing the art of followership, based on your trust that each person is capable, competent, and the expert of their own lives?

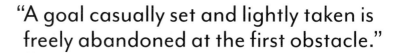

"A goal casually set and lightly taken is freely abandoned at the first obstacle."

19

—Zig Ziglar

In my own life, I have seen a pattern repeat: I set a goal that I think I should have (from either an external or an internal pressure), but then I rarely achieve success because I don't stick with it. I have found more success with goals that have something to do with what I really want, when I feel called forward or pulled, not pushed. I need clarity about why the goal matters or why it is meaningful so I stick with my efforts when the journey gets difficult or uncomfortable. I am most successful when I connect what I want with my heart, my sense of purpose, my desire to help, or my need to gain some kind of freedom.

REFLECTIVE PRACTICE
Have you been struggling with achieving a goal? Is the goal feeling like an external pressure, or is it generated from an internal motivating desire? How can you cultivate and clarify your desire? If you support others in achieving their goals, help them to clarify their motivation to achieve their goal or reframe what they really want. Ask them to tell their story of why their goal is meaningful and relevant to them. If they are not actually inspired by the goal, let them share about their lack of motivation and explore what would make it motivating for them—it might mean modifying the goal or reframing the benefit of accomplishing the goal with something meaningful to them.

Overcoming Challenges to Success

We must have the stamina and perseverance to engage with challenges and to not be stopped or discouraged while on the journey to attaining goals. It is predictable that we will all encounter challenges and obstacles in our lives and professions, and this is not a measure of failure. Reframing hurdles, mistakes, or trials and errors as learning, discovery, and deepening understanding leads to both wisdom and resilience.

20

"If you believe it will work out, you'll see opportunities. If you believe it won't, you will see obstacles."

—Wayne Dyer

Our own beliefs about mistakes, failures, and successes influence our ability to achieve what we want. Our beliefs create the stories we tell ourselves, what we too often believe are facts, if we do not examine them to see whether they are really assumptions and perspectives based in fear. When we shift our attitude about challenge so we see it as an opportunity to learn, we come to tell ourselves a more empowering story, which allows us to positively narrate our journeys. Become aware of what story you are telling yourself, and if you don't like the story, then rewrite it!

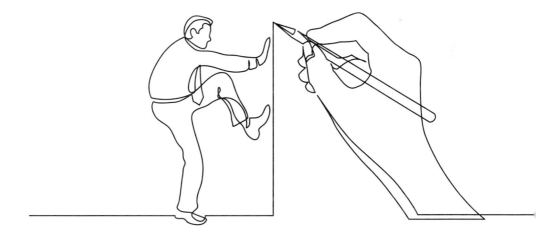

REFLECTIVE PRACTICE
What belief do you hold that is inconsistent with achieving a goal, vision, or dream? How can you rewrite a more empowering story and belief to support your success?

21

"Our vision is only action-able if we share it. Without sharing, it's just a figment of our imagination."

—Simon Sinek

What vision, hope, or goal do you have that you can share with someone to make it more real and actionable? It may cause feel-ings of vulnerability, and it might take some courage to tolerate the discomfort and risk of sharing. Do not let the fear stop you!

"Every vice has its excuse ready."

22

—Publius Syrus

Develop reflective habits to help you discern which challenges engage and awaken you and which overwhelm you. One "forever" reflective question I ask myself when faced with a challenge is, "Is this challenge an internal or an external challenge?" If I am the source of the challenge, then I usually need a mindset shift to reset the tone or reframe my perspective, especially if I am experiencing overwhelm. If I am engaged by a challenge or drawn to something that might feel out of reach, it might be the time to clarify more concretely and specifically what I want and connect with my positive or optimistic attitude. Or it might be the time to break the situation down into detailed, bite-size pieces or small action steps. Establishing and embedding reflective habits can make or break our chances of achieving and maintaining our goals.

A FEW FOREVER QUESTIONS

When facing a challenge and discerning how to engage with it, here are a few reflective habits to embed:

- Identify a few key "forever" reflective questions to ask yourself. Examples: "What is causing this to be a problem or trigger for me?" "Am I willing to take a risk and maybe fail in order to learn? Why or why not?"
- Check your perspective and reframe if it is limiting, disempowering, or single-sided. Is it negative, or optimistic and hopeful? Ask yourself if there might be another perspective or way of looking at the challenge that could shift how you perceive and engage with it. For example, would it be helpful to have a balcony view, seeing a bigger perspective, or a grass-blades viewpoint, examining more details?
- Focus on what you want.
- Be compassionate with yourself. Ask yourself whether the person who loves you the most would talk to you or treat you as you do yourself when you're facing a challenge.

(23) "If we can just let go and trust that things will work out the way they're supposed to, without trying to control the outcome, then we can begin to enjoy the moment more fully. The joy of the freedom it brings becomes more pleasurable than the experience itself."

—Goldie Hawn

Whenever we are trying to exert control—over people, outcomes, or circumstances—it's a symptom that fear is running the show. Fear about the future or how something will turn out usually feels like worry, which then kicks off our controlling habits. It's a constant practice to remind ourselves that there is more freedom in letting go. Our minds in fear mode tell us—actually fool us into thinking—control will make us safer, but it's not true. It's an illusion. We usually feel constriction and tightness from fearful controlling rather than safety. Developing the quality of trust is key. You might need to look at what traps you in your lack of trust. Or you might need to just resist the old habit of falling into fear. It will probably require you to turn within, seeking a higher intelligence and perspective rather than looking to the external world or your fretful mind for solutions. Trust is an internal experience, and it implies not knowing. Trust comes from the heart and comes from within, and it sometimes doesn't seem logically rational, given your mind's limited understanding. Choose to trust and let go and discover a new freedom.

REFLECTIVE PRACTICE
When you fall into fear or when you feel the need for control, consider what you want to feel or experience instead in those moments or situations. You might aim for something as simple as trusting and letting go. Refocus your attention toward what you want and create habits that help you aim for that. Use mindfulness practices, prayer, talking it out with a friend—whatever reflective practice helps you focus on what you want. Your behaviors will follow what you focus on, so focus on what you want. Even if your logical mind doesn't think it knows how to trust or let go, let your heart lead you.

24

"How much happier would you be if you focused your energy solely on what you can control?"

—*Best Self* journal

There's a difference between what you can control and what you want to control. Fear often drives us to want to control circumstances, people, or outcomes over which we have little or no control. To focus only on what you can control is remarkably freeing. Freedom comes from making choices we are actually able to make. Sometimes setting a goal feels challenging since we might not understand or know how to achieve it. You do not always need to know the how—the action plan—to have vision or a dream. The plan can come later, and it will likely require trust and some letting go of control. Letting go is always a choice we make in the moment, not in the future. Use mindfulness reflection to stay present in the moment and appreciate your available choices. Happiness, acceptance, and peace come from the choices you make in how you think, how you permit yourself to dream big, how you respond in any given moment, and how you recover from a misstep. You have choice over yourself.

REFLECTIVE PRACTICE
Make a list of what you want to control. Review the list, considering what you can control and what's not in your control. You cannot control other people, circumstances, or outcomes. Get clear and be honest with yourself: What do you need to let go of the urge to control? Where should you invest your energy?

25

"Don't be afraid. Be focused. Be determined. Be hopeful. Be empowered."

—Michelle Obama

Don't let fear stop you. Move forward despite your fears. Do not assume your fears are true or worth listening to. All too often they are just faulty thoughts and feelings that present as reality. Even when fears are lurking, you can move toward what you want and be hopeful about possibilities and opportunities. You just have to be determined to not listen to the fears—you can't necessarily wait for them to go away. Often they don't go away; we just use our desire and our determination to keep going no matter what and override those disempowering thoughts and feelings. Listen to your heart, trust in hope, and invest in possibility.

think positive

REFLECTIVE PRACTICE
Make a sign that says, "Do Not Let the Fear Stop You!" Put this sign where you will see it every day—at your desk, on your bathroom mirror, on the fridge. Let this empower you, giving you courage to stay in motion toward what you want.

26 "Every good idea is offensive to someone. This is the very nature of good ideas; they are good because they change things. Change is required, otherwise you don't have an idea—you have regurgitation. Ideas, on the other hand, insist on uncertainty."

—Ash Ambirge

It's risky to come up with good ideas because they are untried and uncertain. It takes courage to come up with a good idea and even more to bring it into reality by speaking and sharing it. It takes a lot of risk tolerance to keep investing in your idea with time and effort. Some people will resist because coming up with something new implies that the old isn't good enough and that confronts them. As Ash Ambirge says, "By challenging the old, you're challenging me."*

REFLECTIVE PRACTICE
Do you hold your new ideas back or take no action because you fear resistance or being challenged? As a leader or a coworker, are you open-minded to new ideas, or do you feel challenged by them and resist? How can you not let your fear stop you?

* Ash Ambirge, *The Middle Finger Project* (New York: Penguin, 2020), 87.

"Have patience. All things are difficult before they become easy."

—Often attributed to Saadi Shirazi

Sometimes things just flow and are easy right out of the gate. More often when you are trying to make a change, to grow, or to learn something, it takes practice and endeavor before it gets easier. Having an expectation that change should be easy will only lead to self-judgment and discouragement. Patience includes tolerating the discomfort before it gets easier. The discomfort is usually connected to an internal expectation or disempowering attitude that the situation should be different than it is. Managing your thoughts and expectations is a first step to easing your journey. Patience is what provides the space to persevere until it becomes easy. Practicing relaxation and mindfulness enhances our patience.

REFLECTIVE PRACTICE
In what ways are you being impatient with yourself or someone else? Clarify and acknowledge what your expectations are of yourself or the other person. Take time to explore how to infuse kindness to loosen your expectations, so you expand your capacity to keep trying and not give up.

28

"The more you praise and celebrate your life, the more there is in life to celebrate."

—Oprah Winfrey

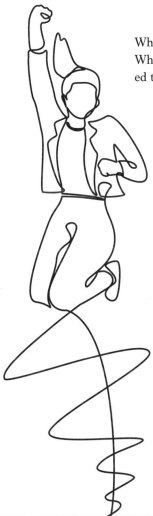

What were your wins for this week? What are you grateful for that contributed to those wins?

29

"True optimism is not about avoiding reality—it's about being able to accept and manage obstacles with the intention of not letting them stop you from enjoying life."

—*TIME* magazine, "The Power of Positive Thinking: Why Attitude Matters"

The antidote to chronic stress is cultivating an optimistic mindset. In a study conducted by Michelle Gielan and Shawn Anchor, the data clearly showed that optimists were more likely than pessimists to be promoted, make more money, and manage their money wisely. The study also reveals that optimists are six times more likely to be highly engaged at work, and five times less likely to burn out than pessimists.* Thus being positive has very concrete outcomes. Optimism is not about ignoring reality or stressful situations but instead staying hopeful that good things will happen. Having an optimistic attitude reminds us that our behaviors and our choices matter. Be mindful of what you think, how your mindset and perspective influence your actions, and how you accept and manage challenges, since it correlates to your ability to achieve goals and outcomes.

REFLECTIVE PRACTICE
Focus on progress, not perfection. Don't wait until you have perfected your plan. Set a meaningful goal and take a small but measurable step toward achieving it. Taking small, incremental steps that you can succeed at will reinforce a positive and hopeful attitude. Each win sends a message to your brain that progress is occurring, and this reinforces an optimistic viewpoint.

* Michelle Gielan, "The Financial Upside of Being an Optimist," *Harvard Business Review*, March 12, 2019, https://hbr.org/2019/03/the-financial-upside-of-being-an-optimist.

30

"So often people are working hard at the wrong thing. Working on the right thing is probably more important than working hard."

—Caterina Fake

Working on the wrong thing or being consumed in working hard but being disconnected from what really needs your attention can derail success. How do you know what you're working on is the right thing? What's your criteria for discerning that? Often we get distracted by social expectations, the pressure to achieve at work, or the need to meet someone else's expectations. Give yourself some space to determine whether what you are expending a lot of energy on is actually moving you closer to the goals you really care about. Is persistently checking your emails or getting notifications throughout the day really serving your greater goals? Or has it become mindless habit or evidence of a fear of missing out? You can choose how to spend your energy, but you will likely have to reflect on whether what you are doing is moving you closer to what you want. Even if you don't know what you do want, you probably have a sense if you're on the wrong track. You don't even need to know how to change anything right now. Just stop and do a heart check: Are you working on the right thing? Is it taking you in the direction you want to go, or are you just working hard?

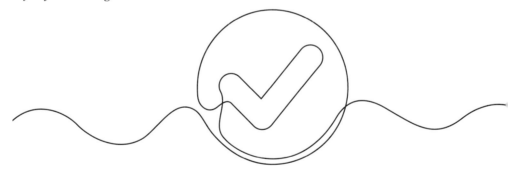

REFLECTIVE PRACTICE
Take five minutes each day for the next seven days and ponder whether what you're working on is the right thing. Is it related to what you want to accomplish or to a goal? What's your criteria for discerning that?

Chapter 6

MOBILIZE: PLAN AND TAKE ACTION

Facilitating sticky change is not a sequential endeavor, but there are a variety of predictable components that I introduce in the *GROOMER Framework for Change™* model. Each of these components will need focused attention to ensure sticky change occurs. Mobilizing, one of those components, is about bridging the gap between ideas, goals, and actions. A good plan can wisely guide our options in terms of what choices we can make, but it's not the same thing as actually implementing an action and practicing those actions over time. To truly change involves making thoughtful decisions and plans, feeling the courage and momentum that comes when we actually take specific actions, and sticking it out through the challenging parts of experimenting with and implementing our actions to reach our desired outcomes.

https://www.redleafpress.org/dre/6-1.pdf

Making Decisions

Creating an action plan for HOW to proceed to attain a specific dream or goal (the WHAT) requires making decisions and committing to a specific direction or pathway. Decision-making is a daily occurrence. It is a worthy investment to examine how you make decisions as a process and embed reflection practices so you maintain healthy decision-making practices.

"Decisions are the frequent fabric of our daily design."

—Attributed to Don Yaeger

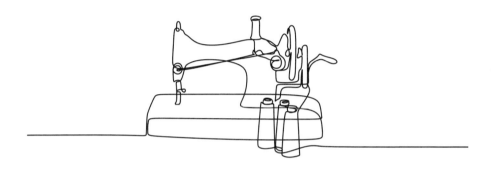

The quality of our life is directly linked to the quality of our decisions. Having a process or protocol that incorporates awareness and mindfulness practices to support your decision-making can be helpful. Do you have a framework or a set of questions you routinely ask yourself that stretches you to consider your rationale and bias and tests your reasoning so you feel confident you have considered all of the relevant factors? (See the list of Forever Questions in the Introduction on pages xviii-xix as a sample.) With reflection and thoughtfulness, you can learn how your views have changed and consider which decisions worked out and why, so you can consistently improve your decision-making skills. You can review using hindsight to assess what worked or didn't about your decision-making process and better inform future decisions to improve the quality of your life.

REFLECTIVE PRACTICE
When you make a big decision, set an alarm or appointment with yourself for six months later to reflect on your decision. What was the outcome of your decision? How did your educated guess stack up to the reality?

2

> "Honest, honest exploration during meditative thinking improves the quality of your life because it activates the wisdom of intuition and higher intelligence. Your soul converses with the Supreme, your soul listens, and then it's up to you, to listen, say yes, and act."

—The Lady*

Consider the process of how we choose which actions we will take. Many people make choices and take action casually, shooting from the hip without much reflection, while others suffer a worrisome, anxious, and repetitive deliberation that is quite fear-based. How do you make decisions? Using meditation to access an inner wisdom, beyond the mind and deeper than emotional reactions, can make a qualitative difference in your life and work. To access this higher wisdom requires being able to slow down and calm the mind and emotions. It doesn't mean you don't think or feel—that's really not possible. But meditation can invite you to explore an inner domain that offers a different experience of time than the material world, beyond the chatter of the everyday mind and the push and shove of emotions. Using meditation as a tool to check in within and access a greater perspective can be a deeply important element to your decision-making process and the quality and accuracy of your actions.

REFLECTIVE PRACTICE
Explore meditative thinking. Do you have a desire to experience this? Be open-minded in how you might approach it, through trying structured meditation or informal meditation, formally learning a specific meditation, or practicing your own type of meditation. Let your desire lead you.

* The Lady, "How to Keep Your Connection Going," spoken March 22, 2006, at Center of the Golden One® Retreat, www.CenteroftheGoldenOne.com.

"There is no decision that we can make that doesn't come with some sort of balance or sacrifice."

—Simon Sinek

Some decisions feel clear and easy to make. Others involve conflicting feelings, doubts, or uncertainty. Some of us fear making any wrong decision, falling into this habitual, disempowering perspective. Taking time and asking yourself some reflective questions can help ease the decision-making process. It's always helpful to consider and view the situation through different perspectives. Consider who might give counsel, who has had a similar experience and can share from hindsight, or who might help you reflect and ask you coaching questions.

REFLECTIVE PRACTICE
Describe your inside view of the decision or problem within your own context. What might an outsider's perspective on your decision look like? Do you have any habitual perspectives that are clouding and complicating your ability to view this specific situation clearly? List all your assumptions about this decision. Where did your assumptions come from? Given your assumptions what needs to be clarified, what questions asked, to not base your decision on faulty information or lack of knowledge? What do you not know, and what missing variables may help you make a better decision? When you're feeling stuck making a decision, contemplate ways to open up possibilities or find additional options. What might an experimental test run look like, and is that possible? What are the alternatives? What's the worst outcome or the most probable outcome? If you had no fear, what would be an option?

4

"Unless we are making intentional choices to slow down, pay attention and live in the present moment, life can be one long to-do list, a day is full of shoulds and musts. We have no time for spontaneous pleasures or good moments."

—Mary Pipher

Consciously deciding how to live your life requires focused attention on the specific choices you make. When we feel pushed around by the winds of life, we lose our power and often feel like we don't have choice or control to make decisions. This can be quickly shifted by focusing on what matters to you, making intentional choices to aim yourself in that direction. Satisfaction and meaning don't happen to us; we create it through making intentional decisions and choices.

REFLECTIVE PRACTICE
Where did you decide to invest your time this week? Was it aligned with your intentions? Ponder how your actions and experiences reveal your decisions and choices, considering how avoiding making decisions and a lack of attention on your choices can impact the quality of your life.

Taking Action and Making Changes

One step, one action at a time, is how we get wherever we want to go. Knowing where you want to go is important, as it guides the direction for each step, day by day. But sometimes just taking the first step to start the journey is a huge accomplishment. Learning how to pace your steps, day after day on a long journey, is also vital to making permanent change.

"The change we want is within us and shall always be within us; the change we can have is in the steps we can take to realize the change we want. Take a step if you want a change!"

—Attributed to Ernest Agyemang Yeboah

Just the act of realizing we want change is a big step forward. Reflecting on what we are doing or thinking that's working and what's not working each day is a simple way to focus on areas that might need our attention. We typically discover what kind of changes we need to make as we get feedback from others or as we intentionally observe our attitudes and feelings and the impact they have on our behaviors, responses, and results. Embedding daily reflective practices is a concrete step we can take to realize the change we want.

REFLECTIVE PRACTICE
Keep a small notebook and take five minutes before finishing or leaving work to jot down what worked today and what did not work today—with the focus on yourself, not others. What were your thoughts, feelings, behaviors, actions, and outcomes?

"Think only about your first step."

— Widely attributed to Shams-i Tabrizi

6

If you have big goals or encounter a big challenge, don't let overwhelm derail you. This is a time to keep your focus small and specific. They say that to eat an elephant (achieve a big goal), you need to break it down into bite-size pieces. You may not know how you are going to accomplish the goal or overcome the challenge; all you need to do is identify one small step. Take that first step. Each step will create momentum, and often that first step will reveal a next step. You don't have to see the whole path, just the next stepping stone.

REFLECTIVE PRACTICE
Think of something you have been procrastinating about. What is just one small step that you could take to be in action? Don't worry about what comes next. Take that first step.

"I never lose. Either I win or learn."

—Commonly attributed to Nelson Mandela

Is there something you realize you need to learn or unlearn from the past week's experiences?

8

"If you can't fly, run; if you can't run, walk; if you can't walk, crawl; but by all means keep moving."

—Dr. Martin Luther King Jr.

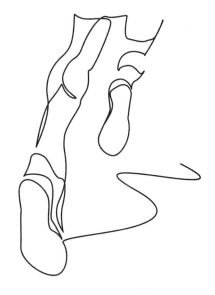

Wanting to be perfect in execution or implementation can get in the way of making change, and you can get stuck in your head. Sometimes the only way to proceed is to just take an action, any action. It can be a very small action or a half-baked action you are not sure about, but taking the action will matter. Movement forward is the point, not the speed or perfection. Stay focused on one day at a time, one step at a time, and just keep going . . . fly, run, walk, or crawl. Don't give up; stay focused on what you want and let that pull you forward. Being clear about what you want becomes an immense motivator.

REFLECTIVE PRACTICE
Write down something you want on an index card. Put it somewhere you will see it every day to help you stay focused. Your desire will generate movement and action toward what you want. Trust your desire, and trust any ideas you have about actions you could take—whether big or small, clear or foggy, write them down. Pick one item on the list and declare a date you will act, and keep yourself accountable by telling someone else too. Just keep moving.

"The most difficult thing is the decision to act, the rest is merely tenacity. . . . You can do anything you decide to do."

—Amelia Earhart

Once you have decided to do something, go for it! Being persistent—continuing to pursue it when things get tough—is the quality you need to go the distance. Your devotion and belief in what you are doing becomes the engine that keeps you going. It also takes practicality as you identify which tasks to do, then specificity as you plan when and how you will do these tasks. Persistence very often requires refining and modifying the implementation plan, being adaptive in the face of obstacles, and figuring out a work-around plan, perhaps creatively reinventing your approach or embedding reflective habits to keep refining and deepening your commitment. Having the leadership quality of persistence in the face of difficulty, combined with devotion and adaptability, is very inspirational to others.

start

finish

REFLECTIVE PRACTICE
Reflect in what ways you may need to be persistent, adapt, refine, or reinvent in order to accomplish a goal. Write down any specific nonnegotiable tasks. Assign times in your calendar to accomplish them.

10

"Simple daily disciplines—little productive actions, repeated consistently over time—add up to the difference between failure and success."

—Jeff Olson

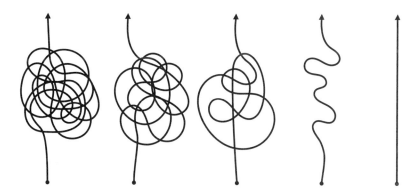

The coach's role as change agent helps coachees tolerate the discomfort and vulnerability of going through the change process, which includes practicing, experiencing failures, trying things out for the first time, taking risks, not knowing what the results are going to be, and taking what might seem like insignificantly small steps. It is these repeated small steps, however, that create sustainable change and foster effective, consistent habits. For a coach to be steadfast in their role as change agent, they need to continuously reflect, learn, practice, and change themselves. The coach must understand and empathize with the feelings of discomfort and vulnerability associated with the change process and creating new habits.*

REFLECTIVE PRACTICE
What is a simple daily discipline in your own professional life or as a coach or leader that you can add to or improve upon to become better at what you do?

* Excerpts from Constant Hine and Robin Levy, "Transformational Coaching: Moving Beyond Goals and Action Plans to Foster Continuous Quality Improvement," *Exchange* (November/December 2019).

11

"In essence, through coaching, the leader facilitates the transformation of possibilities into realities."

—Attributed to Sackeena Gordon-Jones

There is a difference between possibility and action. Both are needed. Some people take action first and possibilities unfold. For others, an incubation of possibilities must grow and then action follows. As a coach and leader, helping people identify and clarify both possibilities and actions is a transformational process and requires focused reflection. When someone takes action first, the coach can use reflective analysis to help them detect what they learned from the action and why it is important, cultivating insights into the possibilities. For those who have pockets full of possibilities, the facilitation may be to help them divvy their ideas into small actionable steps and then encourage them to take an action, however big or small, grounding the possibility into reality. Coaches and leaders facilitate the dance between possibility and action by individually nurturing reflection, critical thinking, and the courage to take the first step.

A FEW FOREVER QUESTIONS
Consider the people you support. Who takes action first and needs support to reflect on what they learned from the action? Facilitate examination of their intent and what happened. If there is a gap between their intent and its impact, help them clarify their goals and illuminate the options. Consider which people have good ideas but find implementation a hurdle. Check whether they have a disempowering attitude about making mistakes or needing to be perfect and help them shift that attitude so they can take action.

"Don't look at your feet to see if you are doing it right. Just dance."

—Anne Lamott

It takes some courage to grow and change. If a person tends to get stuck in their mind or feel an internal pressure to make no mistakes, they can get quite jammed up. To get unstuck, help them identify and name the disempowering perspective or limiting thought in their head. Encourage them to recognize whether the thought is fear-based or trust-based, and choose which type they want more in their life. They might need to make a long list of the worst things that might happen if they do something wrong and consider which ones are realistic and which ones are unlikely or untrue. Then have them write all the potential positive outcomes to consider why it might be worth going ahead and trying, even in the face of failure. A coach or leader can help normalize the discomfort of change by viewing mistakes as learning opportunities. But you can't just tell others this. Through facilitated reflection, they need to unravel it for themselves and learn to reanchor their trust in their ability to learn and adapt, rather than believing that perfect results are the measure of success. It takes trust to just dance. Help them cultivate their trust in themselves.

REFLECTIVE PRACTICE
Recall a time when you were stuck in your mind, feeling fear about doing something wrong (the fear of making mistakes, often related to feelings of unworthiness or "getting in trouble") or needing to be right (perfectionism, needing to prove oneself, or having the need to be right, which often diminishes alternative perspectives or answers). What helped you let go of these disempowering perspectives so that you were willing to take a risk, let go, and trust your body or heart instead? Clarify these helpful things so you can be specific. Be willing to share your own vulnerable, authentic story with someone having a similar experience. And ask what it's like for them.

Focus Choices and Time

Maintaining a focus on our plans, actions, and daily choices will influence our success. How we invest our time can either support or derail our accomplishments and can also affect the quality of the journey.

13

"Without strategy, change is merely substitution, not evolution."

—Glenn Llopis

Moving prematurely to an action plan or strategy without deeper reflection can result in superficial or ineffective change. Change itself doesn't inherently equate to growth or mean that transformation is occurring. You can make changes in your life that don't result in a significant difference. You can, so to speak, just rearrange the chairs on the deck of the *Titanic* in your life, removing one ineffective practice and replacing it with another—but that's not transformational. To foster evolution, transformation, and sticky change, our learning and reflection must tie into a process of constructing and assigning new and revised interpretations or meanings to our experiences to create a perspective transformation, or what is called a paradigm shift. Incorporating routine habits of reflection can help us become aware of, examine, and revise our frame of reference, values, attitudes, and beliefs to achieve transformational change.

REFLECTIVE PRACTICE
Identify something you want to change in your life. Allow yourself space and time to reflect on your desire for this change before taking an action step. Insert reflection as the first strategy. Ask yourself, what has been holding in place this thing you want to change? What is contributing to this being a stuck place or behavior? Do you have a perspective that might need adjusting or reframing? What do you really want? What can you let go of, accept, or forgive? Explore deeply so that your action plan can address more essential and core aspects of the change. This is more likely to result in meaningful, significant, and transformational change.

"If there is no wind, row."

14

—Anonymous

Think of a way you are intentionally taking action right now. If you feel stagnant or have had a difficult week progressing in this area, what does "rowing" mean to you? What are some ideas that might help you gain momentum, to reactivate your plan and actively progress forward? Don't forget, small steps are beneficial and constructive.

15

"Besides the noble art of getting things done, there is the noble art of leaving things undone. The wisdom of life consists in the elimination of nonessentials."

—Lin Yutang

Time is fleeting. If we don't set our focus and priorities and protect our time by making the time for what is important to us, it will slip away or be taken from us, or we will become the victim of circumstances and fires vying for our attention. We need to make intentional choices about how we spend our time and what we spend it on. There will always be more to do than time to do it. Living life by completing a checklist, meeting an expectation, or reducing an inner pressure does not guarantee satisfaction or meaning. Many of us operate from inherited or old beliefs that have become internal expectations. It is time to revisit your values and beliefs and align them with your current goals and desires, shedding those expectations that add pressure and don't contribute value to our current lives.

REFLECTIVE PRACTICE
Consider which things are essential to invest your time and energy in—things that contribute to meaning and purpose in your life—and which things are nonessential or unaligned with what you really want.

16

"The essence of self-discipline is to do the important thing rather than the urgent thing."

—Attributed to Barry Werner

I have been very disciplined for the last decade about creating a to-do list each day. When I started, this was a good plan. But I discovered that how I actually spent my time didn't always play out as planned. There was a gap between what I intended to happen and what actually happened. Earlier in my life, my accountant told me to write down everything I spent for a month so we could analyze where the money was going. I decided to do the same thing for my time. I still made my daily plan. In addition, for a week I wrote down everything I did, the time of day, and how long it took. I mean everything! How long my morning dressing routine took, eating, checking emails, travel time, work projects, meetings, time with family and friends, recreational activities, and getting ready for bed. I called this My Time Review. I discovered that I distracted myself every day with many things that felt urgent at the time—taking a phone call or replying to emails that didn't actually need immediate attention. I worked on administrative tasks that eased the discomfort of difficult high-priority projects. The feelings of urgency, it turned out, dictated a lot of my choices around how I spent my time, and I was unaware until I did this inventory and analysis. Not only do I still create a daily to-do list, but I have incorporated a daily practice at the end of each day to review how effective I was in staying focused. This daily review keeps my attention focused on making better choices surrounding how I spend my time. I am helped by my routine daily reflective practice to make supportive decisions so I accomplish what I want and stay my course.

REFLECTIVE PRACTICE
Expand your awareness and start to examine what is motivating your daily actions. Are you focusing on what's actually important or what feels urgent? Start to prioritize what's important and use awareness and mindfulness to notice what distracts you. Consider the choices you are making about how you spend your time.

17

"You get to decide where your time goes. You can either spend it moving forward, or you can spend it putting out fires. You decide. And if you don't decide, others will decide for you."

—Tony Morgan

People often say they can't find the time for routine habits of reflection they know would positively affect their lives. We never "find" time: We have to intentionally "make" time. I use the My Time Review strategy to collect data about what I plan to do and compare it to how my time is spent. The purpose is to identify patterns that are disruptive and to assess whether you are accurately estimating how long things really take, including all important actions. This inventory helps you make intentional choices and modify them if necessary. It wasn't until I took a long, honest look at how I actually spent my time that I was able to be much more intentional and focused about my choices and improve my planning so it accurately aligned with my goals and the hours available in a given day. I was finally able to create a daily plan that included time for what I wanted, as well as what was important to reach my goals. This radically increased my sense of accomplishment and reduced my stress and overwhelm. I continue this as a daily practice, making frequent modifications so I stay aligned with what I want. The purpose of this reflective practice is not to live in a narrowly defined schedule but to ensure I am creating time and space for what's important to me. It's not about being perfect— it's about continually focusing my attention and making better choices.

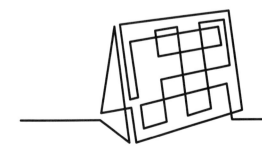

REFLECTIVE PRACTICE

Do a My Time Review study for at least a week and analyze what you are actually spending your time on, including how long tasks really take.

1. Create a list of what you want to spend your time on for each day this week. Include everything!

2. Using a daily time schedule that includes the hours of the day, write everything you need and want to make time for each day to create your daily plan.

3. At the end of each day, compare your plan to what actually happened. Observe patterns of distractions or actions you took based on fear or urgency.

4. Notice if you neglected to include time and space for things you either wanted or needed to do in your schedule.

5. Give yourself a percentage for how accurate your plan was.

Collect and analyze the data without self-judgment. Reflect on any changes you might want to practice. Modify future daily time schedules to make necessary adjustments.

18

"What gets measured gets improved."

—Popular adage

One of the most powerful actions you can take is to track and measure the progress and results of any endeavor. If you are working on your spending habits, collect specific information on how much money you are spending and on what. If you want to get more exercise, track what exercise actions you are taking, on what days, and for how long, and compare it to the results you hoped to achieve. If you have leadership behaviors you want to develop, you may give yourself a hash mark for every kind action you took in a week or for every individualized conversation you had with each member of your team in a month. Taking an honest look at observable data about what's really happening can be eye-opening and powerful in helping us develop more successful improvement plans. Plans can look good on paper, but tracking the actual actions taken and examining the frequency, quantity, or quality of the action adds a great deal of dimension and detail to aid in your success.

REFLECTIVE PRACTICE

Identify an area in which you already have set goals and review any specific actions for how you intend to achieve that goal. Specify what information and data you can track or measure that will inform you about what you are really doing and what's really happening. Are you actually taking those actions and implementing your plan?

Overcoming Obstacles and Improving Continuously

Overcoming challenges and busting barriers is the heart of an effective action plan. Plans, especially first plans, don't always work out, but that doesn't mean you won't achieve the goal. Anticipating unexpected bumps along the way can help us create more thoughtful action plans. Planning for the unexpected by having a plan B or C while also nurturing your ability to respond with resilience can help you create a calm and thoughtful response in the face of challenges, rather than becoming reactive, stressed, or imbalanced. Get used to a preventive reflective planning mindset, in which you consider in advance what the challenges may be and assume obstacles will present themselves, including those internal obstacles you habitually encounter.

19

> "Nothing is trivial if it is standing in the way of the light. The smallest things that you perceive in your way must be removed. It is simply a question of understanding what it is that is in your way. This is very important. You must see for yourself what the obstacles are and deal with them."

—Gourasana*

Identifying the obstacles or barriers is key to developing a strategy or action plan. Often we create an action plan, but when we start to implement it, we bump into unforeseen obstacles and challenges. But don't get discouraged: The bumps are actually progress on the journey to change. Do not judge yourself or blame others because you hit a challenge. When you do encounter a challenge or bump, you then need to create a targeted action plan to specifically address the obstacle before you return to your original goal plan. You can also be proactive and reflect about what possible obstacles you are likely to encounter—you don't have to wait to stumble. But when an unexpected challenge or obstacle interrupts your progress, stop and clarify what the obstacle is—don't just give up. You can't change what you can't see. So stop to see and name the obstacle. Then when options for busting that specific barrier come into focus, you can create a specific action plan.

REFLECTIVE PRACTICE

Think of a goal you currently have and are feeling stuck or somehow slowed down in achieving. Or recall a time in the past that you set a goal and started to pursue it but encountered an obstacle or challenge that stopped you. Name or label the obstacle or challenge. When you name and clarify what kind of obstacle it is, then you can focus on what your options are to address the challenge. Identify whether the challenge is one of the common AAMESS obstacles people encounter, introduced in the GROOMER Framework for Change™**:

A	lack of **A**wareness
A	limiting perspective or **A**ttitude
M	lack of or conflicting **M**otivation
E	triggering or strong **E**motions
S	**S**tress or lack of resiliency
S	lack of a **S**kill

* Gourasana, *Breaking the Cycle of Birth and Death*, #8, www.CenteroftheGoldenOne.com.
** Constant Hine, *Transformational Coaching for Early Childhood Educators* (St. Paul, MN: Redleaf Press, 2019), 43–46.

20

> "Everyone faces challenges
> in life. It's a matter of how you
> learn to overcome them and use
> them to your advantage."

—Celestine Chua

Clarifying the obstacle is the first step in using challenges to your advantage. The second step is creating a targeted action plan to specifically overcome that obstacle. In this way, you can use your obstacles to create a stronger action plan, so you achieve what you want. Then add practice, repetition, time, experimentation, and lots of self-compassion as you learn and grow. I have a client who is a coach who knows she has a habit of talking too much. Her goal was to listen more, and her action plan was to talk less when meeting with her coachees. After trying this for several weeks, she noticed she was better, but she still ended up talking more than she wanted. We then explored and clarified what had her continuing to talk more. She came to understand that her barrier to listening, and what motivated her to talk, was that she believed as a coach she was supposed to have the answers and fix problems. Her targeted plan was to focus on asking more questions instead of talking to advise the coachees and to shift her self-expectation that she should have answers.

REFLECTIVE PRACTICE

Identify a goal you want to achieve—focus on what you want. Think about any obstacles that might get in your way. These could be unsupportive habits or attitudes you know you have, a lack of resources, or a lack of motivation. Whatever it is, clarify the obstacle. You can't change what you can't see. Brainstorm options for how you might overcome or address that obstacle. Then pick one of those options and try it out. Modify and adjust if necessary. Keep practicing and refining.

21

"When we least expect it, life
sets us a challenge to test
our courage and willingness
to change."

—Paulo Coelho

Were there any challenges or difficulties you encountered this
past week(s)? In hindsight, how open were you to embracing that
situation as an invitation for change? What fears do you need to
face surrounding this situation? What will help you increase your
courage to be vulnerable, to face your fears, and to cultivate your
willingness and readiness to change?

"Challenge yourself every day to do better and be better. Remember, growth starts with a decision to move beyond your present circumstances."

—Widely attributed to Robert Tew

Choosing to grow is a decision you want to make consciously and intentionally. You have to accept that most growth often comes accompanied with some discord, challenges, and difficulty; otherwise it would simply be the next step on your current journey. Embracing rather than resisting challenges can influence your experience during the choppy times of growing and changing. Try keeping a higher balcony-view perspective of the purpose, value, and benefit of these times, like keeping your eyes on the horizon to minimize seasickness. Growth is more easily experienced when you can remember what you want and focus on where you are going and why.

REFLECTIVE PRACTICE

Choose one thing about yourself you want to change or improve. Frame this as a positive goal and clarify why it's beneficial. Consider one bite-size next step or simple action that will move you in that direction.

"Strive for continuous improvement, instead of perfection."

23

—Widely attributed to Kim Collins

Striving to be perfect can stop continuous improvement. Continuous improvement is a respect and appreciation that "getting better at getting better" is a process, not an event or outcome. Reflect so you can identify any disempowering perspectives that fuel perfectionism. These thoughts contribute to negative and limited outcomes in our lives, make communication challenging, undermine relationships, and limit how we see opportunities and find creative solutions to problems. The following are the four most common disempowering perspectives I have encountered:

1. **Being Right:** The need to always be right or correct and to prove this to others is an ego position that frequently results in a dominating, arrogant, or dismissive demeanor. This way of thinking does not allow for other points of view and often causes distance in relationships with others.

2. **Not Being Wrong:** This way of thinking is based in fear and the need to show one's worth by proving that you are correct, defending your opinion, or avoiding getting in trouble for being wrong or making a mistake.

3. **Fear of Failure:** This attitude views mistakes and failure as threats or hazards that should be avoided at all costs rather than as learning opportunities. Insisting on compliance, following rules, and needing to have answers can become restrictive and lower one's ability to tolerate the discomfort of change. This often closes one off to other ways of thinking and doesn't allow for flexibility or creative adaption.

4. **Shoulds:** This tendency is tied to judging and finding fault, believing that you and others in your life need to follow a list of rules you have created.

REFLECTIVE PRACTICE
Review the list above and check any of those perspectives you have when facing stress, everyday situations, challenging people, changes in your life, or difficult circumstances. Put a star by the most important perspective you would like to change and reframe that would positively impact your life and help you step out of perfectionistic tendencies.

24

"Every choice you make is a right choice. What is really important is not the choice but the reason why you make it. Any choice made from fear is a disempowering choice."

—Karen Kingston

Overcoming fear, a common obstacle to making choices and taking action, is part of the human process of transforming. Learn to have self-compassion for any missteps or possible failures you make. Often our best learning comes from the very mistakes we make when we don't let fear stop us. Accepting gentle pacing and continuing to move in the face of fear is in itself the win! Focus on just the very next step, however small, to keep going. Find the strength and grit to take that step. Sometimes the next baby step is about going within to your Source, depth, higher power, or prayer (whatever you call it) for the wisdom, truth, faith, and courage to take a step forward.

REFLECTIVE PRACTICE
Carefully reflect on the choices you make in the next week and ask if you are taking an action or avoiding an action out of fear. If you discover you are, what would your choice or action be if fear were not stopping you? How can you shift your perspective, make a more empowering choice, or take a courageous action even in the face of fear?

25

> "The barrier to success is not some thing which exists in the real world; it is composed purely and simply of doubts about ability."

—Franklin D. Roosevelt

All too often we externalize what we identify as barriers, blaming people or circumstances we encounter. It's easy to do this to avoid taking responsibility, to not feel bad about ourselves, or to transfer feelings of overwhelm to external causes. Thinking the challenge or problem is "out there" is much less confrontational than reflecting about ourselves, our feelings of doubt, or our insecurities that are so often the source of our barriers. The irony of this is that we have little control over external barriers or challenges, but we have much more control and choice around how we approach any kind of challenge, external or internal. Exploring how to get out of our own way is a remarkably fruitful inquiry, although it does require tolerating some initial discomfort to reflect and look within. But authentically doing this inner work can make all the difference in creating action plans that really help us achieve our hopes, dreams, and goals. Ultimately it is worth it!

REFLECTIVE PRACTICE
Was there anything that came up this week, a topic of reflection or a problem, that you feel you need to stay with a little longer? Were there any internal narratives about the situation or doubts about yourself that you might want to reframe?

Reflecting on Action

Just taking action is not enough to foster sustainable change. We must be conscious and mindful of our actions, taking responsibility for them and, when necessary, stopping, refining, or modifying them to better achieve what we want. This requires intentional reflection surrounding what we have done and what we are currently doing to guide our next actions.

26

"Slow, soulful living is all about coming back to your truth, the only guidance you'll ever need. When you rush, you have the tendency to follow others. When you bring in mindfulness, you have the power to align with yourself."

—Kris Franken

Being mindful is very connected to pacing and slowing down the speed of our bodies, our minds, and our speaking. Slowing your pace expands your access to a deeper awareness of what's guiding you and informing your thoughts and actions. Are you being guided or internally pressured to respond to other people or circumstances from your material mind, wrapped up in expectations and urgency, or from an emotionally reactive need or habit? When we rush or feel hurried, we tend to be more reactive and less aware of what's driving us forward. Slowing your pace allows you to turn within and tap into your heart and inner guidance. Staying true to yourself and aligning your values with your actions and responses is directly connected to slowing your pace, listening to your internal space, and calmly making conscious, mindful decisions.

REFLECTIVE PRACTICE
Begin to notice and increase your awareness of your pacing. Witness your personal symptoms that tell you that you need to self-regulate your pace and slow down. Become aware of your body's sensations—quick movements, dropping things, an increase in blood pressure. Witness your mind's activity, and notice if you are jumping to conclusions, losing focus, making mistakes in your work, or missing details. Watch your speaking, and observe if you are interrupting people, talking really fast, or saying things that are curt, unkind, or unthoughtful. Use this expanded awareness of your symptoms to guide you to slow down and turn within to adjust your mindfulness.

"Challenges make you discover things about yourself that you never really knew."

27

—Widely attributed to Cicely Tyson

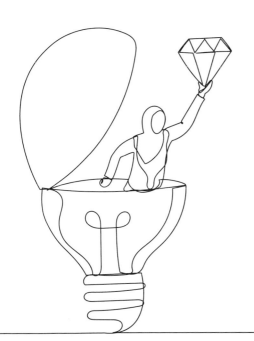

Learning about yourself with an honest desire to become self-aware can be challenging, but it will always offer you a freedom that is well worth the effort. Taking the step to learn about yourself is usually a smoother journey than waiting to get feedback from others. Taking the initiative to self-reflect about what's working in terms of how you think, feel, and behave and what might need changing puts the keys to becoming who you want to be in your hands. With desire, motivation, and consistent reflective practices, you can leverage the discomfort of becoming self-aware and take what you learn to your advantage. Becoming more self-aware and waking up can be uncomfortable, but it's worth it to become more conscious and become who you know you want to be.

REFLECTIVE PRACTICE
Develop a daily reflective practice to review your plan or intention for the day and examine what actually happened as compared to your intention. What worked or didn't? What distracted you or helped you focus? What unexpected things occurred, and how did you respond? At the end of each week, review your notebook and look for patterns. These can reveal attitudes or behaviors you want to work on or habits you want to change. Implementing this reflective habit becomes an action plan for clarifying what you want to change.

28

"Sometimes overcoming a challenge is as simple as changing the way you think about it."

—Anonymous

What was a challenge you encountered this week? Consider your mindset and how you think about that challenge. How might you reframe or shift your perspective? Are you willing to change your perspective?

"To succeed in this world, you have to change all the time."

29

—Sam Walton

Go beyond thinking that setting a goal or outcome or even creating an action plan is enough. A plan is only a map of a journey to get to a desired destination or goal; it's not the same thing as actually taking the trip or accomplishing the necessary actions. During the journey itself, it's important to reflect, learn, and examine what's working and what needs refinement or tweaking. To blindly arrive at a destination is a missed learning opportunity and will not contribute to the ease and quality of future journeys. Reflecting and focusing on the journey while it's happening adds meaningful learning, expands your perspective, and offers opportunities for intentional choices. The process of learning and achieving sticky change requires reflection before, during, and after the experience or the journey. Coaches often make the mistake of thinking that helping someone set goals and create action plans is the core of their work. That is just the tip of the iceberg! The real work is to accompany the person, helping them reflect about the steps they are taking and what they are learning as they accomplish the action.

REFLECTIVE PRACTICE
Keep a progress journal of what you are learning while trying to achieve a goal. If you support others in achieving their goals, help them by facilitating reflective conversations about their progress on implementing their plan and supporting them in documenting their efforts, learning, progress, plan modifications, and achievements. Help them witness their own learning story.

30

"Watch the little things; a small leak will sink a great ship."

—Benjamin Franklin

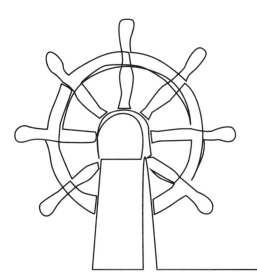

Daily reflective practices are an excellent way to watch the little things. Choose any focus area. For example, focus on how you react to people or circumstances and consider where you have control and can make changes. How do you want to respond or behave? You can also focus on your daily actions and habits and consider which ones support you and which ones distract you. You can also review which routines or habits you know would be helpful but you are not practicing or are perhaps avoiding. Increase your self-awareness to discover the changes you want to make by observing yourself and watching the little things. You can't change what you don't see, and wanting to change something is the best motivation to take a step.

REFLECTIVE PRACTICE
Choose something to pay attention to—something that bothers you or stresses you out, or something that inspires you or you want to excel at. Focus on one thing every day for a month, and reflect by writing, talking, or thinking about what you observed. Don't feel judgment or pressure to take any action; just witness and observe.

Chapter 7

EXPERIMENT AND PRACTICE

The only avenue to success is through implementing new ideas or behaviors; practicing and repeating them over time; and adjusting, modifying, and refining them as challenges, failures, or mistakes happen. Experimenting and modifying your approach requires tolerance for the discomfort of learning from and overcoming obstacles and mistakes, which happen to everyone. Staying focused on motivation and purpose fuels our practice over time. It also takes character, grit, strength, courage, and perseverance to keep going in the face of challenges to achieve success.

Getting Better at Getting Better

It is through practice that we get better at anything. Improvement and mastery are part of a lifestyle of getting better at getting better, more than a one-time event.

"Ideas are easy, implementation is hard."

—Guy Kawasaki

It is the coach or leader's role to cultivate an individual's ability to persevere through implementation. When implementing new ideas, leveraging learning opportunities from trial and error, or having unexpected consequences, people often appreciate some facilitation to help them actively reflect and think critically about their process while they are in the middle of it. Experimentation and refinement based on collected data, previous experiences, and new knowledge is a key part of the change process as we adopt new skills and practices. Making perceptible change requires tolerating the discomfort of not getting it right and not getting quick results, because real growth and change takes time. It takes grit, vulnerability, and motivation to continue to practice new skills, change small daily habits, identify and weed out barriers and obstacles, and use data to inform refinement over time. The goal is not just implementing one new habit or action but allowing the coachee to glean the fruits of their learning, including new professional reflective habits and tools to travel their own future change pathways. It is our role to be a reflective partner with the people we support, empowering them to discover their own answers and learn the process of changing, a necessary lifelong skill.

REFLECTIVE PRACTICE
Are you able to tolerate the discomfort of not giving advice to someone you are supporting and replace this with humble active listening, inquiry, and reflective questions, even when you think you know what they need? Are you able to focus on helping them reflect on how they are approaching their challenges or difficulties rather than trying to fix the issue for them?

2

"When you become comfortable with uncertainty, infinite possibilities open up in your life."

—Eckhart Tolle

Tolerating discomfort is key to growing and transforming. It takes practice to tolerate discomfort while learning, not unlike how an infant or toddler practices saying good-bye to a parent without distress. It takes a supportive setting and transition from adults. It takes experience to learn that it really isn't too dangerous or unsafe to lose sight of a parent. It takes repeated practice over time for children to tolerate the risk and discomfort, but they eventually are strengthened and gain confidence. Tolerating discomfort is developmentally part of growing and learning. For adults, becoming comfortable tolerating uncertainty is significant if we are to become adaptable, grow and excel in life, and experience the world's myriad possibilities. Leaders certainly need to model this way of thinking, so they can advance transformation by encouraging reflective practices, supporting adaptability, and investing in the development of those they serve to cultivate their visions and embrace opportunities even in the face of uncertainty.

REFLECTIVE PRACTICE
Is there something in taking a next step in your work or personal life that feels risky or that you are currently uncomfortable with? What role is the uncertainty of the outcome playing in your feelings of discomfort? How are your thoughts and feelings of discomfort related to not feeling safe? To what degree are these feelings connected to your internal perspectives about the situation, and might you need to reframe them? How might shifting your focus from fearing risk to cultivating courage be a more productive direction? What specifically would you need in order to have courage in this—speaking up, overcoming fear of failure, letting go of control, being honest about feeling vulnerable?

3

> "When we strive to become better than we are, everything around us becomes better too."

—Paulo Coelho

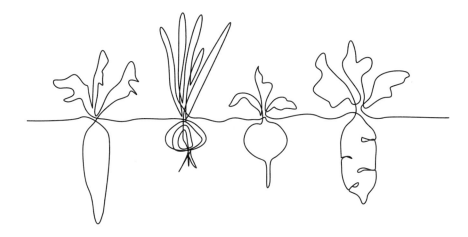

Learning new habits, implementing new work protocols, and transforming how we manage our time won't change overnight. When we turn within ourselves to dig deeper and continue to improve ourselves, we call forth a type of focus, energy, and attitude that inspires others. That's not to say that inspiring others is the reason you do this; it's more like a natural byproduct. Striving to better yourself, even just for yourself, makes a contribution to those around you since you model how to empower yourself, using positive, hopeful attitudes, grit, courage, and mindful problem-solving. We likely also need to turn to others for support, wisdom, and encouragement. It takes vulnerability to lean on others, and through that humility and openness one finds deep strength. This too is a valuable contribution to everyone around you. Our own growth is in itself a contribution to our community.

REFLECTIVE PRACTICE
Who has inspired you to strive to be better than you are? What were the qualities, attitudes, and actions that made them successful and also encouraged you? How did their own growth affect you? How can you apply what you learned from them to some endeavor you are currently undertaking to improve yourself?

"People do best . . . what they like best to do"

4

—Anonymous

In the book *Visual Leadership,* Todd Cherches introduces the Passion/Skill Matrix. He outlines a four-quadrant matrix comprised of the following:

1. **Sweet Spot** (upper-right quadrant)—The things that you like/LOVE doing and are GOOD AT. Spend as much time here as possible.
2. **Growth Zone** (upper-left quadrant)—The things you like/LOVE to do but are NOT GREAT AT yet. These are your primary development opportunities.
3. **Default Zone** (lower-right quadrant)—The things you DON'T LIKE to do but are GOOD at. Here's where you might outsource, delegate, mentor, or coach someone else to develop their skills in this area.
4. **Failure Zone** (lower-left quadrant)—The things that you DON'T LIKE and are NOT GOOD at. Do whatever you can to get out of this box. Consider whether you might not like doing these things **because** you are not good at them. Would improving your skill affect your confidence? Sometimes when we explore, we find that this zone hides a great opportunity. Or it might take some soul-searching to consider a new job better suited to your skills and your passions.

REFLECTIVE PRACTICE · PART 1: CURRENT STORY

Make a list of all the things you do on a regular basis within your job, including all the tasks and responsibilities that come with your role, and then break these tasks up into the four categories:

1. Things you are *good* or *great* at
2. Things that you are not *good* or *great* at
3. Things that you *like* or *love* doing
4. Things that you *don't like* or *love* doing

Next draw a four-box matrix following the Passion/Skill Matrix and place each of the items from your lists above in one of the four boxes. What insights do you gain from doing this categorizing activity? Are there any decisions or actions you might consider? What might you want to reflect more about?

5

"Having a solid base of values and testing them under fire enables you to develop the principles you will use in leading."

—Bill George, Peter Sims, Andrew N. McClean, and Diana Mayer

The ability to implement and modify action plans, persevere while facing obstacles and challenges, and practice new ways of doing things that might need a lot of refining is directly connected to the values you hold and your core beliefs. Are you clear about what your core values and beliefs are? When you are facing difficult or challenging situations, you might be tempted to take actions that seem easier or less confrontational than holding true to your beliefs. It requires mindfulness to make value-based leadership choices.

REFLECTIVE PRACTICE
Through reflection, evaluate whether the behaviors, mindset, and emotional responses you demonstrate while accomplishing what you want are aligned with your values and beliefs. Modify anything that is not your best effort. Clarify what leadership principles are important to you based on your values and your ability to "walk your talk."

6

> "The coach is a 'midwife to skill building,' and is not typically a highly didactic teacher. The coach's most important decision is whether to instruct/suggest or whether to ask a question—or indeed whether to use a style of interaction somewhere between these two extremes."

—Max Landsberg

Helping people find their way, to develop and change, happens as we engage them in thought-provoking conversations to explore what might be possible or desired in their lives or work—and then we help them figure out how to achieve it. Staying present with them as they practice, try things out, and take their plans into action is also part of the coaching role. Learning about yourself, your emotions, and your motivations is a critical step to practice before attempting to help others change, no matter what your job title or role.

REFLECTIVE PRACTICE
Make a list of the people throughout your life who have inspired you most, helped you grow as a person, and helped you accomplish your life goals. Divide your life into sections by significant stages or by decade intervals; for example, birth to mid-adolescence (0–14 years), high school (14–18 years), college/military/early workforce (19–25 years), and so on. For each life stage, write the names or initials of these influential and helpful people who impacted the course of your life.

"Excellence is not a destination, it is a continuous journey that never ends."

—Brian Tracy

Think about an area in which you might push or stretch yourself. Remember that pushing yourself is not always about doing more but sometimes about doing less.

"The key to successful leadership is influence, not authority."

—Widely attributed to Ken Blanchard

The people who influence others demonstrate and practice a pattern of interactions: serving as an inspiration, genuinely caring for the well-being of the person, providing support and encouragement, and facilitating the quest for the dreams, goals, and passions of the people they are helping. Helping people find or remember their true passion deepens their motivation to change and grow. This approach fosters an intrinsically motivated journey, which is more likely to result in sustainable change and growth. This is very different from facilitating a person to accomplish an externally defined objective or meet a compliance expectation.

> **REFLECTIVE PRACTICE**
> Use the list of people who influenced you that you made with Reflection 6. Think of a specific situation in which each of these people helped you. Write what they said or did in those situations, and reflect on how these people made you feel during and after. What did you learn from each person and situation? Review them all looking for patterns or themes in how these people inspired, motivated, or supported you. What did they do that actually helped you? What might you pay forward to help others?

Learning from Experience

Learning happens by reflecting on and leveraging our experiences, not just by having things happen. Learning from experience comes from observing and examining our successes, trials, and errors and determining which actions and modifications produced better outcomes. In this way, we use our past experiences to make more educated and intentional choices in the future.

"Don't let yesterday take up too much of today."

—Widely attributed to Will Rogers

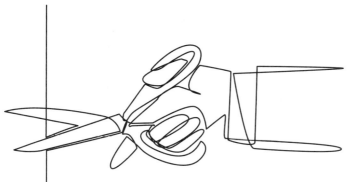

We want to learn from our past so that it informs our future. We don't want to get stuck in the past. Guilt is a sign that we are stuck in the past, not moving toward healing. Guilt doesn't really serve growth. Guilt and regret can take up too much of our current attention and are symptoms that we may have things we need to forgive, let go of, or accept in order to keep moving and growing. This is true for all people. There are often aspects of our past that need to be faced, felt, and healed. This is what growing and transforming looks like. We want to invest in our healing by accepting help from others or by reflecting and witnessing our life with forgiveness, a desire to learn, and an open heart and mind. Doing our self-work and healing is an important investment in our current awareness and in our search for a fulfilling, successful future life.

REFLECTIVE PRACTICE

Identify any areas of guilt or regret you currently have that are taking up too much of today. What do you need to let go of, accept, or forgive? Are there any past experiences that continue to negatively pull at you that need your attention, emotional resolution, or an intentional investment in healing for yourself? What resources or people may you need to do this?

"It makes no sense to worry about the things you have no control over because there's nothing you can do about them, and why worry about things you do control? The activity of worrying keeps you immobilized."

—Widely attributed to Wayne Dyer

The process of discerning what is and what is not controllable can be hard. It takes focus. But worrying about the things you can't control is a total waste of your energy and time, energy that you could otherwise use to focus on what you *can* influence. I spend a lot of my coaching sessions helping people clarify their challenges and concerns, with specific attention on helping them determine what they can change and what they have no or very little control over. For example, we have little control over what other people say or how they behave. So it's better to refocus on how *you* will respond than to complain or worry about what they are doing. To grumble about work policies or procedures, the amount of money you make, bad weather, or people who do not reply to their emails wastes energy. Your complaints indicate where you can look to reframe your perspective. Refocus on shifting your viewpoint: Stop complaining and instead control your response to circumstances or take action where you do have influence. Do you really want to waste your precious time focusing on the wrong things?

> **REFLECTIVE PRACTICE**
> What have you recently worried or complained about that is beyond your control? Separate what you do not have control over, like external circumstances, and refocus your attention on any internal attitudes or strong feelings or reactions you are experiencing that need reframing. Focus on your response, not the situations themselves, and make intentional decisions to change your attitude or actions. Reflect on ways you do have influence or choice in improving a situation. In areas where you do not have influence or in times when you encounter disappointing, uncomfortable, or disempowering circumstances, reflect on ways to regulate your emotional reaction or adapt your response.

"Reflection gives the brain an opportunity to pause amidst the chaos, untangle and sort through observations and experiences, consider multiple possible inter-pretations, and create meaning. This meaning becomes learning, which can then inform future mindsets and actions."

—Jennifer Porter

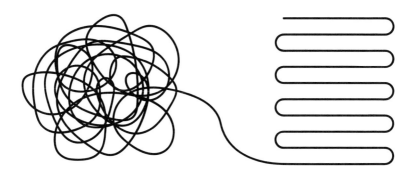

Taking careful time to reflect can reveal uncomfortable feelings, which can be challenging and often need a lot of space and time to unfold. I invite you to sit with those feelings and try to have patience and faith in the reflective process. Slow, consistent, and small shifts make big transformations. It is easier to feel and see progress when you practice careful reflection. Sometimes progress can come more from your way of perceiving things, things that you may overlook if you don't embed reflective practices in your daily and weekly life. Seeing what we need to unlearn is a significant part of this too. Keep investing in your rou-tine reflective habits, and over time you will witness progress and growth.

REFLECTIVE PRACTICE
What might you need to continue to unlearn?

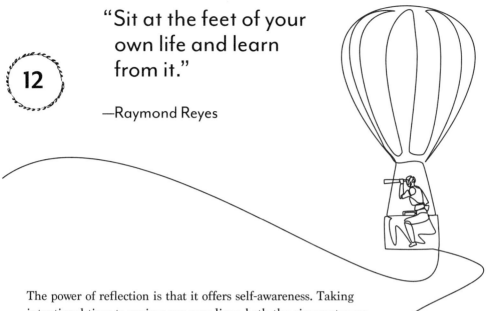

12

"Sit at the feet of your own life and learn from it."

—Raymond Reyes

The power of reflection is that it offers self-awareness. Taking intentional time to review our own lives, both the circumstances and how we responded to those circumstances, offers a great deal of learning. Witnessing our experiences—including victories and disappointments, the hurdles we faced, and how we deal with hurts and hardships—from a vantage point of wanting to learn, not from a perspective of judgment and evaluation, can open many doors and expand our self-awareness in ways that contribute to positive future mindful choices. Take a seat at the feet of your own life to learn from your journey with the same reverence, respect, and kindness you would feel at the feet of a beloved mentor.

REFLECTIVE PRACTICE

Choose a few highlights from your life—some bright spots and some darker moments. Write about the circumstances, people, and events as well as how you responded to those situations and people. Do this from a perspective of inquiry and wonder—don't assume you know. Write and reflect as if you are interviewing yourself in the current moment about your observations of the past, not from the perspective of the person you were at the time. Allow your current awareness to inform how you are witnessing these past times, gathering lessons that might not have been available that are now open to you. Proceed with kindness, forgiveness, and love.

13

"Experience is a hard teacher because she gives the test first, the lesson afterwards."

—Popular saying

People need time to encounter and negotiate complexity, including the opportunity to experiment with implementing actions over time. Tolerating imperfection, learning from our mistakes, examining what contributed to our successes, reflecting about these experiences, and talking about them are all important for meaningful learning. Consider how you might deepen your facilitation practice to assist someone in reflecting about their experiences, successes, trials, or mistakes, or to negotiate complex issues to support meaningful learning so they can appreciate the lessons of their journey.

REFLECTIVE PRACTICE
Do you take the time and have strategies to model this type of reflection? How can you foster meaningful learning using reflection with the people you support this week?

14

"Continuous effort—not strength or intelligence— is the key to unlocking our potential."

—Liane Cordes

What is an area of your life or professional practices that continues to need your focus, effort, and reflection to make needed or desired improvements? How can you overcome your tendency to take your foot off the gas or give up the endeavor? What can you do next week to improve this?

Harnessing Your Habits

Intentionally replacing ineffective habits with routine practices that are positive and motivating is the heart of successful transformation. The step-by-step details of experimenting with and practicing habits are how successful change and growth becomes sticky and sustainable.

15

"Success is the product of daily habits—not once-in-a-lifetime transformations."

—James Clear

Choice exists only in the current moment. We do not make choices for days, weeks, or years—we can make a plan but not the actual choice. When we are thinking about creating new habits, for example, it is only in the moment that you say yes to doing it or not. To build a new habit requires making a choice in that particular moment when you do not want to do it. It takes a little reflection, reminding ourselves why we want to do it and thinking about the value of habit. Why bother? Some mornings I just don't want to meditate. When this happens, I consider the bigger benefit. I remind myself that it doesn't really matter how I feel this second—just do it. I have to override my momentary emotions and my mind's excuses. Only through repeated reflection can I gain the perspective I need, so that in each moment I know how to choose what I really want.

REFLECTIVE PRACTICE
How do you support yourself to consistently make the choice to practice a desired habit? What do you do when you don't want to or if your mind offers excuses?

16

"You can't discover new oceans unless you have the courage to lose sight of the shore."

—Common saying

To achieve success is not just about being focused on a goal, outcome, or result, like always keeping your sights on the shore. Focusing our attention on making tweaks as we experiment and learn from trial and error is much more successful for changing habits than focusing on a goal and feeling the pressure of performance outcomes. Having the focus on the learning process rather than just achieving an outcome can be more motivating to change habits. It takes a learning mindset that focuses on growing, reflecting, and adapting. This requires curiosity and tweaking—making small, mild modifications to habits or ideas—which is also called *iteration*. Research shows that successful people who change habits have highly iterative mindsets. This means the pathway to changing habits looks like: assess where you are; clarify your authentic motivation and desire to change; then practice, practice, practice, trialing as you go. While walking the path, make iterative modifications, experiment, and practice. It's good to know the direction of the journey, but too much focus on the outcome often increases unnecessary unease and distress that can undermine the whole process. Often the most meaningful and significant changes come from immersing yourself in the journey and softening your focus on the destination.

REFLECTIVE PRACTICE
Think of a habitual behavior or a recurring disempowering thought you want to change. Assess how the habit shows up, what it looks like, and how you feel when you do it. Allow yourself to experiment with making small tweaks or modifications to your current habit. Observe what happens as you explore, and ask yourself, "What did I learn from making that small change?" Keep practicing making that change, and if necessary, keep tweaking. Observe with an attitude of discovery, curiosity, and wonder. Do your best to disengage from evaluating your performance and resist making any judgments. Stay focused just on what you learned in the process. Allowing learning to be your focus.

17

"Change is about interrupting the habits and patterns that no longer serve us. If you want to meaningfully alter your life, you don't instantly abandon a dysfunctional habit or belief; you replace it with a healthy one. You choose what you're moving toward. You find an arrow and you follow it. As you begin your journey, it's important to reflect not only on what you'd like to be free from, but on what you want to become free to do or to become."

—Edith Eger

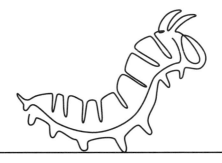

Habit tracking is a powerful practice that reveals the details of your life. Taking regular small steps, repeated over time, is how we create fulfilling, successful lives. There's a lot of research to show that happy, successful people have a routine of positive habits. Focus on the habits you want to see in your life rather than the ones you want to get rid of.

REFLECTIVE PRACTICE
What habit do you need to change? What are some options for a positive replacement habit?

"The golden rule of habit change: You can't extinguish a bad habit, you can only change it."

—Charles Duhigg

Our lives are shaped by our habits. Habits include patterns of action and thought that we choose automatically and repeatedly in certain situations. We often don't even see the habits that shape our lives. We have emotional or physical reactions that become unsupportive habitual patterns, often set off by the same repeated triggers. Often when you want to change or grow, you bump into bad habits. For example, I had learned about the importance of sleep health and decided I wanted more sleep. I created a goal to sleep no less than eight hours each night. Little did I know how many habits I was going to encounter and need to change in order to get more sleep! I have been intentionally focusing on developing better sleep habits for the last five years. I am focused daily, I have specific goals, I track the hours and regularity of my sleep, and I have an accountability buddy with whom I share my results daily. I have needed to routinely examine my habits that diminish my sleep and to keep changing my behaviors. It is a "practice" to consistently get my desired hours of sleep, and I am not by any means perfect. But I don't give up. Some habits take more effort than others to change, develop, and maintain. I'm learning that I require a daily review of my helpful and hindering habits so I remain successful in achieving my goal. Creating the lifestyle of reflecting on my habits has become, in itself, one of my foundational reflective habits.

REFLECTIVE PRACTICE
What is a goal you want to achieve? What habit(s) will you need to examine and change to get there?

19

"Practice isn't the thing you do once you're good. It's the thing you do that makes you good."

—Malcolm Gladwell

Practice, never giving up, and making continual refinements are how you get good at something. Most masters in any field are continuing learners; they rarely sit back and cruise. To be successful in improving my sleep health, I reflect daily about my habitual thoughts and actions that help or hinder my sleep. Each week I assess my progress, and then I make modifications in my action plan as needed. I continually collect data about how many hours I actually sleep and track my bedtime behavior patterns. I reflect on disempowering attitudes that have me dismissing the importance of sleep health. I get honest about the ways I justify my excuses for continuing habits that aren't supportive. And I have significantly increased the number of hours of sleep I do get. Many weeks I am successful in meeting my goals. Each small step and effort matters! So practice it is!

REFLECTIVE PRACTICE
What thoughts and behaviors will you need to monitor to help you override any discouraging feelings or bad habits to continue making small changes as needed and not give up?

20

"You're never in the wrong place. But sometimes you're in the right place looking at things the wrong way."

—Attributed to Abraham-Hicks Publications

When you are in the process of trying to change or create new habits, your perspective is often close to the ground and focused on the details. Our daily attention to the ebb and flow of accomplishments and disappointments can be nearsighted. Sometimes we need to refocus our perspective. You might be doing exactly what is needed but have forgotten that practice takes time—it's not necessarily going to present as distinct gains each day. Improvement can be gradual overall, and when viewed from a balcony perspective, even when there are daily dips or plateaus, the gains are visible. A slight shift in how we look at things or where we look from can make a profound difference and help us to stay the course.

> **REFLECTIVE PRACTICE**
> In what ways might you be looking at a particular situation or at your efforts to change a habit in the wrong way? How can you shift your perspective to look through a more useful lens?

"Habits—the only reason they persist is that they are offering some satisfaction. You allow them to persist by not seeking any other, better form of satisfying the same needs. Every habit, good or bad, is acquired and learned in the same way—by finding that it is a means of satisfaction."

—Attributed to Juliene Berk

Staying focused on what you want will keep you thinking about learning new ways to get there. It takes persistent endeavors to make new habits that offer the true satisfaction of accomplishing your dreams and doing your best. Name a habit you have adopted that you know is supporting your step-by-step journey. Identify another habit or behavior that may be giving you some kind of satisfaction but is not aligned with what you really want.

Trying with Optimism

Key components of optimism include having a hopeful attitude even in the face of difficulties, being confident in your success and positive future, attributing positive events with internal causes, characteristics, or actions one can take, and having resilience—the ability to adjust to and recover from adversity. Optimism can be learned, and practicing optimism entails becoming more mindful, consciously challenging and replacing negative and self-limiting thinking

22

"Always let your reach exceed your grasp."

—Common saying

Playing it safe rarely leads to success. Bold dreams and broad visions motivate the most inventive, inspiring actions and life journeys. Knowing how to accomplish something is not a prerequisite to stepping onto the pathway of pursuing it. Leaders who are led by strong vision and willing to be vulnerable and take risks are deeply inspiring. Too often coaches expect people to set a goal and immediately create an action plan. But the goal and the plan don't always come at the same time. Some people need time and courage to express their hopes and visions. They might need permission to even feel hopeful or to speak specifically and meaningfully about what they feel is possible. Many require encouragement to bring their hopes and dreams to life, especially if they are uncertain of their path. The desire and passion to accomplish something will, with time, birth the next steps, and it's OK if it's a small next step and not a complete plan.

REFLECTIVE PRACTICE
Have you ever had a dream or vision that you let go because you didn't know how to accomplish it? How would you want someone to help you have the courage to set big goals or reach for the stars even if you didn't know how to proceed? What would help you to risk and step forward, and what would hold you back or increase your doubt or fear?

23

"The pessimist sees difficulty in every opportunity. The optimist sees opportunity in every difficulty."

—Common saying

How we view difficulty and challenges sets the attitude and tone of our internal landscape, influencing the lens of our perceptions and how we experience the world and people around us. Too often we think it is external circumstances or other people that "cause" our experiences. Strong leaders know it's the exact opposite! Managing our own perspective is the key to success, and a main focus of a leader is managing the perspectives of the people around them. We do this with intent, by knowing our people and being a model. Coaching is an important tool for cultivating empowering perspectives, which in turn empowers people.

REFLECTIVE PRACTICE
Name several difficulties you encountered in the last week. Did you approach them as opportunities? Were you presented any opportunities to grow or change that didn't feel great at first? How can you shift your perspective by reframing your lens?

24

> "There is something wonderfully bold and liberating about saying yes to our entire imperfect and messy life."

—Tara Brach

Dissolving the disempowering attitude that we should somehow be perfect or mistake-free allows us to accept our imperfect human condition—hello, Human, and welcome! Accepting life, people, and ourselves as is creates a freedom from constricting judgment and comparisons. Like buying a clothing item at a store marked "as is," you are clear about what you are getting and what condition it's in. To accept things as they are doesn't mean you are without hopes, goals, and vision. It just means you are taking honest stock of how things currently are (both flawed and wonderous) so you can freely plan a life journey that you want and make informed choices based on acceptance, not resistance, denial, or shame.

REFLECTIVE PRACTICE

Is there an area of your life where you feel resistance, shame, or avoidance? How can you shift your internal no to a yes by accepting something as is? Where would you need to let go of a binding expectation, judgment, or fear? What freedom would be available or what weight would be lifted if you could do this?

"You cannot change your future, but you can change your habits, and surely your habits will change your future."

—Widely attributed to Dr. A. P. J. Abdul Kalam

Our attitudes influence not only our thought habits but also our behaviors. Thousands of thinking routines are running every day in the brain, and these thought patterns determine how we assess our own abilities and knowledge. They decide whether, for example, you love keeping things in order or consider it important to be punctual. Thought patterns determine whether we perceive rejection as something bad and how we deal with negative news or pain. For example, do we tend to worry too much, or do we firmly believe that everything will be better tomorrow? The truth is that a positive attitude allows us to enter spheres we could never reach in any other way. And it is often our attitude that stands between what we are and what we want to be. Each of us is empowered to become a better person, and the first step in this direction is usually a change of attitude. This means that our attitudes and behaviors determine our whole life and ultimately shape our identity. That's why it is so important to acquire good routines. They are the key to a successful life!

REFLECTIVE PRACTICE
What thought pattern or behavior habit do you want to change so you can have the future you want?

Success and Failure

The dance partner of success is failure. Just don't stop dancing! Having the perseverance to keep going in the face of failure, breakdown, or disappointment is the pathway to achieving success.

"Success is not final; failure is not fatal: It is the courage to continue that counts."

26

—Anonymous

It's helpful to think of success and failure as the ebb and flow of a lifestyle of continuous growth improvement. It's risky to think of success as an event or something that is over and done. Not that successes don't deserve celebration— they do! But if you rest on your laurels and stop reflecting, being curious, trying to improve, and using your successes and your failures to further new discovery, you risk losing out on greater self-discovery and continued excellence for your life, your family, your coworkers, your clients, and your community. Excellence and expansion takes the courage to continue . . . to never give up.

REFLECTIVE PRACTICE
Recall a recent success you had. Did the success end when you "fin-ished," or did the success generate a continued wave of creativity or form a new goal? Did you use the energy of your success to move forward? Do this same reflection for a recent failure or misstep—did you quit, or did you use the learning and energy from that experience to move you forward? What role did courage play with the success and with the failure?

27 "There are three ways to ultimate success: The first way is to be kind. The second way is to be kind. The third way is to be kind."

—Fred Rogers

Kindness is both an attitude and a behavior. How can you strengthen this mindset and nurture your attitude and open heart so it naturally results in kind behaviors? Kindness can be a tool to promote success in yourself and others. Kindness can also be a criterium for assessing whether something was a success, looking at not only whether a goal was achieved but also the manner in which it was achieved.

REFLECTIVE PRACTICE
Make a list of five ways to practice kindness in your workplace and another five ways in your personal life. Do each of them in the next two weeks. Track your progress and be reflective of the difference it makes to you and those around you. How does this influence your perspective on success?

28

"Success is peace of mind, which is a direct result of self-satisfaction in knowing you made the effort to become the best of which you are capable."

—John Wooden

Consider carefully how you define success. How can you incorporate excellence, learning from failure, self-satisfaction, your quality of endeavor, diligence, and being on the path to becoming your best self? Write a definition of success for yourself. For each goal or vision you have, write a specific criteria of success so you can know when you have achieved it. Revise and revisit your definitions frequently to keep them current with what you are accomplishing and learning.

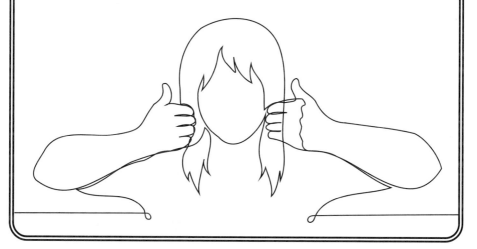

29

"Failure is a feeling long before it becomes an actual result. It's vulnerability that breeds with self-doubt and then is escalated, often deliberately, by fear."

—Michelle Obama

Failure is a perception or interpretation of events. When the lens through which you view situations is laced with self-doubt or fear, often you will declare things to be failures. This fear of failure or making mistakes is alive and operating before any actual event occurs. It's a preconditioned state of mind, thinking a mistake is dangerous, painful, or threatening. When the fear of failure is coupled with an intolerance for taking risks and an unwillingness to feel vulnerable, our choices become limited and reach a dead end at an inner wall. I know for myself that when I've declared something a failure, it is a judgment my mind comes up with as a result of interpreting and feeding off negative feelings and the meaning I've assigned to the circumstance. But I experience my judgment as truth, often not recognizing it as a lens of FEAR—**F**aulty **E**vidence **A**ppearing **R**eal. However, this whole outlook toward failure can be reframed to deliver a very different experience of the same events. Adopting a more inspiring interpretation or mindset toward mistakes or failure is possible. Practice mindfulness to recognize when fear is the driving feeling and use that awareness to choose whether to believe your fear. You can choose to reframe your perspective so that mistakes and "failures" are learning opportunities, knowing that you are capable of and able to recover from temporary setbacks and that having an open heart is worth the discomfort of occasionally feeling vulnerable. The choice is yours, and like any other habit, it will take reflection, desire, and effort to shift your perspective. With desire everything is possible.

REFLECTIVE PRACTICE
What were the messages you received in your early life from your family or culture about failing or making mistakes? Do those messages empower you? Are these messages what you currently believe? If not, what messages and beliefs do you want to hold and carry forward in your life and as a role model for others? Use your awareness to make empowering choices.

30

"FLAWSOME (adj.) an individual who embraces their 'flaws' and knows they're awesome regardless."

—Anonymous

It takes humility, inner strength, courage, and humor to honestly acknowledge the ways we are imperfect without judging ourselves or collapsing in shame. Expecting perfection in ourselves or in others is inevitably going to cause suffering and disappointment. This is something to let go of. Embrace reflection, not perfection. Taking an honest inventory of our flaws is an ongoing reflective practice as we investigate and learn about ourselves—to know ourselves so we can intentionally get better at getting better. Focus on quality, not perfection. There is so much relief to be found by releasing inner pressure and accepting oneself as is—as an imperfect human. At the same time, self-discovery will always lead to ways we can gently yet consistently improve the quality of our life, so we can redirect our behaviors and actions to guide transformation. We continue to try, to learn, and to grow, expanding our awareness to make choices that shape our future.

REFLECTIVE PRACTICE
Share with someone today a funny mistake you made.

Chapter 8

RESILIENCY AND STRESS

Stress is the result of an imbalance between the demands we experience and our ability to respond to those demands. In this chapter, we explore internal and external stressors and how to reduce the demands we can control. Delve into reflective practices to strengthen resiliency, increase your capacity to respond to demands, build your ability to bounce back quickly from difficulties, and help others do the same.

Managing Stress

There are as many potential causes of stress as there are stars in the sky. But learning basic principles and strategies to transform stress and implementing reflective practices can expand your skills and capacity to respond to life's inevitable stress.

"The greatest weapon against stress is our ability to choose one thought over another."

—William James

Stress is caused when the relationship between the demands we face and our ability to respond to those demands is out of balance. It's like a fraction: Demands are the numerator, and our ability to respond is the denominator. To address stress, there are only two options: 1) reduce the demands, or 2) increase your ability to respond to demands. The easiest way to reduce stress is to focus where we have the most control and choice. The good news is we have 100 percent choice and control over how we respond to demands. There are four basic areas in which we can make choices that will increase our ability to respond to demands: physical/body, mental/mind, emotional/heart, and spiritual/soul. The physical/body options are the most commonly offered options for stress reduction, encompassing physical well-being behaviors and habits such diet, exercise, sleep, health, deep breathing, and so on. But perhaps the most significant stress prevention and intervention strategy to promote resilience is to reframe our mental perceptions and attitudes and choose which thoughts we listen to. When you notice negative or limiting thinking that creates worry, fear, anxiety, or overwhelm, be the DJ of your mind and say, "Not that one!" and delete that thought playlist. Replace it by flipping it with a more empowering thought. For example, if you believe you and others need to follow a list of rules and this causes demanding and judgmental thoughts or shoulds, replace them with a thought or question such as, "That's an option; or what's another possibility?" Or, if you are afraid of failing, you can flip that into a replacement thought, such as "Mistakes and failures are learning opportunities."

REFLECTIVE PRACTICE
Identify one disempowering thought or negative attitude you have and flip it! Write down the disempowering thought and then write a few words or simple phrases that are the opposite, or that redirect your attention to a more empowering perspective or thought.

"Gratitude unlocks the fullness of life. It turns what we have into enough, and more."

—Melody Beattie

If you have a negative perspective that focuses only on the bad things in a situation and ignores the good, you are likely contributing to your own stress. Our inner thoughts and attitudes are actually internal demands, and they can create stress for ourselves. This stress is not really coming from our external circumstances. Gratitude changes attitude. Use gratitude to shift a habit of responding negatively to circumstances, other people, or challenging situations.

REFLECTIVE PRACTICE
Write a thought of gratitude every day. Think of anything that you are grateful for, no matter how small or simple it might be. You can write this as the first thing on your to-do list each day. Strengthen your positive thinking like strengthening a muscle by intentionally starting every day with gratitude. Before you go to sleep, say or write another thing you were grateful for during the day. This will create a positive gratitude bookend to each day.

"The more we extend ourselves into a field of time other than the present moment, the more we attenuate our life energy. This leads to increased stress, worry, and more permutations about how to cope with those feelings."

—Imetai M. Henderson

Mindfulness occurs only in the present moment. Choices occur only in the present moment. When we get overfocused on either the past or the future, we step out of the zone of control and choice. Often this increases feelings of worry or being a victim or not having choice or control, which is not empowering, causes stress, and drains our energy. The result is feeling exhausted and tired. Notice the connection between worry, feeling stressed, and being depleted with how frequently you are focused on the past or the future. It can be useful to reflect on the past to bring your attention to what choices you can make in the present moment that will positively influence the future. The key is to examine choices you can make in the present to create a desired future experience and not get stuck worrying about the future. Learn to reel yourself back from the future, to regain your energy and be connected to your life-force source.

REFLECTIVE PRACTICE
Use the simple mindfulness practice of being aware of yourself and being aware of your surroundings in the present moment. Tune into your inner life source through a pause, breath, meditation, or prayer. Focus your attention on the choices you have and determine what you actually have control over in the present moment. Practice saying, "I am choosing to focus on just this moment right now."

Building Resilience

Resilience is having a large enough capacity to respond to the demands and challenges we experience. Building resilience requires us to explore a variety of ways to expand our capacity so we can more easily recover from adversity and respond constructively rather than react adversely. Protective factors that help expand our resiliency include attending to our internal beliefs, including how our feelings and thoughts impact how effective we think we are; strengthening supportive relationships; nurturing initiative to make positive choices and decisions, and take action; as well as practicing self-regulation, which is the ability to experience a wide range of emotions and express them verbally and with actions that are socially and culturally appropriate.

4

"More resilient people tend to embrace love and friendship, count their blessings, and grow emotionally as a result of their hardships. . . . We can learn to 'harness' the impact of stress on our emotions by . . . thinking in terms of challenges rather than threats, seeing our-selves as capable of meeting a challenge and thinking of the search for 'positive meaning' as a skill we can develop."

—Barbara Fredrickson

The following are four basic principles for transforming stress and becoming more capable of responding to the demands of stress in our lives:

1. Become response-able. Increase your ability to respond to demands, especially those demands causing stress.
2. Start where you have choice.
3. Reframe perceptions to empower yourself.
4. Focus on what you want, not what you worry about.

These principles are avenues to becoming more resilient. They build skills so we are able to reduce demands, increase our ability to respond, and reframe disem-powering perceptions. Whatever we focus on tends to consume our attention, so choose to focus on what you want over what you worry about. Keeping your focus aimed on what you want redirects your attention in that proactive direction and will result in a shift in behavior. Reframing our thinking to see ourselves as capa-ble of successfully addressing challenges allows us to make the choice to design a life we want and not be a victim of our circumstances.

> **REFLECTIVE PRACTICE**
> Consider the current stressors in your life and how you are feeling—are you leaning toward feeling like the circumstances are controlling your life, or do you feel empowered to be able to respond? Which of these four principles might be a direction you could take to become more resilient?

5

"More than education, more than experience, more than training, a person's level of resilience will determine who succeeds and who fails. That's true in the cancer ward, it's true in the Olympics, and it's true in the boardroom."

—Dean Becker

What makes some individuals and some organizations more resilient than others? Journalist Diane Coutu concludes in *Harvard Business Review* that three overlapping themes emerge across the many resilience studies of the last forty years. Resilient people and organizations possess three characteristics: They face reality and challenging situations with staunchness and acceptance; they believe life is meaningful and make meaning of hardship instead of crying out in despair; and they have an uncanny ability to improvise solutions, often without proper tools or resources.* The studies indicate that you can bounce back from hardship with just one or two of these qualities, but you will only be truly resilient with all three.

REFLECTIVE PRACTICE
Take an internal inventory to assess to what degree you have these three qualities of resilience—the ability to face reality, the ability to search for meaning in hardship, and the ability to improvise solutions with limited support or resources. Reflect on a time when you faced an extremely challenging situation, and review if and how you displayed any or all of these abilities. Is there one of these qualities you feel you might benefit from developing or strengthening?

* Diane Coutu, "How Resilience Works," *Harvard Business Review*, May 2002, https://hbr.org/2002/05/how-resilience-works.

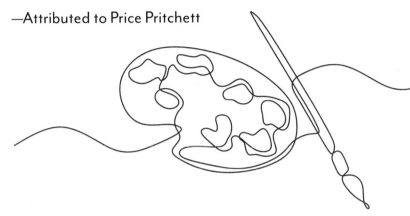

6

"Optimism inspires, energizes, and brings out our best. It points the mind toward possibilities and helps us think creatively past problems."

—Attributed to Price Pritchett

Optimism is a source of resiliency—but only as long as optimism doesn't distort your sense of reality. There is a difference between being optimistic and wearing rose-colored glasses that filter out significant information or aid denial. It takes a type of sobriety, grit, and hard work to face reality so we are prepared to endure and survive extraordinary hardships. Resilient people have an ability to find and create some sort of meaning for themselves and others in their suffering or hardship. This dynamic of making meaning helps us face the challenge of a current situation, modifies any attitude that the present is overwhelming, and points us to the possibilities of a fuller, more purposeful future.

REFLECTIVE PRACTICE
Think of a person you know or a famous person who is resilient. Make a list of their qualities or characteristics. Which of those qualities do you share? Which qualities might you want to strengthen? Choose one quality to focus on strengthening for the rest of the month. Write the quality on a card or sticky note. Put it somewhere you will see it daily. Contemplate the quality and what attitudes, actions, or behaviors embody it. Without any pressure or expectation to change or act differently, allow yourself to just witness how the quality is or is not reflected in your way of being. It's a month of just expanding your awareness and feeling your desire to embody that quality.

"Develop success from failures. Discouragement and failure are two of the surest stepping stones to success."

—Widely attributed to Dale Carnegie

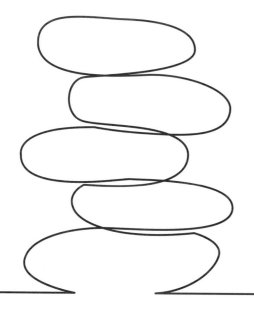

List three failures, mistakes, or missteps you have had in the last month. How might they be a stepping stone to your success?

8 "The key to resilience is trying really hard, then stopping, recovering, and then trying again."

—Shawn Achor and Michelle Gielan

Mistakenly, many of us have a notion that resilience is connected to pushing through challenges and obstacles like a soldier marching through the mud. This concept is scientifically inaccurate. Overwork and exhaustion are the opposite of resilience. When we lack a recovery period, it diminishes our ability to be resilient and success-ful. Stopping does not equal recovering, and rest and recovery are not the same. We build resilience by strengthening our ability to recover from difficult or demanding experiences. Jim Loehr and Tony Schwartz, authors of *The Power of Full Engagement*, have written that if you have too much time in the performance zone, you need more time in the recovery zone; otherwise, you risk burnout. To bounce back quickly, we must create routine habits of recovery time. Consider allowing yourself short periods of relaxation during the workday by having scheduled or unscheduled short breaks, shifting your attention, or changing to other work tasks when your mental or physical resources are temporarily depleted. At home, try not checking emails, looking at texts, watching the news, or even talking with family or friends about work or the demands you have. For many, getting off media entirely for specific periods provides true recovery time. Do things that replenish your energy coffers and intentionally in-corporate actions that create equilibrium and well-being in the body, mind, and soul. Consider putting resting, taking naps, and getting more sleep at the top of your list to physically recharge your brain. Being kinder in your internal self-talk might in itself be the most important act you can take toward recovery. Being kind and gentle with yourself is an act of resilience.

REFLECTIVE PRACTICE
Make a list of possible restorative actions that you can take. Con-sider a variety of things in each of the four domains of body, mind, emotions, and spirit. Start to intentionally incorporate at least one of these actions this week. Don't approach this like a to-do list; think of it as a menu of lovely dessert items to choose from.

9

"Cultural responsiveness is an essential protective factor for building resilience."

—Jill McFarren Avilés and Erika Amadee Flores

Your own cultural rituals and practices are the foundational, familiar threads of your life's fabric, and they can help protect you from risk and adversity and increase your resilience. Identify and nurture the qualities and behaviors you have that protect you from risk and adversity. When you are supporting other people in strengthening their resilience, be very mindful, curious, and inclusive of the many different qualities and cultural approaches individuals may identify for themselves. Be mindful of how culture contributes to what people experience as stressful. Dominant culture can be quite ignorant of diverse kinds of challenges individuals face and can make assumptions about how to best handle such situations. Be very aware of any ways you might not appreciate, honor, or even consider the diverse cultural approaches that people use to care for themselves and deal with stress or challenges. Learn more about the barriers different cultures encounter in considering self-care important or even a possibility.

> **REFLECTIVE PRACTICE**
> What are some of your own cultural values or approaches that hinder or help you deal with stress and adversity and build resilience? Be curious and ask friends and colleagues this same question.

Well-Being: Body, Mind, Heart, Spirit

True well-being must be holistic, incorporating all dimensions of ourselves. We can develop our internal and external healing and improve our practices through reflective attention.

10

> "The practices of self-reflection and self-care are critical in these times to ensure that we can be healthy and whole in our service to those who need us."
>
> —Ann McClain Terrell

Self-care is not selfish. Many of us have disempowering concepts or perspectives saying that investing in yourself with self-care practices is somehow selfish or taking away from the care of others. We receive many messages from our society, media, and culture that productivity is the cornerstone to success. In the book *Rest Is Resistance*,* Tricia Hersey, the founder of the Nap Ministry, addresses how we have subjected our bodies and minds to work at an unrealistic, damaging, and machine-level pace she refers to as the "grind culture." She elevates rest as a form of resistance and a divine human right. Eating well and getting enough sleep are human needs, and not about needing to be worthy enough to deserve them. Explore self-care as a human right. The truth is you cannot care for anyone else if your own health, well-being, and energy are depleted. It would be like trying to fill others' water glasses when your own pitcher is empty. Our ability to be fully present and available to others is dependent on the care we provide ourselves. It takes self-reflection to expand your awareness and mindfulness, so you know what you need and when.

REFLECTIVE PRACTICE
Do you have the belief that self-care is selfish? Is there an area of your life in which you know you would benefit from more self-care? What are the barriers or challenges that keep you from taking the needed steps to care for yourself? Either write down your thoughts or have a conversation with a friend about these questions.

* Tricia Hersey, *Rest Is Resistance: A Manifesto* (New York: Little, Brown Spark, 2022).

242

11

"I go to nature to be soothed and healed, and to have my senses put in tune once more."

—John Burroughs

For many folks, time in nature reconnects them with themselves. It helps them reframe their perspective and become more reflective. It's important to know how to regenerate yourself and invest in your well-being—emotionally, mentally, physically, and spiritually. All four of these areas need deposits in order to nurture the ability to keep going, to revisit values and our sense of purpose and "why bother," and to avoid burnout. If it's not time in nature, then be clear in what other ways you nurture yourself.

REFLECTIVE PRACTICE
How can you invest in yourself today? Is there an extra step you want to take, a request you could make, or a way to carve out time for yourself?

12

"The time to relax is when you don't have time for it."

—Sydney J. Harris

Often I hear people say they don't have time to slow down and do self-care. This is more of a perspective issue than a time issue. Thinking that you don't have the time is creating the stressful reaction when demands come your way. This is exactly when you most need to relax. Relax your mind, body, and spirit. You might have to reframe what relaxing looks like.

REFLECTIVE PRACTICE
Today, list five ways to relax that take less than ten minutes. List another five ways to relax that could take longer. Do one of them today.

13

"Breathing in, I calm body and mind. Breathing out, I smile. Dwelling in the present moment I know this is a wonderful moment."

—Thich Nhat Hanh

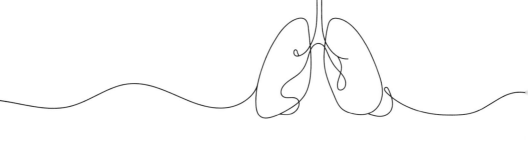

Self-care doesn't have to be a huge time or money investment, like having a spa day. (Although don't rule that out!) The small acts of self-care you do daily add up over time to strengthen your coping strategies for those times you start to feel emotionally overwhelmed or physically drained. Two simple examples are to take deep breaths and to pause for mindful moments in your day. Pause breaks can just be one minute when you suspend "doing" and become aware of your body, your mood, and your thoughts—just be in the moment. Becoming mindful in the moment allows the opportunity for a quick reset if necessary. It might be that your body needs to move. You might become aware that you are overwhelmed or anxious or are experiencing some negative or judgmental self-talk. Taking a deep breath alleviates the symptoms of stress by lowering your heart rate and helping you concentrate. A deep breath can create a little inner space where you become present, letting you make a conscious choice to reset your perspective and attitude. This is a reflective habit that doesn't take a lot of time but can be a big investment in your well-being, even if you take only five minutes a day!

REFLECTIVE PRACTICE
Today, practice taking mindful moments and deep breaths several times throughout your day. At the end of the day, review whether this practice was valuable. Did this expand your self-awareness, create a little more space to make mindful choices, or help you reset?

"Live by design rather than by default."

—Common saying

Given your own self-care practices, in which areas do you need to be more intentional and design a life that will not only support your own well-being but also be an investment toward achieving what you know you are here to give and contribute? What physical, mental, emotional, or spiritual practice or habit do you need to change or embed in your regular routine? Develop a first draft of an action plan and share it with someone.

15

"We sacrifice sleep in the name of productivity, but ironically our loss of sleep, despite the extra hours we spend at work, adds up to 11 days of lost productivity per year per worker."

—Arianna Huffington

There has been a great deal of research on the importance of sleep health, including its role in being resilient, relieving stress, keeping emotions in check, restoring the immune system, keeping weight under control, and helping brain function. What seems most important for health, renewal, learning, and memory is the amount of time in REM (rapid eye movement) sleep, not just the hours spent asleep. Most sleep physicians believe that the average adult needs seven to nine hours a night, with seven hours being the minimum for almost everyone. When you read that, do you automatically think you are an exception and it's not applicable to you, or feel that it just isn't possible? Sleeping less than seven hours per night on a regular basis is associated with adverse health outcomes, including weight gain and obesity, diabetes, hypertension, heart disease and stroke, depression, and increased risk of death. Sleeping less than seven hours per night is also associated with impaired immune function, increased pain, impaired performance, increased errors, and greater risk of accidents.

Are you dismissing hard research and using excuses or justification to ignore the science because you are not currently practicing sleep health and don't want to change; don't know how or feel discouraged; or feel defeated because you have tried and haven't been successful? For everyone, there are likely times in life when this is challenging for some duration, for example, when parenting newborn babies, when temporarily traveling long distances, or when dealing with a specific health challenge. In all circumstances, it remains important to develop routines that will contribute to better sleep habits. Making better habits will likely not happen quickly or easily. Motivation matters. Do a little research to connect the dots between any stress, health issues, emotional distress, mental fatigue, or memory issues you have and the impact of sleep.

> **REFLECTIVE PRACTICE**
> Take an honest look at your sleep health and habits. Just observe without any pressure to change anything. Collect actual data rather than holding a vague notion or interpretation—have the grit to witness how much sleep you are really getting and consider the habits that support or hinder this. For a week, track the hours of sleep you are actually getting each night. Start to watch which habits you have that contribute to getting less sleep. Start to list your excuses or justifications for not getting enough sleep. Are they related to busyness, distractions, social media, food or drink, emotions, or thought patterns? Expand your awareness to eventually make some choices that better support your resiliency and ability to respond to stress.

16

> "Lack of direction, not lack of time, is the problem. We all have twenty-four-hour days."
>
> —Zig Ziglar

We need to provide our brain opportunities to continually restore and sustain well-being. We want to intentionally incorporate certain actions that create equilibrium and well-being in the body and practice those until they become a habit, part of our lifestyle. When we get out of balance from overworking, we waste vast mental and physical resources trying to balance before we can move forward. Waiting until we are out of balance to do something is using an intervention approach, after the fact, which requires more energy and is not as effective as being proactive. Build proactive and preventative actions and habits to avoid falling out of balance in the first place. Getting realistic and intentional about planning your time and schedule is an essential way to avoid exhaustion, burnout, and falling out of balance. For example, do you intentionally plan recovery time after a big project or even after a joyous occasion like a wedding? Even joyous events can be demanding and stressful and require recovery. Planning for recovery time after predictable events or projects that are stressful or require more energy than usual will support your well-being and maintain your ability to perform with excellence. Being an influence leader who models self-care and resilience brings light and encouragement to others.

> **REFLECTIVE PRACTICE**
> Review your upcoming plans and schedule for the next month. Consider creating more recovery time if you have big projects or events. Also consider how to embed intentional space and moments in your everyday life, like transition time between meetings or even transitioning from work to home. These habits will help maintain your resilience so you bounce back more quickly and smoothly when stretched.

Meditation and Reflection

Reflection is the thoughtful consideration of something you are focusing on. Meditation is an introspective contemplation that can range from moments of slowing down and quieting your mind to deep, soul-searching concentration or prayerful attention. The range of practices are diverse, but the focus is within.

17 "To calm down means just that, you're not striving for a spiritual experience and nor are you striving to stop all your thoughts. You just want to become still and calm and undisturbed as much as possible, even while there may be many thoughts racing in your mind. Just be still and keep going deeper into a prayerful quietness, openness, with no expectation, just a quiet, calm state."

—Kalindi*

It can be simple to slow down, pause, and take a calm moment. We have preconceived ideas that to calm or meditate is hard or that there are rules for calming. Practicing how to become still within yourself can happen in small increments and start when you have just a few minutes. As you start to trust your desire for calm and explore the benefits of becoming still and turning within, you can lengthen the time you spend in quiet. Recognize that the goal is not to eliminate all thoughts but to quiet the busyness and external focus, turn within with an open mind, and step aside from worries. Having an attitude of exploration and wonder rather than expectation can make a big difference in our experience.

REFLECTIVE PRACTICE
Go somewhere quiet and close your eyes to block external distractions. Experiment with using calm music or just being in silence. Start with five to ten minutes, and as your comfort increases add more time in increments until you can maintain the routine you want. This allows you to deepen your desire for calmness and experience the benefits of turning within, which in turn helps you be successful. Desire is everything! It's more important to create a routine for developing the practice of calming and turning within than it is to dictate the length of time you should be practicing each day. Scaffold yourself into a daily routine, ideally at the same time during the day, by experimenting with ways to calm yourself. You might want to meditate first thing in the morning or just before bedtime.

* Kalindi, Goursana Meditation Practice Series, www.CenteroftheGoldenOne.com.

18

"You should sit in meditation for twenty minutes every day—unless you're too busy; then you should sit for an hour."

—Zen-inspired adage

Taking the time to slow down, just to slow your pace, is the first step toward being reflective and mindful and making intentional choices. When we listen to our inner voice when it tells us that we don't have time to slow down, it's important not to believe that thought is true—rather, it's just your current interpretation. Going nonstop, going too fast, actually costs us time as we tend to make more mistakes. It also takes more energy as we get caught in cycles of stress that make us less effective and efficient. It even puts our greater resilience and well-being at risk. If you are trapped in this mindset that you can't pause, take a breath, or take a few minutes to go within, like the quote above says, you probably need to take more time to go within than you think. Don't confuse your assumption that you don't have time to slow down with an internal resistance to doing so. Overcoming resistance to slowing down might take a little deeper reflection, as it might be more connected to motivation, not understanding the value of slowing and quieting your body and mind, or fearing that you don't know how.

REFLECTIVE PRACTICE

List ways you often go too fast for your own good. What attitudes or thoughts keep you from slowing down enough to take a breath and step out of the fray of the chronic buzz and pace of the material world? Talk with others about how they pace themselves and how they take quiet time for themselves.

19

"Mindfulness is a collection of practices nowadays, aimed to help most of us cultivate moment-to-moment awareness. You're not only aware of your body; you're aware of your surroundings and your world. It forces you to pay attention to life [rather] that get caught up in your head with anxious thoughts, worries and ruminating about the future."

—Monica Vermani

Science is showing that practicing meditation can actually change the brain. Mindfulness is "commonly and operationally defined as the quality of conscious or awareness that arises through intentionally attending to present moment experience in a non-judgmental and accepting way."* According to the American Psychological Association, "mindfulness influences two stress pathways in the brain, altering brain structure and activity in regions that regulate attention and emotion."** People who practice mindfulness and meditation reportedly are less likely to have negative thoughts or unhelpful emotional reactions when facing stressful situations. There are many kinds of meditation, and finding a type that is best for your body and mental state can make the difference to your success. Some styles of meditation involve being still and quiet, some are active and dynamic, and some are specifically focused on mindfulness, while others use music or guided meditations led by a teacher or audio recording. Yoga is one type of active body-based meditation. There are even laughter meditations. Research online, ask friends, or search phone applications, as there are now many options available. Experiment and explore!

REFLECTIVE PRACTICE
If you don't currently have a preferred meditation practice, explore several different types this month. Ask others or do a little online research, and you will likely find many options. If you are a beginner or feel cautious, perhaps begin with just five minutes and build up. Take action, even if it's small steps.

* J. Kabat-Zinn, cited in Jenny Gu, Clara Strauss, Rod Bond, and Kate Cavanagh, "How Do Mindfulness-Based Cognitive Therapy and Mindfulness-Based Stress Reduction Improve Mental Health and Wellbeing? A Systematic Review and Meta-Analysis of Mediation Studies," *Clinical Psychology Review* 37 (April 2015): 1–12, www.sciencedirect.com/science/article/abs/pii/S0272735815000197.

** American Psychological Association, "Mindfulness Meditation: A Research-Proven Way to Reduce Stress," APA.org, October 30, 2019, www.apa.org/topics/mindfulness-meditation.

"Take the perspective of watching your mind chatter like you are watching a film every day."

—Kalindi*

Humans are meaning-making machines. The meaning we give things comes from our internal frame of reference, the lens through which we interpret all our experiences. It's important to make the distinction between our perspective and our lens and what's true and real. A great deal of our thinking is not only inaccurate and not based in fact, but actually something we have conceived in our mind with unsubstantiated assumptions we have made about ourselves and others. This nonfactual thinking can stimulate stressful emotional reactions. We often think something external is stressing us when it's actually our own mind and perspectives. Learn to watch your thinking, to simply witness your thoughts, without attachment and without judgment. Take time to reflect and become aware of which thoughts are worth believing and which are unsupportive perspectives or disempowering thoughts. This mindful practice can greatly transform your experience of stress by revealing where you have control to reframe your mindset. Is it really the external circumstance itself, or is it your reaction stemming from an internal perspective that judges the experience as bad or stressful that results in more reactive thoughts and behaviors? Reframing your perspective can drastically alter the amount of stress you experience.

REFLECTIVE PRACTICE
Develop the quality of noticing and merely watch your thoughts. Do not judge them or do anything about them. Just witness and observe them so you grow aware of the voices in your mind. Discern disempowering thoughts or attitudes that cause stress and are not supportive. Later you can make some choices about them. First, just start by becoming aware of your thinking. You can't change what you can't see.

* Kalindi, Break-Free Message, www.CenteroftheGoldenOne.com.

21

"If you concentrate on finding whatever is good in every sit uation, you will discover that your life will suddenly be filled with gratitude, a feel ing that nurtures the soul."

—Rabbi Harold Kushner

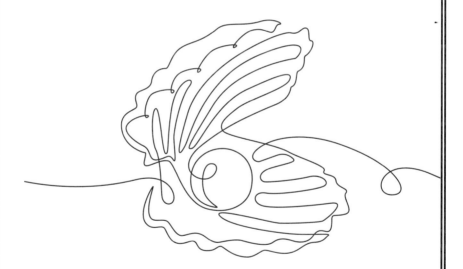

At the end of each day for one week, ask, "What good things happened today? What were my wins for the day? What good came from difficult situations?" At the end of the week, write a list of what you are grateful for, given your experiences from the week. Continue this as a regular practice if it's helpful for you, and discover how gratitude changes attitude.

22

"The world is full of magical things, patiently waiting for our senses to grow sharper."

—Eden Phillpotts

To sharpen our senses, we need to go at a slower pace so we notice the present moment—being in our bodies, using our senses with awareness. It takes intentional choice to slow down to experience more joy, connection, delight, and pleasure. Life can become one long to-do list, full of internal pressure and "shoulds" that speed up our pacing, reducing spontaneity and our appreciation for good moments and even our ability to acknowledge our accomplishments and successes. Simple human rituals can reconnect us to deep-seated sources of pleasure. Communal meals, lying on the ground watching clouds, star-gazing, making angels in the snow, playing music or singing with others, taking a slow walk in nature, cuddling with a child, turning your face to the sun and soaking it up with a smile and gratitude—these simple examples reconnect us to magical moments.

> **REFLECTIVE PRACTICE**
> What are some small treats and human rituals that would sharpen your senses so you more fully experience the magical delights around you? How can you shift your pace to slow down and reconnect with yourself and sweetly shift your attention?

Inner Strength

Identifying and nurturing the inner qualities that strengthen our character will help us be resilient. Some of us need support to even recognize our strengths and trust those inner qualities when adversity hits and not wallow in self-doubt when we are stressed. Others are clear in knowing what inner qualities and strength to turn to and reliably do so.

---

23 "What lies behind us and what lies before us are tiny matters compared to what lies within us."

—Henry Haskins

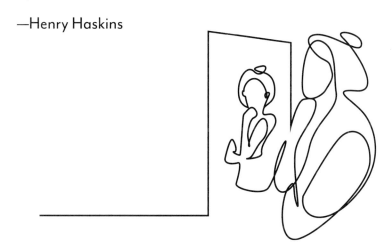

Turn within to find your source of authentic power. This is where you are your truest self, most connected to love and the spark that feeds your faith and trust, and where you touch the divine (however you might define or experience that). Turning within is one of the most important acts that will help you in your life. This turning within is unlocked through reflection, contemplation, mindfulness practices, meditation, calm and quiet time, and prayer. These essential inner qualities are a source of great refuge when the going gets tough: desire, trust and faith, courage, determination, humility, inner strength, and the ability to be in action. By cultivating and immersing yourself in these qualities, you will change, you will overcome obstacles, and you will reap the rewards of living a meaningful, resilient life.

REFLECTIVE PRACTICE
Name one quality you have that you know is strong within you, one that is reliable and can be counted on. Identify one quality you would like to strengthen, and reflect on ways to learn more about and cultivate that quality.

24 things I cannot change, the courage to change the things I can, and the wisdom to know the difference."

—Attributed to Saint Francis of Assisi

Being able to discern where you have choice and control and where you don't is really important in order to take responsibility for yourself and your attitudes, to let go of control and worry in areas where you do not have a choice or control, and to stop wasting your energy and time. Doing this is not a one-time event. This is a living, active, and ongoing discernment often needed multiple times in a day. It takes humility to accept people as they are and to recognize that we really do not have control over other people's behaviors and reactions. At times it requires awareness and letting go of feeling that our viewpoint or opinion about a situation is "truth" and the only valid perspective. It takes strength to resist the temptation to overreach with our actions and second-guess motivations and outcomes, so we can create respectful space for the differing voices and choices of other people. It takes persistence to shift our attachment to our personal perspective, and it takes courage to change our own habits of mind, emotional reactions, and behaviors.

REFLECTIVE PRACTICE
Choose a situation or a person around which you are experiencing frustration, anger, worry, or disappointment. Examine where you really have choice and control and sort out what is not within your control or lies beyond your scope of influence. Ask yourself what choices are available to you. What might you need to change in yourself or in situations that you do have control over? What might you need to accept, let go of, or forgive?

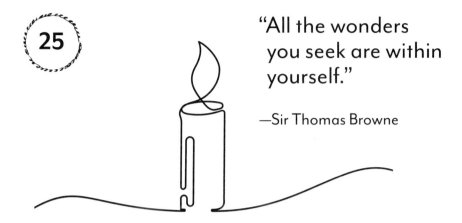

25

"All the wonders you seek are within yourself."

—Sir Thomas Browne

The ability to bounce back from misfortune or change is resilience. The strengths that help resilient people bounce back are called protective factors. You can strengthen your internal protective factors throughout your life. The Devereux Center for Resilient Children (DCRC) has created a tool for adults that can help them strengthen their internal protective factors to become more resilient. The Devereux Adult Resilience Survey (DARS) provides adults the opportunity to gain valuable insights in the following four protective factors: relationships, internal beliefs, initiative, and self-control. In the book *Building Your Bounce: Simple Strategies for a Resilient You*, authors Mary Mackrain and Nefertiti Bruce Poyner state, "Our protective factors have an impact not only on ourselves but also on the people with whom we interact on a daily basis, such as our family members and co-workers."* They offer practical strategies to strengthen each of the four protective factors.

REFLECTIVE PRACTICE
Download and complete the free Devereux Adult Resilience Survey (DARS) and develop an action plan to strengthen any areas that would benefit you. (https://centerforresilientchildren.org/wp-content/uploads/Devereux-Adult-Resilience-Survey-DARS-Packet.pdf).

* Mary Mackrain and Nefertiti Bruce Poyner, *Building Your Bounce: Simple Strategies for a Resilient You*, 2nd ed. (Lewisville, NC: Kaplan, 2013),8.

"Accept what you can't change."

26

—Karen Reivich

Sometimes persevering and never giving up are the qualities we most need in order to achieve what we want. Yet sometimes acceptance is the graceful solution to situations that have caused us stress or disappointment. Take time to reflect on whether you can realistically change the situation. When we get caught in a loop of trying to fix something or someone and our response is frustration, it can be a sign that we are exerting effort where we really do not have any control, even if we wish we did. It takes an inner softening and acceptance to have the humility to recognize when we can't change something. It is a general rule that if you are trying to change someone else you will become frustrated, because you simply don't have the control to change any other living person. In this area, we must always practice the art of acceptance and letting go. Self-expectations surrounding what you think you "should" do or change can contribute to trying too hard, when the true course may well be to accept our own human limitations.

REFLECTIVE PRACTICE
Identify an area in your life that has been the source of frustration. Take time to contemplate or meditate about whether you have any control over this situation or power to change the other person. What might you have to accept about the other person, the situation, or yourself? How can you begin to gracefully accept this with compassion and kindness?

"Some of us think holding on makes us strong, but sometimes it is letting go."

—Widely attributed to Hermann Hesse

We can know inside ourselves that we have an unsupportive habit or an opinion, a position we have taken, or a judgment that is problematic—but somehow, we can't let it go. We might have fears about what will happen, maybe that we will lose face, or we are attached to it and our ego just wants what it wants. Letting go happens on the inside first. To let go takes trust and courage. When we let go, we let go of our need to be right. Letting go allows us to change how we view what's happening. Quite often what's needed is a shift in perspective. The benefit of trusting and taking a risk is that it allows us to see the same thing in different ways. This can loosen our tight hold, which in truth makes us brittle, hard, and often exhausted. That is not strength. Often strength is found more in being able to bend and be flexible, adaptable, and cooperative. To be resilient is to have the strength to be able to bounce back rather than break.

REFLECTIVE PRACTICE
Review your life and think of times in the past when letting go seemed difficult but, with trust, you were able to do so. What supported you to take the risk and loosen your grip? Think of people in your life who demonstrate great strength by being resilient and letting go.

28

"You must be the change you wish to see in the world."

—Commonly attributed to Mahatma Gandhi

What change do you wish to see in the world? In what ways are you being that change, or what do you need to practice more to step closer to being who you want to be?

"Sometimes when things fall apart . . . well, that's the big opportunity to change."

—Attributed to Pema Chödrön

There have been many times in my life that something fell apart or didn't go as I planned, or when something I thought was so important just crumbled around me, and my first perspective was to freak out and think it was a really big problem and bad news. However, I have learned that my first response and interpretation is often not my best, as I am too close to the situation and do not have perspective. Over time I've learned that about myself, and I can now respond differently because I have seen a pattern: Often those experiences have ended up being the beginning of a whole new venture or chapter in my life. Getting fired ended up being the biggest blessing and opened doors to writing my first book. Having a health issue created havoc with my work plans but ended up affording me some deep rest that was way overdue and helped me tap into a deep creative thought process that changed the direction of my company. I could not have accessed that creativity without the rest. I am learning to examine the assumptions I am making, and now, with curiosity, I ask myself a lot of questions. I have learned I often have to give myself space to grieve when I let go of what I thought was going to happen. I am much more gracious about letting myself just have and feel my feelings without making up stories in my mind and without needing to hang on with attachment. I am much better at not assuming that when things go off the rails or fall apart it's going to be awful. I can lean forward to wonder whether there is opportunity. I am not perfect about this and sometimes I forget, but I turn around much faster these days. It's taken practice over time, watching for patterns, being intentionally reflective, and recognizing when negative perspectives want to capture my attention, and then just saying no. I remember the power of metaphor and the legend of the phoenix rising from the ashes; I remember that what seems like a falling-apart change can hold hope and possibilities.

REFLECTIVE PRACTICE
Reflect on the big disruptions in your life, the times it felt like something was falling apart. What was the eventual outcome? Did any new horizons open that you may not have discovered otherwise? What helped or hindered you to respond resiliently rather than resisting? If you could go back in time and support yourself, what would you tell yourself to help trust the process?

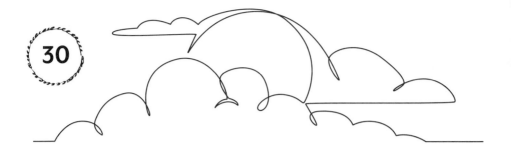

"There are uses to adversity, and they don't reveal themselves until tested, whether it's serious illness, financial hardship, or the simple constraint of parents who speak limited English, difficulty can tap unexpected strengths."

—Sonia Sotomayor

When I read this quote, I think of the saying that God doesn't give you more than you can handle. When I am faced with what feels like overwhelming hardships, how often in my mind's eye I think I am not capable or able to cope with whatever is in front of me. Yet repeatedly, somehow, I find a way. I am rarely alone, with adversity often teaching me to ask for help from others. Sometimes it has simply driven me deeper within to access connection with Source for wisdom, comfort, and solutions. When adversity expands my capacity to handle a situation, even just to muddle through, whether mentally, emotionally, physically, or spiritually, it always feels like a miracle. Adversity and even failures seem to be the best stimulus for transformation and growth, even though I can rarely appreciate it while I'm in it. That positive perspective comes after the stretch and after I find a way through. And I am always left being more than who I was at the beginning.

REFLECTIVE PRACTICE

What helps you to trust, go deeper within yourself, connect to Source, or turn to others for help when facing adversity? What are your practices now to help yourself be ready, adaptable, open, and prepared for difficult times or circumstances?

Chapter 9

EMOTIONS, FEELINGS, AND SELF-REGULATION

Emotions are what we experience in the present through our bodily sensations. Feelings are more a result of our thoughts and interpretations surrounding the emotional bodily sensations. Being mindful of our emotions coupled with understanding our feelings and how we react or respond to our emotions is the key to emotional intelligence. Growing our capacity to consciously practice positive ways to self-regulate and express our feelings all contribute to the development of self-management habits and skills that empower ourselves and others.

Understanding Our Emotions and Feelings

It takes some courage to examine our emotions and tolerate the discomfort of what we might discover in the process. Becoming self-aware is the first step to understanding our emotions and feelings.

"There is no separation of mind and emotions; emotions, thinking, and learning are all linked."

—Eric Jensen

Emotional well-being influences the brain's capacity to learn. Feelings are most often the result of our thoughts and perceptions. Sometimes our feelings cause us to interpret or judge situations, people, or experiences as "good" or "bad." They are so intertwined we often miss the correlation between thoughts and feelings. Reflective practices that help us examine this relationship foster our ability to live mindfully. When we have strong negative feelings, it often throws us into a stressful emotional reaction where the brain's response is to fight, flee, or freeze. Our ability to access our frontal cortex, where reasoning, decision-making, and high cognitive processes happen, is literally cut off in those moments. Essentially this stressful emotional reaction prohibits thinking and hinders the ability to intentionally respond, putting us into reaction mode. Clearly emotions and feelings have a foundational impact on our ability to learn and make mindful decisions. We want to facilitate our coaching partners to be able to grow, learn, and change. Tending to their emotional well-being and helping them become more resilient when experiencing stress, whatever the cause, is a part of our role. We are ineffective when we try to work around their feelings and expect them or us to compartmentalize ourselves. In today's environment, helping people deal with stress and using reflective strategies to help them become more self-aware of their emotions, thoughts, and feelings will be necessary to foster their learning and growth.

REFLECTIVE PRACTICE
Focus on the connection between what you perceive your role to be as a coach or leader—a change agent facilitating reflection or a content expert who should have answers. Examine any concern or hesitancy you might have about discussing emotions, feelings, or stress with the people you support. Clarify whether your own feelings are causing an emotional reaction or stress within you and if this is perhaps contributing to any reactive or unfounded conclusions. Practice self-awareness to witness the relationship between your feelings, thoughts, and perceptions and your own behaviors.

2

"Affective knowing—developing an awareness of feelings and emotions in the reflective process—is inherent in critical reflection."

—Jack Mezirow and Edward W. Taylor

Develop a practice of checking in with yourself once a day to get an overview of your thoughts and emotions. Becoming aware of how you are feeling creates a bit of space to diminish the feeling's intensity because you are actually observing it, like putting a wedge in a door before it slams shut, rather than instantly reacting and being overwhelmed by it. Some people find it difficult to identify how they feel. If this is true for you, you might start with first recognizing what your bodily sensations are. Then you could also start by observing what you are thinking, even if you don't know what you're feeling. It's a chance to take a moment to look at the thoughts that accompany the feelings and also interpret your emotions and by-bodily sensations. You might find that often the thoughts are creating the feeling. Once you sort it all out by tapping into your body to identify your emotions and by witnessing any connections between your feelings and thoughts from day to day, you will start to see the benefits. This differentiation helps prevent emotional upheavals if a crisis strikes. You can witness the emotions and thoughts that cause reactive feelings, rather than being run by them. A reflective practice lets you decide whether you need to do something about your emotions—for example, do you need support or just need to feel and accept them? Identifying your feelings will help you see a connection between cause and effect so you can direct your life toward what you want.

REFLECTIVE PRACTICE
Check in with yourself at the beginning of the day or around the time you start your bedtime routine. Just five to ten minutes is enough time to get a quick summary snapshot of your emotional body, thoughts, and feelings.

> "Respect other people's feelings. It might mean nothing to you, but it could mean everything to them."

—Attributed to Roy T. Bennett

To respect other people's feelings first requires a level of attention and being present. Listening is a powerful way to show respect, as you are taking the time to truly hear their story, their perspective, and their feelings. It doesn't matter if you agree with or approve of their feelings or behaviors. Respect comes from really granting that their life and who they are is no less or more important than your own. Your agreement is not required. To treat all people with the awareness that you are not better than them is an act of both humility and respect. If you are a parent or educator, learning how to truly listen and respect a child's emotions and feelings is one of the single most important actions you can take for developing trust and demonstrating the kind of respect you hope to receive from them as well. They will do as you do. Model respect through listening, acknowledging how they feel, and not judging them. This doesn't mean you may not need to provide guidance or consequences, but coming from a respectful place can be a game changer not just for your relationship but for their lifetime.

REFLECTIVE PRACTICE

Recall an adult who truly listened to you when you were a young child or teen and think about how you felt. If you do not have any memories from your youth of an adult listening, then think of a person later in life who was in authority or had power or whom you admired who listened to you with respect. Recall the impact it had on you.

4

> "To do nothing is to hold yourself still so that you can perceive what is actually there."
>
> —Jenny Odell

Try slowing down, taking things in, and simply looking to make sense of the world. To witness, to be mindful of the present moment and what's happening, requires staying still and being present without doing. Cultivating an interest in what's around you helps you focus and either zoom in or take a wide-lens look. Simple activities like bird-watching, stargazing, watching a sunset without taking a photo, or field sketching in nature are examples of ways to calm yourself, wind down, and become mindfully present. It may feel uncomfortable if it's difficult for you to "do nothing" and your mind is yammering that it's a waste of time. Practicing taking moments like this will build your comfort, so you can manage your mind and finally give yourself permission to find pleasure, joy, and fulfillment in being fully present in simple moments. Embed pleasurable, mindful moments into your daily life and explore their benefits.

REFLECTIVE PRACTICE
Choose ways to slow down and pay attention to simple moments during your day, enjoying the pleasure and peace this allows without any advance planning time. Watch a squirrel, observe children playing, hear the birds, or just listen to a song.

5

> "The ultimate measure of a man is not where he stands in moments of comfort and convenience, but where he stands at times of challenge and controversy."

—Martin Luther King Jr.

It's important to not repress our feelings but rather to accept the wide range of human emotions we feel. Knowing how to express all of our feelings in ways that are not harmful to ourselves or others is equally important. Our mental health and our responsibility for our actions require that we not stuff down or avoid our feelings using substances, checking out, or acting out in socially unacceptable ways when we are afraid, angry, or stressed. Our ability to self-regulate our emotions means we have self-awareness of our feelings and thoughts, we make appropriate choices for how to acknowledge our emotions and express our feelings and intense energy, and we mindfully choose our actions, especially when we feel challenged or are engaged in conflict situations. This sophisticated balance requires reflection and practice, and it develops emotional maturity, strong character, and inspiring leadership.

REFLECTIVE PRACTICE
Start by naming and labeling your emotions and feelings. Some of us are good at identifying more pleasant feelings, like happiness, joy, love, or gratitude. But we may have to take more time to stay present with other emotions to really identify and label what we are feeling. Using specific labels can help both with acknowledging how we feel and with actually feeling it—is it loneliness, sadness, anger, disappointment, agitation, grief? Some of us do better by clarifying where in our body our emotion is located. Stopping to identify, locate, and name the emotion can give a great deal of awareness. Releasing intense feelings through moving, cleaning, shooting hoops, or walking can help. Sitting down with tissues and having a good cry is an appropriate release for many feelings. It turns out that tears and sweat are the body's natural response to stress!

6

"Emotions act as a trigger for the reflective process, prompting the learner to question deeply held beliefs."

—Unknown

Feelings are not good or bad in themselves. Whether we react and act out in challenging ways when we are emotionally triggered or whether we are able to observe with awareness what the emotional triggers are and mindfully respond with conscious, intentional actions is a large part of emotional intelligence in action. The social-emotional well-being of a person has everything to do with how well they perform at school or at work. Emotional intelligence is an essential skill for meaningfully contributing in the workplace both as an employee and as a successful leader. Emotions can be a doorway that reveals disempowering beliefs or unexamined values that may be causing negative or judgmental responses to oneself or others. In this way, emotions are an opportunity to focus and facilitate reflection to expand one's awareness.

REFLECTIVE PRACTICE
Strengthen your own emotional intelligence as a foundation to stand on to support others. Over the next week, intentionally focus on and become aware of and name the emotions and feelings you are having. Reflect on the underlying belief, thought, or value associated with each feeling, especially for any feelings that result from a triggering experience. The intention of this reflective practice is to discover the connection between your perspective, your emotional reactions, and your behaviors. Are you reacting or mindfully responding? Write a list of questions to ask yourself to better understand your emotional triggers. Just ask questions—do not try to answer them now. Let curiosity lead you from one question to another. After you do this exercise, ask yourself what insights you gained.

7

"Observer-self is a term used to refer to the practice of metaphorically stepping back and neutrally observing your active engaged self. It heightens awareness and supports more intentional choices."

—James Bradford Terrell and Marcia Hughes

Did you take the time to practice self-observation surrounding your emotions this week? Did you stop if you encountered discomfort while examining your emotions, or did you demonstrate and strengthen your ability to observe your emotional self and behaviors? Take time now to assess and observe your own emotional energy this past week. How did you express and receive emotional energy in ways that either strengthened or diminished your connection and relationship with others?

Emotional Intelligence

Emotional intelligence requires that you remain aware of your emotions and triggers and manage your emotional responses in a positive way. Taking time to reflect, observe, and inspect our emotions increases our ability both to acknowledge our feelings and to express them in healthy ways for ourselves and others. To choose intentional, effective behaviors that are responsive, not reactive, requires awareness and self-regulation.

"We define emotional intelligence as the subset of social intelligence that involves the ability to monitor one's own and others' feelings and emotions, to discriminate among them, and to use this information to guide one's thinking and actions."

—John Mayer and Peter Salovey

To be able to monitor emotions and feelings requires the self-awareness to identify the emotion and some level of an acceptance that feelings are not good or bad but human. It's more helpful to monitor our emotions from the perspective of a neutral witness, rather than with opinion and judgment. Our overall relationship with and attitude toward emotions and feelings sets a tone for how we use our awareness to guide our thoughts and choose the most fruitful actions.

REFLECTIVE PRACTICE
Today, work on accepting your stubbornness or resistance. Use it to learn what you are afraid of or what unmet needs you have. How can your insights help guide you in the future?

9

"Coaching for emotional and social effectiveness is a process of helping others learn how to express and receive emotional energy in ways that strengthen their connection with others and build more effective relationships."

—James Bradford Terrell and Marcia Hughes

One of the purposes of coaching is to help people reflect on the intent of their behavior or choice and consider the actual resulting impact. This includes when you or someone you are supporting becomes triggered and reacts emotionally. This takes practice and requires reflecting and talking through the connection between emotions, values, thoughts, and perspectives that trigger feelings, behaviors, and habits, especially as related to professional effectiveness. Practicing what happens when you feel triggered and learning to mindfully respond rather than react is essential in order to compassionately and authentically help others. Strengthening emotional intelligence is not the same as therapy, which is to treat, provide relief from, or heal a disorder. Fostering awareness and understanding emotions is a natural part of the coaching relationship. It is foundational to supporting the social-emotional well-being of individuals and expanding their awareness, so they make positive choices to be successful in the workplace and in their personal lives.

REFLECTIVE PRACTICE
Think of a time you were triggered at work and had a strong emotional reaction. Did you justify your reaction or blame the person or situation? Shift your viewpoint: Entertain the notion that the situation or the person that triggered you is not the source of the problem and wanting them to be different is not in your zone of control. You are the one who has the button that got pushed. Keep your attention focused on where you have choice and control. Your feelings and underlying thoughts are in your control zone. Deepen your self-reflection and look at the feelings that the trigger brought up. What was your interpretation of the situation, or what did you think that led to your interpretation? Being triggered is connected to some meaning or interpretation we assign, and it's this interpretation that causes the rush of feelings.

"Knowing what matters to us may be one of the most valuable benefits of self-awareness."

10

—Daniel Goleman

Self-awareness is a core competency of emotional intelligence. Self-awareness is the skill of being aware and mindful of our emotions, thoughts, feelings, and values from moment to moment. We are all called to lead at one time or another. Self-awareness allows us to show up in this role with authenticity, integrity, and resilience. Leaders need to inspire others with their vision and make them feel comfortable with change. Through self-awareness, leaders can move forward themselves with authenticity and integrity and, in turn, better lead others and organizations. Korn Ferry research found that "among leaders with multiple strengths in Emotional Self-Awareness, 92% had teams with high energy and high performance. In sharp contrast, leaders low in Emotional Self-Awareness created negative climates 78% of the time."* In this way, emotional intelligence is more important than IQ or business skills and strategies. A leader must continue to invest in their emotional self-awareness and developing their emotional intelligences as a lifestyle. It's not some end point one achieves and then stops.

> **REFLECTIVE PRACTICE**
> Adopt a daily mindfulness practice. Research has found that a short daily mindfulness practice leads to changes in the structure and function of the brain that enhances self-awareness. Some studies show that even just ten minutes a day of daily mindfulness for five weeks increased the leader's self-awareness up to 35 percent.**

* Daniel Goleman, "What Is Emotional Self-Awareness?" Korn Ferry, www.kornferry.com/insights/this-week-in-leadership/what-is-emotional-self-awareness-2019.

** Rasmus Hougaard, Jacqueline Carter, and Marissa Afton, "Self-Awareness Can Help Leaders More Than an MBA Can," *Harvard Business Review*, January 12, 2018, https://hbr.org/2018/01/self-awareness-can-help-leaders-more-than-an-mba-can.

11

"CEOs are hired for their intellect and business expertise—and fired for a lack of emotional intelligence."

—Daniel Goleman

Don't mistake productive efficiency and accomplishing goals as the main focus of a leader. In order to accomplish any measure of success, the leader must carefully attend to and invest in the well-being, development of respectful relationships, and expansion of human consciousness of the people in their care. The human resources are the heart and soul of any organization, and procedures and managing systems will not replace adaptive leaders who are present to effectively communicate with and develop authentic relationships with people. Adaptive leaders are responsive to the organization's people and are the employees' creative partner to inspire, stimulate, motivate, and have consideration of their needs, hopes, challenges, and strengths.

REFLECTIVE PRACTICE
Which of the following five emotional intelligence characteristics do you need to further develop: self-awareness, self-regulation, empathy, motivation, or social skills?

12

"When you stop expecting people to be perfect, you can like them for who they are."

—Donald Miller

Having expectations about others is a common cause of relationship struggles and conflict. Contemplate the unspoken or even spoken expectations you have had in any relationship where there has been strife and discord. Expectations are based in a person's beliefs and hopes, which are often not honestly assessed and rarely agreed upon—in both personal and professional relationships. Perfectionism is a disempowering attitude that breeds judgment, unkindness, and discord toward others and self. People who have attitudes of perfectionism usually suffer great pain on the inside from the expectations they have of themselves. Accepting who people are, just as they are, is the foundation of kindness, compassion, and unconditional love. Self-acceptance of oneself is the foundation of freedom. Dismantling perfectionism is one of the most empowering and transformational changes you can undertake to deepen relationships and your own self-esteem.

REFLECTIVE PRACTICE
What are your expectations for yourself or others? Write your expectations down so you can think very clearly about what they are. Are any based on expecting yourself or others to be perfect or needing to do things right or not make any mistakes? Where do those expectations come from? Are they spoken and agreed upon between you and the other person, or are they unspoken?

Facing Our Fears

Learning to normalize the challenges of the change process, to grow and transform, requires you to tolerate emotional discomfort. Fear is a common reaction to change. Learning to become aware of our fears, to reframe and shift limiting perspectives and change how they influence our feelings, decisions, and actions, involves developing the art of self-reflection.

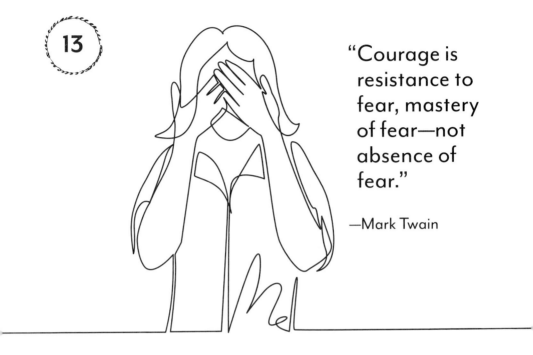

13

"Courage is resistance to fear, mastery of fear—not absence of fear."

—Mark Twain

Everyone faces fear many times in a lifetime. Success and leadership are born of not letting the fear stop you. It takes setting your intention to face the fear when it comes up—and it will. Think about how the mind creates a story or perception that is feeding the feeling of fear, your belief that something is dangerous or unsafe, or that you are not capable of handling it. Drawing from within yourself or a higher power and staying connected to what is most important to you is how you can find courage to proceed even when you feel fear. Courage is not about waiting for the fear to go away—it is acting anyway.

REFLECTIVE PRACTICE
List four ways doubt or fear has gotten in your way. What stopped you? Think of what you can do to not let that happen again. How can you go within, tap into the qualities you need, and find the trust needed to move yourself through it?

14

"You can conquer almost any fear if you will only make up your mind to do so. For remember, fear doesn't exist anywhere except in the mind."

—Dale Carnegie

Fear is a result of our perspective. As humans, we are meaning-making machines, always assigning meaning through the framework of our thoughts, values, and perspectives. Become mindful of how your lens and viewpoint is assigning meaning to the experiences you have. What is an area in your life you experience some fear about? Think about why you are afraid. Ask yourself what you are making this situation mean. How is your mind interpreting the situation such that you feel fear? How can you use this awareness to reframe your perspective and not let your fear stop you?

15

"As long as we operate from places within us that have no power, or that feel powerless, we will always strive for control. The sad part about control is that without true, neutral power backing it, it eventually becomes domination. Power struggles occur only when we feel powerless."

—Imetai M. Henderson

The primary reason we strive for control is fear, and often what we fear is being powerless. It might seem logical or rational that exerting control is the best solution, but that is a faulty perception because it is not logical but actually emotional. There is not any true power that comes from an emotional reaction to fear. But it often becomes a habit to operate from fear and dominate others in order to feel safe, often unconsciously. Become aware that whenever you are engaged in a power struggle, whether with a two-year-old or a colleague at work, the struggle for power sits on a fear of something. It is more useful to become aware of the fear, admit what it is really about, and find ways to better meet your needs, or to explore the fear and pay attention to the assumptions and perceptions that contribute to it. This might take some deep healing or this might mean reframing an attitude. Controlling is not the most caring and respectful way to make sure your own needs are met nor for respectfully interacting with others. Self-awareness is the first step!

REFLECTIVE PRACTICE
Examine the areas of your life in which you tend toward being controlling or wanting control. Identify any relationships where you engage in a power struggle. Look beneath that compulsion, desire, or habit to control. What do you think control will alleviate? What is your concern or fear of being without control or without power, as you perceive it? Reflect on whether this controlling behavior is coming from a place where you feel or fear you do not have power unless you are dominating.

"Change has a considerable psychological impact on the human mind. To the fearful it is threatening because it means that things may get worse. To the hopeful it is encouraging because things may get better. To the confident it is inspiring because the challenge exists to make things better."

—Attributed to King Whitney Jr.

Perspective and mindset have a remarkably powerful impact on human feelings. Our feelings are not disconnected from our beliefs and perspectives. Fear is most often created by the perceptions we hold. We all have perceptions that cause us to feel fear, and it's human to have fears. Our human power comes from our ability to mindfully choose perspectives and beliefs that empower us to not let fear stop us. We can even shift our attitudes so that something that used to cause fear, like change, can be transformed into a feeling of excitement for possibilities and opportunities. The choice is ours. Desire motivates us to make those kinds of perspective shifts, and reflection and practice keep us anchored in new mental, emotional, and behavioral habits.

REFLECTIVE PRACTICE
What is your typical first response to change? Does it present in your mind and heart as fear, hope, or excitement? How do you want to respond to change? What perspectives contribute to your current typical response to change, and what thoughts, assumptions, or perspectives need reframing to shift how you respond?

17

"The secret of success is learning how to use pain and pleasure instead of having pain and pleasure use you. If you don't, life controls you."

—Tony Robbins

We have the ability to learn from difficult and painful experiences, but we have to look for the learning, rather than falling into complaints and bitterness. Cultivate an attitude that continuous lifelong learning includes bumps and valleys— it's the nature of the journey. The ups and downs are not a sign that something is wrong. Rather, bumps mean there is a change or a challenge you need to deal with. Build your belief that you are capable of facing whatever comes your way.

REFLECTIVE PRACTICE
List three things you have learned from hard times. Write each of these on an index card or create a sign, then post them where you will frequently see and be guided by what you have learned.

18

"Always do your best. Your best is going to change from moment to moment; it will be different when you are healthy as opposed to sick. Under any circumstance, simply do your best, and you will avoid self-judgment, self-abuse, and regret."

—Don Miguel Ruiz

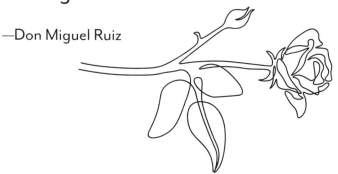

A hospice nurse who spent years supporting the dying reports that these are the five most common deathbed regrets:

1. "I wish I'd had the courage to live a life true to myself, not the life others expected of me."—This is the most common regret of all.
2. "I wish I hadn't worked so hard."
3. "I wish I'd had the courage to express my feelings."
4. "I wish I had stayed in touch with my friends."
5. "I wish I had let myself be happier."

End-of-life regrets are an extension of how we live each day. Don't wait until the end of your life to look back and review your past choices and actions.*

> **REFLECTIVE PRACTICE**
> Declare your mission to have no regrets at the end of your life, and start today. Are you currently making choices that will likely lead to any of the five regrets listed above? What choices can you change, let go of, accept, or forgive?

* Bronnie Ware, *The Top Five Regrets of the Dying: A Life Transformed by the Dearly Departing* (London: Hay House, 2011), ix–x.

Self-Regulation and Self-Control

Learning to redirect our impulsive or reactionary patterns requires strong reflective practices to recognize, understand, and accept the underlying motivations of our habitual behaviors, thoughts, and emotional responses, in order to make mindful and effective choices in our lives and work.

19

"Be curious, not judgmental."

—As heard on *Ted Lasso*

Curiosity is the antidote to judgment! Judgment is a result of thinking we know, often without any supporting information. It is really just an opinion stated as fact, or an arrogant statement based on false assumptions. Judgment causes separation and pain, and it is an attitude worth shifting. Judgment is disempowering not only to others but also to yourself when you aim the judgment inward. Judgment creates an attitude of separating yourself or thinking you are different from others, often referred to as "othering," and is often connected to strong personal and cultural beliefs and values that create both explicit and unconscious biases. These beliefs and biases are typically learned at an early age from our family of origin or those who raised us, which can be generationally and culturally ingrained. It takes purposeful reflection to become aware of generational, cultural, and personal biases. Whatever the reason or the cause, judgment and bias interfere with relationships and diminish kindness and love. It is helpful to identify your own symptoms that pop up when you are judging so you can change the habit. Symptomatic indicators might be feeling righteous, feeling yourself take a position, thinking "they are wrong!," feeling like you want to either defend or make a point. Judgment has a domineering or bullying quality and tone. Curiosity can unhook the claws of judgment, false assumptions, and bias.

REFLECTIVE PRACTICE
When you feel one of the symptoms of judgment taking hold, practice curiosity by asking yourself the following questions:

- What do I know?

- What am I assuming?

- Why do I think this way?

20

"The emotionally intelligent person is skilled in four areas: identifying emotions, using emotions, understanding emotions, and regulating emotions."

—John D. Mayer and Peter Salovey

For the most part, our society and families have not guided us well in acknowledging our emotions and managing feelings. Most of us feel we were never taught how to give emotions a positive space to feel them in ways that are respectful, healthy, and safe for ourselves and others. Regulating emotions does not mean repressing or dismissing feelings. It's more about being tuned in enough to know what you are feeling. Unfortunately, many of us don't have self-awareness of our emotions and feelings until after we have been triggered and are in an emotional reaction. It can help to understand how triggers are symptoms of emotions bursting forth. We can learn to be aware of what experiences or thoughts tend to trigger our emotional responses. With focused attention we can be more proactive, so our responses are regulated and do not cause harm to ourselves or conflict with others. How we respond to our own emotions and feelings is worth examining with curiosity, without judgment. This reflection is important so we can use and regulate our feelings and behaviors in healthy and empowering ways.

REFLECTIVE PRACTICE
Which emotions are you familiar with or do you usually give yourself permission to feel? With which emotions are you uncomfortable or unfamiliar? What do you think or do when they come up? Do you feel justified or proud, or do you praise yourself for these feelings? Why? Do you minimize them, stuff them down, or judge yourself or others rather than feel them? Where or how did you learn to respond that way? How does that emotion or response benefit you, or what does that cost you?

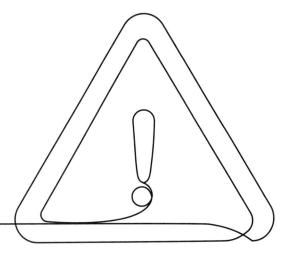

"We are dangerous when we are not conscious of our responsibility for how we behave, think, and feel."

—Marshall B. Rosenberg

As you review this week, how are you feeling? Did you have any strong feelings? How do your feelings inform you? How do you hope to feel next week? What practices or actions will you need to implement to get the results you want?

22

"It is not necessary to react to everything you notice."

—Anonymous

Become aware of and watch for the three Ts—Threats, Triggers, and Traps—that tend to grab or hijack your feelings. When we feel *threatened* or unsafe, or believe something carries danger, we often have an instinctive emotional reaction. When we are *triggered*, we often react defensively or aggressively. When we have strong reactive feelings, we can *trap* ourselves in old emotional neural-response patterns that we may know are not helpful or effective but that, even so, have a deep emotional response that bypasses our rational decision-making skills. Becoming mindful in the moment so you can recognize the emotional and/or physical symptoms and cues that you are having a reaction—such as a flushed face when embarrassed, tightness of your jaw when angry, or pain in your stomach when afraid—increases your ability to self-regulate and choose how you respond. With practice, you can intervene before reacting or acting out. I have learned to identify and listen to my physical cues when I am triggered—a tightness in my chest, a clenching of my jaw, a physical sensation of wanting to growl. I often feel and act defensive: I want to explain myself, build a case about the person or situation in my head, withdraw socially, or start to talk over other people. I have learned to simply stop and notice what my bodily sensations are, put my hand on my chest, and take a breath to calm myself before speaking or acting. This creates a pause for me to witness what's going on inside myself so I can make mindful choices. Sometimes I can do this in the moment, and sometimes I miss the moment and do it afterward. Mindfulness is the key to self-regulation. Having options and a plan for how to handle yourself when you bump into any of the three Ts is how you can regulate your emotions and feelings without repressing or stuffing them down in unhealthy ways.

REFLECTIVE PRACTICE
Write a list of the most common situations, people, or things that activate your three Ts. What makes you feel threatened or triggered, or traps you in a negative or unempowering thought or behavioral pattern? What is your most typical emotion when each of the three Ts happen? Do you feel self-judgment, or do you try to justify your actions when you experience any of those emotions?

23

"When we are less aware, we are identified with a feeling—I am frustrated, I am depressed—and we do not see its temporary nature: we believe it is how we are."

—Don Richard Riso and Russ Hudson

You have the power to create your experience of your life rather than being a victim of your circumstances, your own negative thinking, and your triggered feelings. Notice your feelings as well as the sensations in your body that are a response to your emotions and understand how feelings are so often a result of something you are thinking. This body, mind, and heart connection is well worth paying attention to. We can intervene in this cycle at any point through adjusting our attitudes or thoughts, paying attention to what the body is reacting to, and questioning what triggered us or activated our feelings. When we pause between experiencing feelings and quickly reacting to them, we can chase our thoughts away by realizing they are not facts. We can witness what the negative thoughts are, without harshness or self-judgment, and simply turn away and choose a different perspective. This takes repetition and practice! Watch how your emotions and physical well-being can be directly impacted.

REFLECTIVE PRACTICE
Having a morning positive-thinking practice to intentionally prepare for the day is like practicing emotional and mental sobriety so you can choose in the moment to not indulge in or believe the negative thoughts and triggered feelings. Adopt a daily practice to set yourself up positively for the day. Options might include writing three things you are grateful for; writing down qualities, attitudes, or behaviors you want to focus on for the day; or writing what you are excited about or looking forward to. Use this practice to nurture your ability to stay in the present moment, focus on one day at a time, and turn away from negative thinking, breaking the habit of getting stuck in guilt about the past or worrying about the future.

24 "Courage is what it takes to stand up and speak. Courage is also what it takes to sit down and listen."

—Unknown

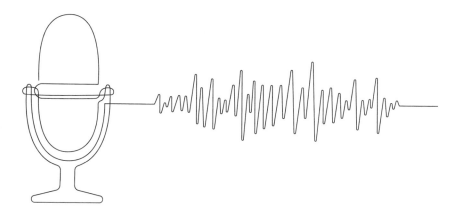

Exercising self-control requires self-awareness and mindfulness, and also an ability to discern what action is or is not needed in a specific moment. The challenge might be to take action, or it might be to refrain from acting. When a person feels afraid, it takes courage to take action, to speak up, to take a chance. When we need to restrain ourselves from doing something, such as not speaking or expressing an opinion, it takes courage to be humble and not press forward from the ego or a desire to make a point, and to create space and time for others as we authentically listen and learn.

> **REFLECTIVE PRACTICE**
> What kind of courage does it take for you to refrain from taking action? Is there a pattern of situations or temptations that require you to practice self-control and not act or speak up? What helps you in these situations?

25

"Emotional agility can help people alleviate stress, reduce errors, become more innovative, and improve job performance."

—Susan David and Christina Congleton

Minimizing or ignoring your thoughts and feelings serves only to amplify them. Self-regulation is not about repressed control but rather making mindful choices. We all have challenging thoughts and feelings, like self-doubt, fear of failure, judgments, irritation, and overwhelm. To assume you're not supposed to have these types of thoughts and feelings adds unnecessary pressure and unrealistic expectations on yourself. Mindfulness is the key because that's where we can interject choice. Identifying and labeling our thoughts and feelings helps us witness rather than react to ourselves or others with judgment. The opposite of control is acceptance: responding to your ideas, thoughts, and emotions with an open attitude, paying attention to them and at the same time letting yourself acknowledge and accept that they are happening, without resistance. It's a way to own your own thoughts and feelings, so they don't trigger you and have to be acted out, and also a way of showing yourself compassion. Paying too much attention to our negative internal chatter or judging ourselves just wastes valuable energy and cognitive resources that could be put to better use. Leaders need to practice this kind of emotional agility to alleviate stress and leverage mindful awareness so they make intentional, productive choices.

REFLECTIVE PRACTICE

Is there an area of your life that often generates negative thoughts and feelings? Use your awareness to identify and label the feelings and identify the specific thoughts—the actual voice in your mind. Become a nonjudgmental witness of these thoughts and feelings, watching for any patterns when they occur. Note how you have habitually reacted. This observation will offer new insights and expanded awareness so you can catch them and then make mindful alternative choices and reframe your thoughts.

26

"Every behavior satisfies a need."

—Edith Eger

If you want to help others (or yourself) grow and change their behaviors and unsupportive habits, clarify the underlying need driving the behavior and explore alternative options to better meet that need. Working with children, I discovered that when they have tantrums it is usually an emotional reaction to some trigger. It might be as simple as being hungry and becoming short-fused, and food will meet their need. Or they might get mad when they don't get what they want. In this case, usually the solution has something to do with offering alternatives. Choice is power and freedom. Lots of people act poorly when they feel like they don't have a choice or are in a power struggle. When working with children, we want to transfer the power to children as often as possible. As leaders, we want to do the same with those we work with. Adults will get stressed out, resistant, or passive-aggressive when they feel they have no choice. To be more successful working with people, don't fixate on a challenging behavior or judge them—this makes it worse. Look more deeply and compassionately to the need that is causing their behavior. Exploring alternative behaviors to better meet needs is a much more successful first step than trying to "fix" behaviors or offering consequences. If you help them identify their underlying need so they can make better choices, then behaviors will change. Focus on the desire and curiosity to uncover our underlying needs. When you reflect about your own needs and behaviors through journaling or talking, you will be better able to facilitate the reflection of others.

REFLECTIVE PRACTICE
Recall a time you acted out with a behavior that did not reflect your best self. Perhaps you regretted it or got feedback about it. What was the feeling that created the behavior: anger, fear, loss, rejection? What was your perception in the situation? What were you not getting enough of or getting too much of? What did you want or need? Would it have made a difference if you were more aware of and perhaps able to express your needs? Imagine an alternative way of getting your need met rather than emotionally reacting with a challenging behavior.

Internal Beliefs

Beliefs are a key component of our social-emotional effectiveness and well-being. The intricate and dynamic relationship between our emotions, how we interpret emotions, and the thoughts or stories we tell ourselves about a situation or an emotion generates reactive feelings and behaviors that require our continuous attention and self-awareness. It's a lifestyle shift to pay attention to our internal beliefs and their impacts so we can develop and strengthen social and emotional competencies in ourselves and others.

"I believe that every person is born with talent."

—Maya Angelou

Internal beliefs are the feelings and thoughts we have about ourselves and our own effectiveness. When you have positive internal core beliefs about yourself, they help you navigate difficult situations, accept compliments, and cope with life's predictable highs and lows. We often reflect on what we want to change or ways we could be better, and this certainly has its value. But it is equally as important to be able to acknowledge and keep our strengths, inner qualities, talents, and gifts in clear view and use them to solve problems and guide choices. Many of us grew up with messages that it was not OK to think good things about ourselves or to acknowledge our strengths. We have to learn to override those old messages and strengthen our positive ideas and beliefs to honor ourselves, so we can be resilient and support others.

REFLECTIVE PRACTICE
Make a list of your strengths, inner qualities, talents, and gifts. It could be cooking, sports, dancing, being optimistic, writing, drawing, caring for children or elders, being flexible, being grateful, or what have you. Whatever it is, even if you haven't done it recently, write it down. If you are uncertain or find it difficult to list things, ask people who know you well to suggest things you can add to your list, but add them only if you can acknowledge them as strengths. Keep this list handy and turn to it when you doubt yourself. Consider ways to increase the time you spend practicing and cultivating your strengths to invest in yourself.

28

"The strength of character and emotional intelligence to face your failures and learn from them are at the core of success."

—Robert Kiyosaki

What did you learn from mistakes or failures this week?

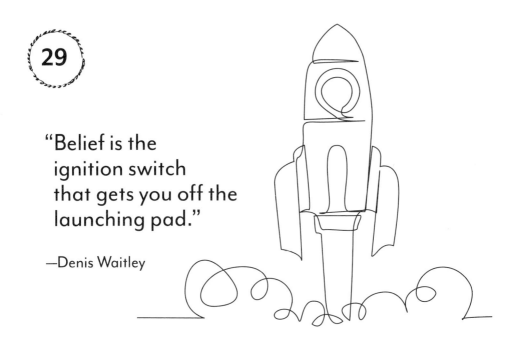

29

> "Belief is the
> ignition switch
> that gets you off the
> launching pad."

—Denis Waitley

Our internal beliefs aim our actions. The ability to imagine possibility, to believe in excellence, to know that solutions are possible even in discord, and to believe that you are capable and competent will aim your life toward what you really want and maximize your choices and actions. Fulfillment starts in the belief that achieving fulfillment is possible. Your desire to achieve what you want coupled with optimistic attitudes and positive internal beliefs will take you the distance.

REFLECTIVE PRACTICE
Identify something you want but have some doubt or limiting internal beliefs about. Allow yourself to visualize putting those doubts and concerns in a closet for a week. You can always go get them later if you want. In this week, encourage yourself to explore the possibilities and to clarify what you really do want, with no limitations. Get concrete and specific. Write it, draw it, or talk about it with someone you trust. You do not have to know how—give yourself a permission pass to just imagine it. Let the possibility grow within you. After a week, intentionally choose to continue nurturing the possibility that you can make this happen, or else choose to drag your doubt and limiting beliefs out of that closet. Your choice!

30

"Whatever the mind of man can conceive and believe, it can achieve."

—Napoleon Hill

The powerful truth of this statement is remarkably inspiring when we aim high and imagine boldly and bravely. But it is equally true that if we conceive and believe negatively that something is not possible, our minds will aim downward and we will not achieve it. Your internal beliefs govern your success—not circumstances, past experiences, failures, or mistakes. Clarify what you believe success is. Is it merely achieving a goal, crossing a finish line, or achieving outcomes? Does it include the quality of the effort, being flexible and responsive to necessary modifications, and maintaining hopefulness in the face of challenges and obstacles? The power of desire, passion, and belief is truly unlimited when we get out of our own way. It's not just the ability to conceive and imagine but the investment in the belief that it's possible that sustains our focus and energy to move toward our goal, in easy or challenging times.

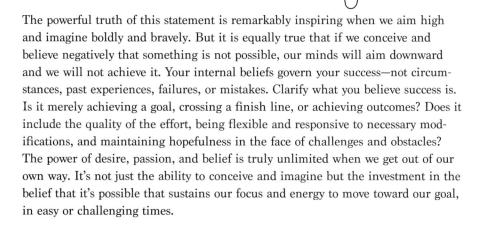

REFLECTIVE PRACTICE
What is something you once imagined to be possible about a relationship, a work or business idea, or a desired goal or change of habit but that, somehow, you backed away from? Perhaps you settled for what you already had instead of going for what you really wanted. Maybe it seemed rational, or external pressures or other people told you to be grateful for what you had, even if it does not fulfill you or truly align with what you want. What would you need to let go of, forgive, or change to reopen this possibility? Allow yourself to dream and focus on what you want and let that energize you to push past any fear. What you think and believe matters, so focus on what you want.

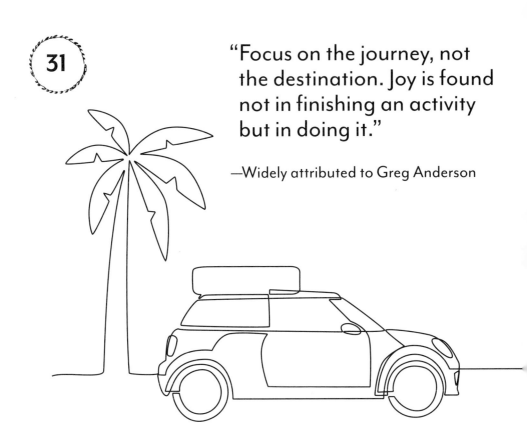

31

"Focus on the journey, not the destination. Joy is found not in finishing an activity but in doing it."

—Widely attributed to Greg Anderson

Surrender to the flow of an endeavor, appreciating the process of becoming and the expansiveness of being fully present in the moment. This opens windows for joy to enter, take over, and fill you. Focusing on accomplishing tasks or achieving future goals can overpower us and decrease the quality of our lives if these accomplishments become the only measure of success and purpose. Be mindful of the remarkable opportunities available in the present moment and appreciate the gift of the here and now to add wonder to your life. Increase joy in your life through simple daily attentions—by shifting a thought, smelling a flower, taking a deep breath, smiling at someone, or learning something wonderous.

REFLECTIVE PRACTICE
Make a list of things that increase your joy. Practice them intentionally and often!

Chapter 10

EFFICACY AND INFLUENCE

Change agents, or those who are supporting others to grow,

learn, and transform, should be mindful of how they influ-

ence others and make sure they are empowering them. We

must impart the value, worth, and contributions each person

brings to ensure they know the difference they can make.

Authenticity and Inspiring Others

Being authentic and vulnerable and sharing in one's personal journey, laced with failures and successes, is how leaders build trust. Staying present, listening, and being familiar with individuals' strengths and needs is what inspires them.

"Authenticity is a state of conscious awareness that enables you to make choices that align you with your world and support your physical, mental, emotional, and spiritual well-being."

—Pamela Bond

People tend to trust leaders more when the leaders share the challenges they face and are transparent about mistakes they have made and learned from. There is great strength in being vulnerable. Being transparent in this way takes humility, which builds respect and trust. It takes courage to be vulnerable, and this is inspiring and motivational for others. Authenticity is being honest about all aspects of yourself, without hiding or misrepresenting things. It is the alignment between what you value and how you behave. Not only does this build connection with people but it also builds self-integrity, which supports your own well-being. Create time to routinely reflect and check in that your behaviors are aligned with your values.

REFLECTIVE PRACTICE
List two ways you can be more transparent and honest with the people who follow or look up to you.

"People who are truly strong lift others up. People who are truly powerful bring others together."

—Michelle Obama

The influence we have on others is a testimony of our leadership—not roles, titles, or rank. Inspiring others, helping them see themselves as capable and able to make a difference, comes from understanding the power of a collective whole and investing in others, rather than relying only on ourselves and focusing on self-advancement. Transformational leaders invest time and energy to help others to see their strengths, hone their skills, and give their gifts. They also stand by individuals to encourage them to stretch when necessary and cultivate the resilience to rebound in challenging times. This happens by being with them, side by side, accompanying them through the messy middle, not telling people what to do from the balcony. They bring people together to authentically practice trust, to tolerate the discomfort of being vulnerable, and to embrace diverse voices and perspectives as a contribution, not a challenge. Leaders bring this about by modeling the same behaviors and sharing an inspiring vision that invites and makes space for each individual to step in and step up.

REFLECTIVE PRACTICE
How do you know if you are lifting others up and bringing them together? What are demonstratable indicators of your success or shortcomings? What implications does this have for your actions in the future? What are you most committed to putting into action?

3

"The power to inspire others exists in all of us. We just have to choose to be present to use it."

—Tanveer Naseer

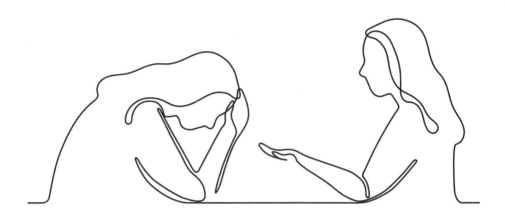

The word *inspire* means "to draw forth or bring out"; the word's Latin root *inspirare* means "to breathe or blow into." It does not imply that someone is empty or void and can be filled up like an empty pail—quite the opposite. To inspire others requires that you see them and their gifts and the potential within them. To do this, one must be very present and intentionally focusing on discovering and calling forth the unique splendor and contributions within another, like blowing on a small spark to ignite the deeper flame. To make a difference and inspire others, whatever our role—leader, coach, teacher, parent, colleague, or friend—we each can be purposeful in our choice to witness the glory and gemlike qualities within each individual.

REFLECTIVE PRACTICE
What's stopping you from choosing to be present to others to inspire and draw others out? What might inspire you to do this more, no matter the obstacles you might encounter?

4

> "If you're trusted, then people will allow you to share their inner garden—what greater gift?"

—Fred Rogers

Leading with heart includes perceiving and trusting what you might not understand with your mind. Being connected with purpose and passion serves as an inner compass directing your actions and choices. This sense of purpose is a cradle for nurturing heartfelt, meaningful relationships that nourish trust, allow vulnerable authenticity, and open us for sharing and receiving honest feedback that pilots the leader's journey.

REFLECTIVE PRACTICE
Think of all the people you're glad have shared their inner garden with you. Think of those who have helped wisely steer your passage as a leader. Add them to your gratitude list. Start telling them today.

"[The 125 leaders interviewed] did not identify any universal characteristics, traits, skills, or styles that led to their success. Rather their leadership emerged from their life stories. Consciously and subconsciously, they were constantly testing themselves through real world experiences and reframing their life stories to understand who they were at their core. In doing so they discovered the purpose of their leadership and learned that being authentic made them more effective."

—Bill George, Peter Sims, Andrew N. McLean, and Diana Mayer

In order for your leadership to emerge from your life story, you first have to identify and clarify what your life story is. Have you told your story to yourself, perhaps through writing or sharing with someone? Think about a mentor, an elder, or another person of influence in your life who has helped you. Think of what they said to you or a story they told you that mattered. There is a special power in the oral tradition of telling stories, both in retelling someone else's story or telling one of your own stories. Some of those stories might be about the value of wandering off the path, the times you tripped and how you recovered, or things that kept you going. Some of the most impactful stories are not about successes but about overcoming obstacles.

REFLECTIVE PRACTICE
Retell a story someone told you and the impact it had on your life and your work.

Mindsets, Power, and Conflict

Embracing a mindset of facilitating change rather than being the expert with all the answers requires humility and curiosity as you intentionally transfer power to others as often as possible. Including diverse perspectives, making space for a variety of voices, and orchestrating healthy conflict are essential areas for reflective practices.

"Leaders do not avoid, repress, or deny conflict, but rather see it as an opportunity."

—Warren G. Bennis

Healthy conflict is an important tool for all leaders and anyone working in teams. Both avoiding conflict and being aggressive erode trust and cause separation. Many people have the false idea that avoiding conflict is positive and better than being aggressive. But avoiding conflict can strongly undermine team building. Leaders who do not fear conflict see it as an opportunity to flesh out authentic perspectives when there are diverse differences of opinion. We can share our authentic voices only when the culture cultivates trust and facilitates healthy conflict. Unhealthy conflict is the result of an inability to tolerate the discomfort of diverse perspectives. Leaders can facilitate discussions with diverse opinions and viewpoints by focusing on sharing ideas and avoiding blaming, judging, and personalizing differences about people. Strong leaders help people gain awareness that ideas and perspectives are not truths but rather one person's perception. Not every thought you have is true; most thoughts are just opinions. It takes owning one's perspective as just that, their own viewpoint, and understanding that each person's perspective is equally important to hear. Agreement doesn't make perspectives true either; it just means that two or more people agree on a certain viewpoint. A group that agrees their perspective is the right or correct perspective can lean toward tyranny, divisiveness, oppression, and bullying.

> **REFLECTIVE PRACTICE**
> What did you learn about conflict from your family of origin? How does your early learning about conflict currently influence your approach to conflict in the workplace?

7

"Remember, teamwork begins by building trust. And the only way to do that is to overcome our need for invulnerability."

—Patrick Lencioni

When you read this quote, what feels affirming and inspiring and what feels like a stretch or a challenge for you? Why? How does overcoming your need for invulnerability affect your work or relationships? What implications does this have for your actions in the future?

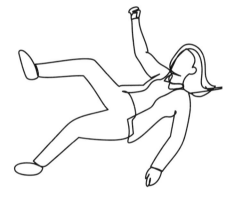

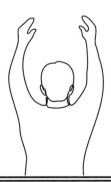

8 "Coaching is an art and it's far easier said than done. It takes courage to ask a question rather than offer up advice, provide an answer, or unleash a solution. Giving another person the opportunity to find their own way, make their own mistakes, and create their own wisdom is both brave and vulnerable."

—Brené Brown

Being a transformational coach requires a mindset of being a change agent rather than someone with all the knowledge or information. Our attitudes and beliefs about coaching and helping people create our coaching behaviors and actions. Consider the belief or attitude behind each coaching behavior: the behaviors of offering your knowledge and experience; the behaviors of teaching; the behaviors of facilitating as someone reflects on their actions in light of their intentions and desires. For example, what belief or attitude is behind your coaching practice of giving advice or providing answers to find solutions or fix problems? It's important to align your words and desired actions with new beliefs to change your course and embrace coaching as an art, not just a procedure. By adopting a set of behaviors and using language that is inconsistent with or challenges your old belief, you make it less possible for your old belief to persist and gives space for your new belief and actions to grow.

9

"The ability to observe without evaluating is the highest form of intelligence."

—Widely attributed to Jiddu Krishnamurti

The human brain's basal ganglia, referred to as the primal or reptilian brain, has instinctive responses and focuses on survival, self-preservation, and defense. It tends to assign things that are familiar as "safe" and things that are not familiar as "dangerous." This unsophisticated evaluation is often misleading and undermines our efforts to change or try new things. It's an important function; yet it offers only simplistic, instinctive, and basic responses to experiences. The neocortex, which is implicated in conscious thought, self-awareness, language, reasoning, and decision-making, can offer more complex and refined responses to our environment and experiences. We must access these executive functioning abilities to be able to observe without evaluating. A benefit of reflection is that it can move us from an "in the weeds" perspective to a "balcony view" vantage point. This expansion of awareness helps us recognize that our thoughts and perceptions are not necessarily true or accurate. To have an attitude of wonder and curiosity requires us to suspend evaluation so we can inquire with an open mind and open heart.

REFLECTIVE PRACTICE
Pay close attention to what others say and question your assumptions. The brain wants simplicity. When we are busy, the brain defaults to pattern recognition and automatically looks for what it has heard before and eliminates what is new. You risk getting stuck in a brain that only listens to and believes your familiar inner voice. Make an effort to listen, not speak, when you are with other people. Become aware of the voice that comments on everything you hear. Practice ignoring it or setting it aside, patting it on the head and saying, "Not now!"

10 "Constant kindness can accomplish much. As the sun makes ice melt, kindness causes misunderstanding, mistrust, and hostility to evaporate."

—Attributed to Albert Schweitzer

Leaders must strive to be kind in the face of discord and uncertainty. Kindness comes from a deep connection within. Behind gentleness is always confidence. Harshness is triggered by fear and multiplies fear in others. Ruthlessness and hard-heartedness are actually displays of weakness and a misguided understanding of power. Kindness is a demonstration of true strength and leadership.

REFLECTIVE PRACTICE
What are your beliefs and perceptions about the relationship between kindness, vulnerability, and powerful leadership? Are your current behaviors and actions aligned with kindness and your beliefs?

11

> "Coming together is a beginning. Keeping together is progress. Working together is success."
>
> —Edward Everett Hale

Team building always sounds good. But to really come together and stay united as a team takes trust and the ability to navigate conflict. We must be vulnerable, take risks, and overcome our individual habits of dealing with conflict. Most of us resort to either denying, avoiding, and withdrawing in conflict or becoming dominant, aggressive, or coercive. To really stay together as a team relies on each person's increasing their risk tolerance and willingness to face their own habits that either help or hinder their ability to navigate conflict. To really work together as a team also requires that everyone commits to goals, responsibilities, or roles to support the greater good, not just individual gain and glory. This might require either stepping up or letting go of some degree of control. Everyone must support one another in being accountable for the agreed commitments, which can mean speaking up (even to the leaders) and sharing perspectives of what's working and what's not. Each team member must listen with an open mind to consider challenging or diverse voices and perspectives. Team building doesn't happen by drafting mission statements or team agreements, although those are early steps. It requires leaning in and demonstrating a willingness to trust, not just tolerating the discomfort of conflict but really adopting healthy conflict behaviors and letting go of ineffective habits. You must change and grow, without resentment and with your eyes cast ahead toward possibility and opportunity for yourself and the team as a whole.

REFLECTIVE PRACTICE
What is one tendency of thought, feeling, or behavior you demonstrate when faced with conflict that is ineffective and doesn't really help all parties involved? What are possible alternative thoughts, feelings, or behaviors you can consider? You don't need to commit to changing right now. Just practice the art of brainstorming and give yourself several options to choose from.

"Wherever there is a man who exercises authority, there is a man who resists authority."

—Oscar Wilde

Our notion and beliefs about authority are anchored in our culture and family. Different countries have very different perspectives around authority, including whether people with authority are to be trusted or challenged. This can vary between generations as well. I grew up in the revolutionary 1960s, and my relationship to authority was very different from that of my older brothers, who grew up in the more conformist culture of the 1950s. The values of authority are embedded in workplace cultures, usually set by the leadership's beliefs, and can greatly influence the working of teams, the success of coaching initiatives, and the commitment and buy-in of individuals. Foster conversations with teams and individuals you work with to gain a better understanding of social and cultural influences on authority and the differing attitudes and beliefs each person has about authority and how this impacts their behaviors. This examination of cultural frameworks will provide avenues for more inclusion, honoring diversity and unraveling assumptions (especially the assumptions of dominant perspectives), so everyone can have deeper insights into and appreciation of one another.

REFLECTIVE PRACTICE

Examine for yourself your own values and beliefs about authority. Facilitate conversations with your teams to discuss the following question, suggested by my colleague Margie Carter.*

My family and culture taught me to view a person in authority as

- someone to always be respected
- someone to be suspicious of
- someone to count on for help
- someone to maneuver around

How does this impact your work and your work relationships?

---

* Margie Carter, "Principles and Strategies for Coaching and Mentoring," in *The Art of Leadership: Leading Early Childhood Organizations* (Lincoln, NE: Exchange Press, 2019), 65.

13

"For a coach, choosing relationship over control is all about shifting to a focus of really trying to understand the coachee's perspective instead of attempting to convince him or her to make a different decision or choice."

—Dathan D. Rush and M'Lisa Shelden

It's worth really looking at how we as coaches position ourselves in authority, power, and control just by implying we have answers and by giving advice. Trying to convince someone of anything is a symptom that we are slipping into a position of authority and power. Instead, let's practice investing our energy and actions toward truly trying to understand the coachee's perspective, through listening, paraphrasing, and questioning. At times this might require biting our tongue when we think we have a really good suggestion, even when we have the best intentions—to save them time or shorten their journey of trial and error. In order to really discern what's going on with their understanding, their rationale for an action, and how they learn from their experiences, we must seek to understand, not to be understood. The point of coaching is not only to achieve a desired outcome in a specific situation or goal but to facilitate coaches' reflective and critical thinking so they can better choose successful pathways for any situation they may face in the future. We can hone our own coaching skills by routinely reflecting on how our coaching approach, actions, and attitudes are transferring power to the coachee through facilitation, rather than by telling, advising, and convincing.

REFLECTIVE PRACTICE
Consider the experiences, conversations, interactions, successes, frustrations, or disappointments you are having as a coach. What's working? What are your challenges or concerns as a coach?

14

"To be aware of a single short-coming within oneself is more useful than to be aware of a thousand in someone else."

—Dalai Lama [Tenzin Gyatso]

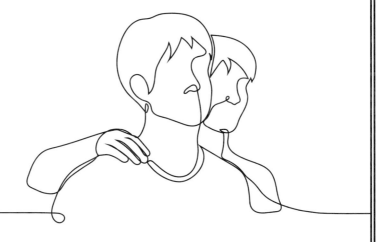

Reflect on the times this week you were focused on someone else's short-coming. Take a moment to consider any tendency or habit you have to focus on others' behaviors. This is in itself a shortcoming you can now become more aware of in yourself; then consider how to mindfully interrupt that tendency or habit. As you do this, practice more compassion for others and for yourself, just observing and not judging.

Being Self-Aware

Self-awareness is a foundational skill that requires routine self-reflective practices, no matter what your role is in your family, work, or community. Your manner of being—how you bring yourself to what you do and how you impact the people around you—will always need your attention and refinements so you stay true to who you want to be.

15

"No doubt emotional intelligence is rarer than book smarts, but my experience says it is actually more important in the making of a leader. You just can't ignore it."

—Widely attributed to Jack Welch

We can develop several emotional intelligence (EI) competencies to improve our relationships and life conditions. One of the foundational EI competencies that helps leaders deal with challenges, lower stress levels, and react less emotionally is self-awareness. Self-awareness is being conscious of your own feelings and your thoughts about them. This puts you in charge of your feelings, rather than letting your feelings run your behaviors and decisions. Self-awareness combined with self-control is strengthened by the regular practice of simple but powerful mindfulness exercises. Mindfulness practices train your brain to resist the overwhelming flight, fight, or freeze response of the amygdala and instead strengthen the prefrontal cortex's capacity for planning and strategizing to exert control over the amygdala's reactionary responses. But it takes routine mindfulness practices to strengthen this overriding system for self-regulation. Emotional intelligence is an integrated system of competencies, including self-awareness and self-regulation, that takes time and practice. But the payoff will be well worth the work.

REFLECTIVE PRACTICE
Explore mindfulness practices—there are many accessible with a quick online search. Start one practice this week, even if for only ten minutes, to invest in your self-awareness and self-control.

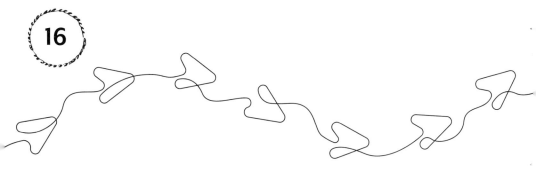

16

"The work of social change requires a commitment to personal change. Leaders must be self-aware, noticing how they are being influenced and changed, in both positive and negative directions."

—Margaret Wheatley

Being self-aware of circumstances that are likely to be challenging for you or behaviors that trigger you is an equally essential leadership skill as knowing how to inspire people. Being aware of how we instinctively respond is necessary in order to stop and override a negative knee-jerk reaction. Having the humility to acknowledge your triggers and unconscious reactions is a foundation of transformational leadership. Small daily actions can influence great gains in shifting obstructive habits and thought patterns.

REFLECTIVE PRACTICE
Take regular breaks. Under pressure, we default to doing what we have always done. Short breaks of even a minute get you out of habitual thinking and behavior and provide space for awareness, so you see things more clearly and from a more mindful perspective.

17

"Authentic leaders demonstrate a passion for their purpose, practice their values consistently, and lead with their hearts as well as their heads. They establish long-term, meaningful relationships and have the self-discipline to get results. They know who they are."

—Bill George

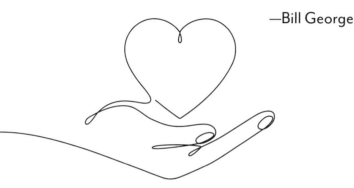

Leaders who know who they are have reflected on what their values are and what matters to them and examined whether their behaviors reflect what they believe. Leadership is a complex combination of heart, soul, and mind, with each aspect informing the others. It takes trust to follow passion, intention to practice what you believe, and courage to be authentically vulnerable and acknowledge mistakes and learn from them. Consistent reflective practices are the underlying tools and small actions that pave the road to authentic leadership.

REFLECTIVE PRACTICE
Take an authentic look in the mirror to expand your self-awareness. Clarify and write your most important foundational values. List several actions or behaviors you reliably practice that are testimony to each of your foundational values. Continue to cultivate those things. Identify any attitudes, behaviors, or habits you have that are not aligned with your values. Choose which of those contradictory actions you want to focus on to improve first. Let your desire lead you.

"As a leader, it's a major responsibility on your shoulders to practice the behavior you want others to follow."

18

—Himanshu Bhatia

Transformational leaders are resilient and reflective, taking precious time to contemplate new or deeper perspectives in changing circumstances. It is not unusual for all people to revert to familiar habits when stressed and challenged, even if those habits do not work effectively and are not what is really needed or intended. Leaders are self-aware of what challenges them and their ineffective habits when stressed. They make mindful, calm, intentional decisions for these situations. Leaders model resiliency by continually expanding their capacity to self-regulate and respond to overwhelming demands and challenges. Transformational leaders are an idealized influence, charismatically walking their talk with open-minded and authentic curiosity regarding the needs of the organization and their followers. They constantly reflect on how to be a role model for others, engage in ethical and mindful behaviors, instill pride and motivation, acknowledge both the value and significant contributions of others, and earn respect and trust among followers through the authentic demonstration of their behaviors.*

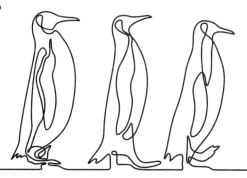

REFLECTIVE PRACTICE
Identify the ineffective habits of thought, feelings, and behaviors you turn to when you are stressed or challenged. Do you revert to old habits or stop self-care habits, compounding your stress rather than reducing it? Clarify which practices support you when you are stressed or challenged and embed these in your daily habits so they are always part of your life and work and are strengthened by daily use.

* Excerpts adapted from Constant Hine and Robin Levy, "Transformational Leadership in Turbulent Times," *Exchange* (September/October 2020).

19

"Discovering your authentic leadership requires a commitment to developing yourself. Like musicians and athletes, you must devote yourself to a lifetime of realizing your potential."

—Bill George, Peter Sims, Andrew N. McLean, and Diana Mayer

Self-awareness requires self-reflection. It requires courage and honesty to examine your experiences as a person and a leader. How we frame our perceptions as well as the meaning we give to our experiences plays a huge part in being self-aware. Our perceptions and how we interpret our life experiences have everything to do with the direction we steer our lives, including our motivation, our passions, and the values we use to navigate our actions and behaviors. Self-awareness and self-reflection hone that inner compass that guides our decisions and actions as we move forward in our life journey and as a leader.

REFLECTIVE PRACTICE
Practice the habit of reflection at the end of each day by asking yourself some thought-provoking questions. For example:

What did I do well today?

What could I have done better?

What should I stop doing in the future?

How could I have felt happier?

Was I kind and compassionate?

How did I leverage my time?

What opportunities did I squander and why?

20

"We committed ourselves to transformational organizing, which does not mainly denounce and protest oppression or mobilize Americans to struggle for more material things, but challenges us as Americans to evolve or transform ourselves into more human human beings."

—Grace Lee Boggs

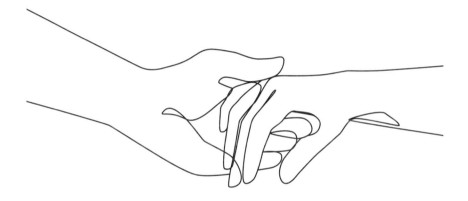

Transformational leaders consciously attend to the alignment of their own and their organization's values and actions, frequently considering whether their actions are embodying their values and determining when shifting tactics and strategy is necessary. They decide when it is time to rest and reorganize or time to seize the moment and push forward. To be responsive, leaders must be self-aware, committed to personal change, and mindful of values. Leadership that focuses on transformation keeps an eye on the human factor and everyone's well-being to ensure it is not lost in the name of progress, profitability, and change.

REFLECTIVE PRACTICE
What are your core values, and how are they demonstrated in your actions and behaviors with other people? Are your values aligned with your organization's values, and as a leader are you aligning organizational decisions with values?

21 "Self-awareness is the starting point of leadership"

—Bill George

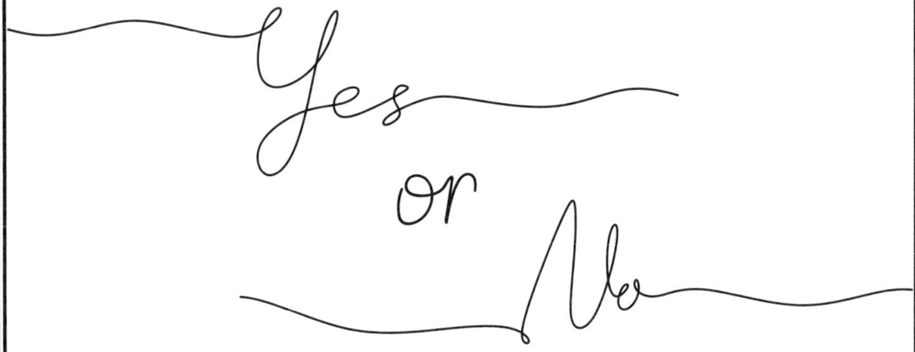

Yes or No

What are you saying yes to that you should be saying no to?

Servant Leadership and Humility

Pursuing the goal of becoming a more human and compassionate being will guide a leader's actions and behaviors to ensure they treat people holistically, respectfully, and compassionately. Focusing on and investing in others with humility creates a powerful and purposeful path for all types of leaders.

22

"I slept and dreamt that life was joy. I awoke and saw that life was service. I acted and behold, service was joy."

—Rabindranath Tagore

Giving opens the heart and soul. It's remarkable how being in service to others offers a way to get beyond ourselves, beyond our self-importance, fear, self-absorption, stress, and isolation. When I find myself caught up in the stresses of life, isolating myself, being self-absorbed, or feeling blue, finding ways to give to someone else or to do some kind of service shifts my soul focus and I find a great deal of unexpected solace. When I'm stressed, I often think there is no way I can do even one more thing. Yet when I can shift my mindset and heart from fear to trust, it's like a miracle happens: My heart calms and opens and my capacity expands. Service is not really about doing; it's more about having an open heart that flows over and wants to give. In that is joy and reward. It might be a simple touch on someone's shoulder, volunteering for a cause close to your heart, or just listening to a child, an elder, or a friend. The joy of life and of service isn't experienced so much from the task itself as from the love flowing.

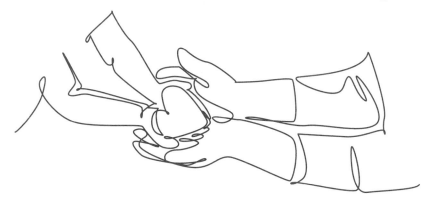

REFLECTIVE PRACTICE
Explore what you think service is. How could mundane tasks be reframed as service by shifting your mind and heart's perspective? How might you shift your perspective of work so it can encompass joy and a heart-filled openness? What helps or hinders your ability to do this?

23

"The servant-leader is servant first. . . . It begins with the natural feeling that one wants to serve, to serve first. Then conscious choice brings one to aspire to lead. That person is sharply different from one who is leader first, perhaps because of the need to assuage an unusual power drive or to acquire material possessions. . . . The leader-first and the servant-first are two extreme types. Between them there are shadings and blends that are part of the infinite variety of human nature."

—Robert K. Greenleaf

Servant leadership is a nontraditional leadership philosophy that places the primary emphasis on the well-being of those being served. A servant-leader focuses primarily on the growth and well-being of people and the communities to which they belong. While traditional leadership generally involves the accumulation and exercise of power at the top of the pyramid, servant-leaders share power. They help people develop and perform as highly as possible, becoming healthier, wiser, and freer, and this in turn cultivates others' likelihood of becoming servants. Servant-leaders attend to the inclusion of all stakeholders and consider the effect of decisions on equity and the least-privileged members of society. The servant-leader doesn't pay less attention to the positive and effective outcomes for an organization than traditional leaders, but they are more mindful to include the well-being of all people in the definition of success. One might start from a desire to serve and move toward leadership, or one who is already leading might discover that service is the truest purpose of leadership.

REFLECTIVE PRACTICE
Do you aspire toward servant-leadership? In what ways are you embracing and behaving as a servant-leader? In what ways do you want to continue to grow, and what changes might you want to make?

24

> "Humility is not thinking less of yourself, it's thinking of yourself less."

—Rick Warren

A leader's focus is not on themselves, wanting to prove themselves or take credit for accomplishments. True leaders are humble yet self-confident, willing to be vulnerable and take risks while trusting their vision and commitment to the people they serve. In the spirit of servant-leadership, they have their attention on the well-being, development, and advancement of those around them as the criteria for success.

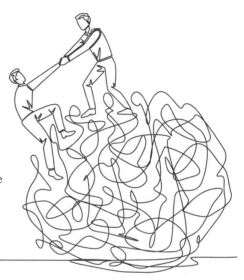

REFLECTIVE PRACTICE
What helps you to think more about the people around you, without losing sight of your own self-care and responsibilities? What causes you to turn your attention back on yourself, to become more self-absorbed or fearful?

Reaching Our Full Potential

To reach our own full potential or to assist others in doing the same requires embedding reflective habits as part of our lifestyle. Becoming all of who we want to be requires a process of getting better at getting better at whatever is important to us. It is a learning process, not a one-time event.

25

"People are seeking feelings of personal significance. . . . People (in all jobs and roles) want to feel that they matter and that the work they do matters."

—Mark C. Crowley

Transformational leaders offer followers something more than just working for self-gain; they provide followers with an inspiring mission and vision, and they empower followers to create an identity and to contribute to the greater good. Because a follower's emotional connection to their work influences their level of engagement, commitment, and willingness to take risks, it is important for leaders to acknowledge the significance each person brings to the whole organization. Acknowledgment helps followers recognize that each person contributes to the shared vision.* To build a work culture that demonstrates that what each person does matters and is a contribution, create meeting protocols that include time for acknowledgments.

REFLECTIVE PRACTICE
In meetings, make a point of acknowledging the contributions that individuals have made to recent projects or to a shared vision. Be sure these acknowledgments are concrete, specific, and unique to each person or team you are highlighting. Track your acknowledgments to ensure each person or every team is included over a month or quarter. Reserve time in meeting agendas for you and team members to acknowledge the small and big victories of their peers and colleagues.

* Excerpts adapted from Constant Hine and Robin Levy, "Transformational Leadership in Turbulent Times," *Exchange* (September/October 2020).

26

"Coaching is unlocking a person's potential to maximize their own performance. It is helping them to learn rather than teaching them."

—John Whitmore

Coaching is really the art of helping people reflect and think critically for themselves to make intentional choices so they achieve what they are aiming for. Too often people combine coaching with being the expert and offering people advice, suggestions, and helpful ideas. That is really the role of a consultant or technical assistant, to help fix problems or find solutions. When we offer advice or suggestions, it doesn't necessarily contribute to the person learning and building their own skills for addressing their current or future challenges. When we consider the role of the coach to be a change agent, helping people to learn how to problem solve, then we are investing in the person's ability, not just addressing one current issue. Raising people up, building on their strengths, and inspiring them is the focus of leaders and coaches. There is a difference between learning and instructing. Facilitate learning and minimize instructing to influence sustainable change in others.

REFLECTIVE PRACTICE
Recall a time recently when, as a coach or leader, you helped someone by offering advice or imparting what you thought was helpful information. Did the person achieve lasting results? Consider this without any self-judgment or defense. Reflect on whether it helped the person in the short term with a specific issue, invested in their ability to solve problems, or unlocked their potential for the future. How might you modify your approach to better invest in their problem-solving abilities rather than offering a solution or fixing a single issue?

27 "What differentiates true experiential learning from simply learning by doing is the reflective processing that takes place after the doing."

—North Carolina Cooperative Extension

There is a difference between teaching and learning. Someone can teach all day, but it does not guarantee that someone else learned. Educators maximize learners' sticky learning when reflection is embedded in their teaching pedagogy, for example using a Do, Reflect, and Apply method. Learning really happens when learners engage with the content, not just passively receive information. After sharing information and offering engaging activities for learners, teachers and adult educators can build in a reflective process for learners so they focus on the value and application of what they learned. This might include asking the learner open-ended questions about how the content is meaningful and relevant for them. Just like when teaching young children you might ask how they built a tower or what might help the next time they build, you can ask your coachee what they notice about what they're doing. This is where a lot of the learning will be anchored. Helping learners reflect while they're learning increases the depth and meaning of what they're learning. There is a difference between knowledge and understanding. Knowledge is easy to lose; understanding is hard to forget. Understanding will come with reflection and engaging with information.

REFLECTIVE PRACTICE
Think of a simple thing you want to teach another person. For example, consider teaching a preschooler how to pour a glass of water by themselves, a teenager how to drive, or an adult how to use a new application on their phone or computer. Think of ways to help them be actively engaged with the content and reflect about what and how they learned and what made a difference for them. You could ask open-ended questions like these: Was that as easy or hard as you thought? What helped? What didn't? How might you use this information? What do you think is the most important tip to help you next time?

28 "You cannot get through a single day without having an impact on the world around you. What you do makes a difference, and you have to decide what kind of difference you want to make."

—Widely attributed to Jane Goodall

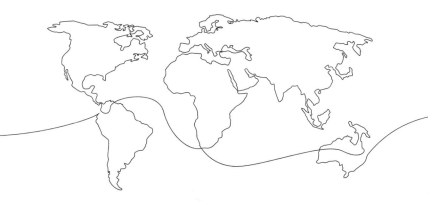

Understanding that everything we do and everything we leave undone has an impact, heightens our awareness of the importance of being intentional. Intentional about who we want to be and how our values inform our actions, aligning our minds, hearts, and behaviors with what we want. Who you are makes a difference every day. What kind of difference do you want to make, and does your current footprint align with your desire? Start each day next week reading this Weekly Reflective Practice quote—how might it influence your choices for the day? To expand your awareness of the difference you make, at the end of each day write down or talk to someone about what you did to make a positive or negative difference that day.

29

"Coaching is not about telling people what to do but giving them a chance to examine what they are doing in light of their intentions."

—James Flaherty

Becoming an agent of change requires that we facilitate reflection in others so that they become skillful in critical thinking; clarifying their goals, actions, and challenges; and finding their own pathway for learning. It really is essential to shift our own mindset away from being a content expert, thinking we are supposed to have the answers and fix people's problems. If we really want to empower others to become thoughtful and successful professionals, we need to help them learn how to fish rather than habitually give them a fish. In order for a coach or leader to transfer power, they must help people reflect, examining and analyzing for themselves what they are doing and considering whether their current professional practices are effective in light of their intentions.

REFLECTIVE PRACTICE
Think about your own coaching or leadership strategies you use when supporting an individual or a team. Do you approach them as a change agent, facilitating their own reflection and critical thinking, asking open-ended, empowering questions, and helping them reframe perspectives? Or do you tend to give advice and suggestions, approaching them or their issue with a fix-it style? Over the next few weeks, observe your approach and gather some data that tracks your habits. You can list possible strategies or actions to achieve or avoid and then hashtag the number of occurrences of your actual actions and behaviors. Or you can use a Likert scale of one to ten, with telling, advising, fixing behaviors at one (far left); observing, giving feedback, modeling, sharing personal experience with no agenda at five (middle); and listening, paraphrasing, asking open-ended questions, reframing, facilitating critical thinking and reflection at ten (far right).

30

"If your actions create a legacy that inspires others to dream more, learn more, do more and become more, then, you are an excellent leader."

—Dolly Parton

The role of the transformational coach is that of a change agent, a thinking partner, a facilitator of growth, and sometimes an accountability partner. A coach's role is to empower people to learn how to reflect and how to thoughtfully make data-driven decisions to improve their practices, solve their own problems, and be responsible for their own learning by learning how to change. The intention of this approach is to groom the coachee's ability to change and learn about any content with skill and, hopefully, some grace and joy. This requires our partnership to accompany them while they are in the messy middle of their learning process. When we approach coaching from the perspective of a content expert, we frequently and often unconsciously position ourselves above our coachees in a power stance of knowing more. This is not empowering and often has the opposite effect, making people feel less competent and more dependent on the coach for answers. Fostering continuous improvement is often more important for a coach than simply being a content expert, with the ultimate goal of promoting real change and growth over time.*

> **REFLECTIVE PRACTICE**
> If you find yourself leaning toward professional practices that aim at giving suggestions, giving advice, fixing problems others bring to you, or being a content expert, ask yourself what values or beliefs are holding these habits in place. Observe whether these practices actually result in sustainable change. Does the person take initiative the next time they are having difficulty? Reflect whether it's emotionally more comfortable for you to help as a content expert or it feeds your ego of being helpful, rather than tolerating the discomfort of being a change agent focused on helping people learn to change for themselves and being their partner during their messy middle.

* Excerpts adapted from Constant Hine and Robin Levy, "Transformational Coaching: Moving Beyond Goals and Action Plans to Foster Continuous Quality Improvement," *Exchange* (November/December 2019).

Chapter 11

PERSONAL AND SOCIAL IDENTITY

Becoming aware of our personal perspectives and the influence of culture and bias is foundational to understanding our personal and social identity. This understanding is key to successfully navigating living and working with others in a culturally diverse society.

Reflecting for Self-Understanding

Routine reflective practices that examine our perspectives, values, and behaviors are essential to understanding ourselves and our needs as we grow and encounter new and diverse experiences, people, social situations, and life demands. Along our journey as we change our work or roles, experience new demands, or achieve our goals, reflection helps us stay current with our changing perspectives and how they influence our behaviors and decision-making.

"We cannot change what we are unaware of, and once we are aware, we cannot help but change."

—Sheryl Sandberg

Intentional reflection expands self-understanding and self-awareness, the foundation for open-minded, respectful, collaborative, and inclusive relations and equitable policies. Reflection is the strategic means for examining and expanding one's awareness of and ability to be responsible for one's own frame of reference, cultural values, social identity, and individual bias that influence personal perspectives and behaviors. Reflection is a pathway for learning about yourself, diffusing triggered and impulsive reactions, and offering a mindful pause to choose more empowering and respectful responses. Intentional reflective practices are essential to "know thyself," which allows you to respectfully interact with people who are different from you or who have diverse viewpoints. Implementing reflective routines requires the qualities of courage, grit, and commitment, the ability to tolerate discomfort, and the vulnerability to look honestly in the mirror.

REFLECTIVE PRACTICE
Use a variety of vantage points when reflecting on any given topic, choosing viewpoints that will stretch your perspective and awareness and deepen your curiosity. There is no right or correct way to reflect. A variety of approaches to reflection are discussed in the introduction of this book.

2

"Expanding awareness of how you uniquely take in information from the world and how you process and react to that information creates your foundation for conscious choice."

—Pamela Bond

According to Howard Gardner, there are different ways of being intelligent. We each have all of the multiple intelligences but in our own unique blend. He states that human intelligence is open and dynamic, not fixed and static, and that both biological and environmental factors contribute to intelligence. Intelligence is how we organize content knowledge and make sense of our experiences. Being self-aware of your own ways of intelligence can offer insight into your strengths as well as aspects of yourself that are not as developed. You can learn to be more intelligent in any of Gardner's types of intelligences. Many people who are not aware of their intelligences are often unconsciously operating from the notion that the way they are naturally smart is how all people operate. This easily becomes a strength-based bias. If you are strong in verbal-linguistic intelligence, you might think everyone organizes and processes information and experiences this way, and when they don't, it's quite easy to judge or criticize them for not getting it. But just because people do not take in or process information like you do doesn't make them less capable, intelligent, or productive. Imagine a person who is very visual-spatial who cannot understand your project outline very easily because you have presented it only verbally, or perhaps you presented it in a linear outline format that seems logical to you because your strengths are logical-mathematical. When you assume your way of understanding and processing is the same for all people, you are unintentionally not honoring diverse ways of being and not being respectful of individual needs.

REFLECTIVE PRACTICE
Complete the Multiple Intelligence Qualities Inventory to discover your own intelligence profile. What are your strengths and what are less-developed areas you may wish to strengthen?

https://www.redleafpress.org/dre/11-2.pdf

"We see what we believe rather than what we see."

—Alan Watts

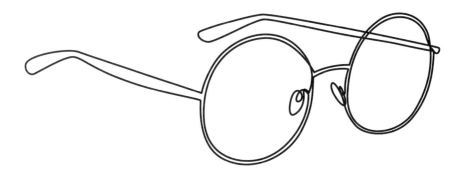

Humans tend to believe what our brain tells us 100 percent of the time and rarely, if ever, question our first hunch or instinct about what we're observing. It takes self-awareness and intentional reflection to realize that just because we have a thought doesn't make it true. It also requires a willingness to pause and use different parts of our brain. When we give ourselves space and permission to see more than what our eyes and conditioning tell us, we give ourselves a chance to step beyond our bias and see a bigger picture. Then we can choose actions that expand our self-awareness and lessen our unconscious bias.

REFLECTIVE PRACTICE
The next time you feel strongly about something or you are very sure your perception of an interaction or situation is accurate, ask yourself these questions:

1. What actually happened, or what did I actually observe?
2. What meaning or interpretation am I applying to what happened?
3. How might someone else or the person I'm interacting with have seen and experienced the situation differently?
4. With alternative possible interpretations, what is the most productive way to deal with the situation that fosters connection and respects diversity?

"When a flower doesn't bloom, you fix the environment in which it grows, not the flower."

—Widely attributed to Alexander den Heijer

When someone is different from us, or they approach dealing with problems or conflict in a different manner than we do, all too often we automatically think that something is wrong with them or that they are doing something wrong, and we judge them or perceive them as "other." It takes remarkable self-awareness and conscious intention to not instinctively respond this way. But if we are willing to continually self-reflect, grow, and change, we can learn to be more mindful, sensitive, and inclusive. As leaders, we monitor whether the work environment, including people and policies, is inclusive and consider whether someone is not blooming because of our work culture, not because they are somehow not performing. To develop the reflective habit of examining and assessing the environment before personalizing the issue with a person takes intention, practice, inquiry, and constant persistence.

> **REFLECTIVE PRACTICE**
> Is there someone you currently work with, or have worked with in the past, who may not have bloomed to their full potential due to the work environment?

Respecting Diversity and Understanding Culture

Having a better understanding of culture can help us move toward greater sensitivity in our responses to the many people with whom we interact, work, and serve whose backgrounds are different from our own. Review and identify any bias or roadblocks to your ability to engage and work with others.

5

"Diversity is valuing difference because it makes a difference: we see more when there are more of us seeing. We know more when everyone's perspective is sought and incorporated into our learning."

—Margaret Wheatley

Differences in ethnicity, culture, religion, language, and a variety of other factors all play a role in the workplace. The practice of ensuring that all people experience a sense of connection and encouragement is referred to as *inclusion*. Dismantling in ourselves and within our teams the idea that there is only one right way is important if we are to embrace inclusion and respect diversity. Shifting our mindset to appreciate more eyes, offer more perspectives, and listen to different voices as a contribution rather than a challenge demonstrates servant leadership in action.

REFLECTIVE PRACTICE

When you notice people do things differently or have a different perspective, be mindful of your temptation to disagree or defend your position. Pause and check your reaction—intercept the urgency to act in the moment. Try shifting to an attitude of inquiry to understand better rather than to be understood. Ask questions. Reflect on how those differences might contribute to or improve your own approach.

6

"The path to diversity begins with supporting, mentoring, and sponsoring diverse women and men to become leaders and entrepreneurs."

—Widely attributed to Denise Morrison

Investing in human resources improves organizational health and well-being and strengthens individuals. One of the secrets of success is to consistently help others succeed in their goals. Remember all the people in your own life who have guided or helped you. This might have been overtly and intentionally or perhaps they didn't even know they were a role model for you. I have a colleague, a woman of color, who attended many of my trainings and said she considered me a mentor. At the same time, her perspective on so many issues really inspired me as our paths overlapped, and she has since become a friend and a mentor to me in turn. I asked her to coteach a workshop with me. I was deeply affected by her perspective, personal insights, and experiences on this topic I often teach, and she expanded my understanding of the topic and my awareness of how my own privileged perspectives had the quality of a single-sided story. This experience reinforced the incredible value of having multiple perspectives when teaching, and I now always teach this topic with a person who is culturally different from me. Your own learning and growth will benefit from being mentored by or mentoring people who are different from you. In order to mentor diverse people, you need to expand your circle to include people of all genders who are not just like you—people who are different from you racially, ethnically, economically, and socially and who may have very different viewpoints, voices, talents, and styles than you do. Make yourself available to give to others what you have received.

REFLECTIVE PRACTICE
Are your current personal and professional circles of people diverse? Make an effort to expand your circles to meet and interact with a wider variety of people. Are there professional groups or meetings you attend where you might seek out people you less typically talk to or associate with? When you attend professional development opportunities (conferences, webinars, or community events), make a point of meeting and talking with at least one person who is different from you: who dresses very differently than you, who is significantly older/younger, who is racially or culturally different, who has a different job role, who shared something you might not agree with, and so on. Explore meet-up groups or book clubs on a topic of interest. Seek conversation cafes in your area.

(7)

"Own your biases. Don't be owned by them."

—Abhijit Naskar

Think about why it is important to actively explore your own bias. How are your biases connected to your life and work?

8

"Our lives can be considered coherent constellations of cultural practices that may dynamically change over time, over social and environmental settings and across generations."

—Adapted from Barbara Rogoff

Understanding cultures other than our own is important in creating connections. We want to share our culture with others such that we are creating connection and bridging diversity to help them understand others' perspectives and values. We don't want to use our culture as a shield or defense to hold people away or to shut down discussion and exploration. Taking a defensive or aggressive stance about one's culture is not in the spirit of creating understanding and connection or bridging diverse perspectives. Our perspective and sense of cultural identity doesn't have to be an either/or stance or attitude. It is worth remembering that cultural practices and perspectives change over time, through the generations, and across social settings. We want to be respectful in our exchanges about culture. We need to examine how and why we are sharing and discussing our culture. When we share a personal perspective or our culture, we should not assume it's the truth but acknowledge that ours is not the only perspective.

REFLECTIVE PRACTICE
Explore the fluidity of your own culture. How have your own personal or cultural values or practices changed over time, over generations? How have your sense of culture and identity or rituals changed as you've added people to your family (births, marriages, adoptions) or when you have lost people (deaths, divorce, alienation)? How about when you have moved to a new area or different country?

9

"Culturally responsive coaching begins with understanding yourself, including your values and practices."

—Jill McFarren Avilés and Erika Amadee Flores

Coaches and leaders need to be mindful of their own values and cultural perspectives and not make the mistake of assuming others share their values and perspectives or agree with them. It isn't the leader's or coach's role to impose their values or perspectives on others, and at times it may not even be relevant to share them. It takes mindfulness to consider the situation and discern whether it's helpful or necessary to share your vantage point. Being mindful of particular issues or perspectives that tend to elicit a strong reaction within you requires self-awareness and self-regulation, so you can respond rather than react and avoid posturing with an attitude of authority or a need to be right. Often it takes great humility to continue to listen, to keep an open mind, and to mindfully monitor yourself when you are triggered or when strong feelings based on values or culture present themselves.

REFLECTIVE PRACTICE
Whenever you feel 100 percent sure of your interpretation of an experience, situation, or person, try asking whether there is another way to interpret the interaction.

10

"Tolerance, inter-cultural dialogue and respect for diversity are more essential than ever in a world where peoples are becoming more and more closely interconnected."

—Kofi Annan

Time and energy are culturally specific. We want to be mindful of the dominant culture in this country and its relationship to time and energy. Yet we must understand how another person's relationship to time and energy can vary due to their culture, disposition, age, or generation. For example, perhaps you have heard the phrase that someone seems to be on "island time," which refers to a different culture's pacing and connection to time yet often carries a derogatory implication. Our current dominant social culture in the United States prioritizes being on the clock, constantly checking our messages, and scheduling every minute of the day, which is very different from slower cultural paces. Be mindful if you are pushing expectations or imposing pressure or anxiety on others based on your own attitudes and behaviors, as well as those of the coaching initiative or dominant culture. Our expectations about the pacing of a coaching session or work meeting can impose anxiety and interfere with learning for some. If we model and create a culture that values pausing, taking time to reflect, and engaging in meaningful, deep conversations, then our colleagues, coaching partners, and children will learn the value of taking time. Being self-reflective is unfamiliar for some individuals and cultures, and asking coaching partners to self-reflect and think through a challenge might cause discomfort if they are expecting answers from a perceived authority figure. I worked with an agency where most of the employees and clientele they served were of Chinese heritage. When the coaches began coaching child care providers, the providers viewed the coaches as authority figures, especially because they were highly revered as educators, and expected the coaches to just tell them what to do and they would comply. The coaches had to set the foundation so the coaching relationship would be a partnership. They needed to be patient as the providers gradually learned that this approach was not disrespectful, then took more initiative and came to value self-reflection and analysis in a shared power dynamic. Investing in these new kinds of relationships took time to develop so both the coach and coaching partners could accept and engage fully as partners.

> **REFLECTIVE PRACTICE**
> How is your own personal and cultural relationship to time and pacing influencing your own anxiety or reflective practices? How is this positively or negatively impacting your coaching relationships or the people you support in your workplace?

> "Diversity is anything that's different—it goes beyond race and ethnicity to different ways of thinking, doing and behaving. We take an approach that enables people to understand, respect and appreciate differences. When they do this, they are able to work with other people on their terms—and other people are able to work with them."

—Attributed to Enrique Garcia Bejar

There is a lot of media advertising and social stereotyping about self-care being mainly for women, in particular wealthy white women. These messages have also reinforced the characterization that self-care is indulgence. Many folks are unaware of current science and research surrounding the importance of self-care and don't know what self-care practices and habits include. It's not just taking bubble baths and having a spa day. Share with others the information and research about the importance of self-care and following habits that promote resiliency, encompassing physical, mental, emotional, and spiritual practices. But providing information alone may not make the difference. Be culturally responsive when coaching or supporting others regarding self-care. Be mindful that people from marginalized groups often think it is not OK to care for themselves. Some families and individuals that participate in certain types of work or trades (for example, farming, ranching, mining, and so on) may have a cultural perspective that self-care is not OK, self-indulgent, or nonproductive, or that it might put one's livelihood at risk. Our current social messaging in the United States is embedded with dominant values that being productive is essential, that being busy, working hard, and working more are rewarded, and that being available 24/7 is required to be successful. Examine how these values often result in burning out, treating people insensitively as if they are machines, or valuing the completion of tasks more than attending to the human needs of individuals. We are at a threshold of needing to reexamine and shift our social values to also recognize the importance of self-care, introspection, reflection, and the social-emotional well-being of individuals and employees, so that we are investing in and valuing our human resources.

338

REFLECTIVE PRACTICE
Have conversations with colleagues, staff, and people you support to discuss attitudes, perspectives, and biases surrounding self-care, resiliency, and the pace we live our lives. Discuss where they learned their perspectives, what assumptions they have, and what facts they know. When supporting coachees who are stressed and overwhelmed, you may need to individualize conversations to help them explore underlying beliefs that inhibit them from implementing self-care and resiliency practices. Inquire about and listen to their beliefs. Don't assume your role is to convince them to change or do something differently.

12

"It is not our differences that divide us. It is our inability to recognize, accept, and celebrate those differences."

—Attributed to Audre Lorde

When coaching or supporting someone from a different culture, you may find that they act or react differently from what you are used to. Cultural differences are not just related to national, racial, language, ethnic, or religious backgrounds but also include how people are influenced by the culture of current or past work situations. Cultures—both national and organizational—differ along many dimensions. These organizational cultural differences can result in different perspectives on performance, differing needs for or acceptance of feedback, varying adherence to deadlines, greater or lesser desire for creativity or taking initiative, differences in following protocols, and the weight one puts on compliance. Investing time to get to know individuals and building respectful relationships based on inquiry rather than assumptions sets the tone for all successful coaching relationships. It is especially important when working with individuals from a different culture than yours or who are new to your workplace culture. It is essential to intentionally discuss the understandings, hopes, and concerns about change, learning, and growth you all hold. Be mindful of and ideally have explicit conversations with individuals about the implications of cultural differences. In *The Tao of Coaching*, Max Landsberg offers the suggestion that when coaching individuals or within organizations, consider the following four cultural dimensions that frequently require cultural responsiveness:

Directness (getting to the point versus implying the message) can influence your style of feedback.

Hierarchy (following instructions versus engaging in dialogue) requires you to clarify the relationship, roles, and responsibilities of coaching, as well as other positions within the organization. For example, it is important to clarify that what is discussed within a coaching conversation is confidential and not shared with supervisors.

Consensus (accepting disagreement versus requiring agreement or compliance) requires that you draw from a repertoire of facilitation techniques, especially about asking and telling.

Individualism (independence versus interdependence) influences whether the focus of coaching is on teamwork or not, as well as how individuals are motivated to succeed.

REFLECTIVE PRACTICE

Recall the last time you worked with someone from another culture (or someone who was new to your organizational culture) with whom you had difficulty or didn't feel as effective. What went wrong, or which of these dimensions might have been overlooked? How might you shift your approach to avoid a similar problem or challenge in the future?

Working through Bias

With ongoing reflective review, we can become more self-aware by examining our own explicit and implicit biases and identifying our personal areas for improvement, noticing where we may need to shift, adjust, or deepen our personal awareness and sensitivity.

13 "Recognizing that you have biases . . . is essential to personal growth."

—Attributed to Mikaela Kiner

We need to take active steps toward revealing and unraveling our biases. It doesn't just happen—it takes effort. Not only do we need to look within and examine our perspectives but we also need to have the courage to talk with others about bias (including our own) and discuss the impact of bias on our interactions, decisions, and actions. Work to differentiate between opinion and perspective based on assumptions and awareness based on facts and comprehension.

I have two brothers who are a decade older than I am, and we grew up in very different social generations. We have always been at opposite ends in our perspectives and values. We learned over the years to simply avoid political discussions, which helped us evade conflicts. We love each other but don't really know each other well. I found myself over the years starting to adopt an attitude that my way of thinking was better, healthier, and "right." But as we are aging, I wanted to be more connected, so I planned a trip to visit them. I decided that if I wanted to get to know them better, I would explore one of their passions; I have learned throughout the years in my coaching practice that this helps create connection. My brothers are avid hunters and gun collectors, while I have always had a negative attitude toward guns. But I decided to ask them to teach me how to shoot on this trip. They were ecstatic when I asked them. On the big day, my brothers and nephew showed up at the shooting range with over fifteen kinds of guns. I was amazed! So I shot every one of those guns with their careful guidance. And I had fun! Turns out I was a really good shot. I can relate to the satisfaction of being skillful in hitting the target. They were beaming with pride, bragging to fellows at the shooting range about my skill, and I was delighted with their attention. Climbing into their world and seeing it from their perspective helped me know them better. We had a conversation about gun rights and I was able to ask, listen, and learn about their values and why guns were important to them. We didn't try to convince each other to change our views or values, but we tried to better understand each other and our differing points of view with interest and kindness, without having to agree. We are definitely more connected now.

REFLECTIVE PRACTICE · PART 1: CURRENT STORY

Invite someone to do this reflective practice with you so you can discuss it. Review the following five examples that commonly trigger a bias perspective.

Choose one of the examples you have a strong opinion about or reaction to. Or identify another topic that would trigger a strong reaction for you. Feel your response.

1. Tattoos and/or facial piercings
2. Bright or multicolored dyed hair
3. Saggy pants that reveal underwear
4. Bumper stickers or political signs in yards
5. Loud, demonstrative speaking in a public place

Reflect on the following three questions for the issue you picked.

1. What do I know?
2. What am I assuming?
3. Why do I think this way?

Discuss with a friend or colleague the topic you picked and why. What were your initial perspectives or assumptions? What did you discover by reflecting on the three questions?

WEEKLY REFLECTIVE PRACTICE

14

"A diverse mix of voices leads to better discussions, decisions, and outcomes for everyone."

—Sundar Pichai

In your organization, which voices are overly heard and which voices are not well represented or are left out?

15

" WHILE DOING *THE RESEARCH, KEEP* IN *MIND THERE ARE ONLY TWO KINDS OF FACTS... THOSE THAT SUPPORT MY POSITION... AND INCONCLUSIVE.* "

CartoonStock.com

Usually confirmation bias is unconscious. At the same time, it is becoming more common for individuals, companies, organizations, and governmental agencies to intentionally fund or find research that supports their preferred perspective or position. Pay attention to the source of data and research. Increase your awareness of your own tendency to settle for the research or data that just proves your point or helps to build a case or a single-sided story in your favor, without thinking critically about the source of facts or information or keeping an eye on a broader perspective and diverse points of view.

REFLECTIVE PRACTICE
As a general best practice, find three reputable sources that verify the information you hear or read. Learn to question the sources of cited research. Was it peer-reviewed? Who funded the research, and were the numbers in the control groups or people studied representative of our society at large? Act like a scientist and try finding sources that disprove your assumptions.

"What we do see depends mainly on what we look for."

16

—John Lubbock

In the article "What Is Confirmation Bias?" Terrell Heick defines confirmation bias as "the tendency to overvalue data that supports a pre-existing belief. . . . The pattern is to form a theory (often based on emotion) supported with insufficient data, and then to restrict critical thinking and ongoing analysis, which is, of course, irrational. Instead, you look for data that fits your theory."* It can sound so extreme in this definition, and yet we all engage in some degrees of confirmation bias, and it's important to expose where you might be doing this. When have we formed an opinion, found data to support that opinion, and become more convinced and emotionally sure we are right? Then perhaps we also discounted and discredited new or better data because then we'd have to reconstruct our belief system, apologize to people, or admit we were wrong. Consider whether you have ever built a case about someone, such as deciding that a colleague is irresponsible or disrespectful. You collect evidence to prove that your perspective is accurate and make this a blanket statement about the person, rather than assuming the best of the person or considering that it might have happened only one time. Did you actively look for evidence to disprove your opinion? Consider the news sources you choose. We typically choose sources that continue to support and justify our views, yet this can contribute to confirmation bias.

REFLECTIVE PRACTICE

Moving forward, use data to inform your theory formation instead of using your theories to inform your data seeking. Intentionally look for data or research that disagrees with or offers a differing perspective from your theory.

- Frequently reevaluate what you believe you know. Ask yourself how you know it. Do you have data to support your belief?
- Know how to differentiate fact from opinion and separate accurate data from inaccurate data. Verify the original source of the data—don't just accept data or research as reported by others
- Insist on the highest-quality data and consider all data equally. Watch out for any tendency to minimize or disregard data you disagree with. Know who funded the research. Pay attention to the context of how the research was conducted and whether it meets industry standards for unbiased results.

* Terrell Heick, "What Is Confirmation Bias?" TeachThought, July 9, 2018, www.teach thought.com/critical-thinking/confirmation-bias-definition.

17

"As long as you have certain desires about how it ought to be, you can't see how it is."

—Adapted from Ram Dass

Having strong opinions or viewpoints or simply being accustomed to a status quo furthers an effort to maintain the right to be comfortable holding your current perspective. Confusing a strong belief for a black-and-white truth creates a judgmental criteria and sets up blanket expectations for how we believe other people should think, feel, and behave. Because we are comfortable with our values and beliefs, we assume that is how it ought to be for everyone. This can hinder us from seeing and acknowledging how others have had different experiences of the world and may not have a shared perspective or value—often limiting our ability to understand and respect who they are, as they are, or worse, resulting in judgment and polarization. Unfortunately, this can contribute to an unconscious adherence to dominant norms, creating unsafe spaces for those who do not adhere to those norms. Which does not equate to them being wrong! When we are situated in dominant norms and culture, we often do not see how the things really are for those in marginalized groups. It's important we recognize that power is a privilege and does not grant us the right to comfort.

We can be part of dominant culture in some areas and be marginalized in others. It's not all or nothing—it's complex. We each must look for ourselves to understand in which areas we are part of dominant culture and examine how it impacts our perspectives, our relationships, and our leadership. We each need to commit to deepening our knowledge of institutionalized racism and other forms of oppression and how our actions or inactions contribute to the suffering of others. That might not be comfortable, yet it is needed.

REFLECTIVE PRACTICE

Clarify in which areas of social or personal identity you are part of the dominant culture. You can take social identity assessments that are available online if you are not clear. Educate yourself about racism and other social forms of systemic oppression. Identify areas or groups of marginalized people you are not familiar with and intentionally educate yourself by reading, watching documentaries, listening to podcasts, or talking with friends and colleagues. Set goals, make an educational plan, and take action. Learn to tolerate the discomfort of becoming more aware and less biased toward others.

18

"Get used to that uncomfortable feeling that arises when you discover that perhaps your privilege is hindering your ability to truly understand or address an issue. Get used to the pang of guilt that comes with realizing yet another area of life where you've benefited at the expense of others. It will not kill you. You can withstand it. You want to be more comfortable with this, so that when you are confronted with your privilege in a stressful situation . . . you will be able to limit your defensiveness enough to listen and learn."

—Ijeoma Oluo

We all must actively work to dismantle defensiveness in ourselves and in the teams we work with and serve. Defensiveness is often connected to the fear of losing power, comfort, or face. A desire to maintain an identity, a sense of ourselves, or a perspective can trigger defensiveness. Noticing and naming our fears when we feel defensive is an act of self-awareness that can deeply affect our choice of actions. Become mindful by examining and reflecting on the ways you are defensive or resistant to new ideas, especially if they get in the way of your vision and mission.

REFLECTIVE PRACTICE
Recall a recent time you reacted, felt defensive, or wanted to prove a point. What was your underlying fear, or what did you feel you needed to defend? What was it you wanted to maintain or not be questioned about? Why was this so important to you? How might this affect your ability to lead or to be open to diverse perspectives and needs of others?

"We all see only that which we are trained to see."

—Robert Anton Wilson

Most people in the dominant group are not consciously oppressive, but they don't often examine their attitudes or values or interrogate how they adopted them. Individual acts of oppression or aggression commonly happen when there is institutional permission for individual members of the dominant group to personally disrespect or mistreat individuals in a marginalized group. Dominant group members have internalized the negative messages about other groups and consider their own attitudes normal or socially accepted. Continue to educate yourself through reading, research, personal conversations, and discussion groups. Increase your tolerance for discomfort so you can have conversations about race and other social identities that have an effect on privilege and oppression, including ability, age, gender, socioeconomic status/class, religion, sexual orientation, and ethnicity.

In my early years as a preschool teacher, I had a young Black boy in my classroom. When I had a parent conference to get to know his family, I met with his mother. She shared with me that she would appreciate if I would use a strong disciplinary approach with her son. I was uncomfortable with her request. On occasion, I had observed her style of discipline during drop-off and pickup times. She spoke with a stern, sometimes loud voice, insisting he pay attention and listen to her and sometimes taking his arm to get his full attention. From my perspective, I was concerned about her approach, and I felt she was too authoritative and harsh in her disciplinary technique for a preschooler. I honestly thought my well-educated understanding of best practices about positive guidance and discipline were true and necessary for this mother. As I gingerly shared my views, trying to "educate" this mother during our conference conversation, she listened, then took a deep breath and shared her very different cultural perspective. She had the grace and patience to share with me, a very privileged young white woman, her concerns for the safety of her young Black son and his older brother when they walked out the door every day. She told me how important it was to provide strong guidance to keep her kids safe in their neighborhood and in our dominant white culture. This was the first time I had been exposed to this world view of many Black families, needing to keep their children safe in a dominantly white culture. I was actually shocked at what she was kind enough to share with me. I really had to rethink my very entitled views about discipline and what was "right" or the "best way." I was humbled. We were able to discuss what I was comfortable doing in our classroom and what I wasn't. We found common ground, but I was forever changed. I learned that, as an educator, it is not appropriate for me to take the stance that I know better than the families, that my training as an educator doesn't make my views more important or valuable than theirs, and that my professional "best practice" recommendations are not laws to follow without consideration of the individual and cultural values and needs of each family.

REFLECTIVE PRACTICE

Increase your awareness in areas in which you have the benefits of privilege. Clarify any disempowering perspectives or false empowerment you may have learned from others, society, or the media. Ask yourself how you came to learn the beliefs and values you have. Get help or coaching to examine and expose your beliefs and values so you can change your actions and habits as needed.

20

"I think unconscious bias is one of the hardest things to get at."

—Ruth Bader Ginsberg

Implicit bias is not just about race. Our unconsciousness can touch many groups and individuals without our awareness. When people take unconscious bias assessments, it's not uncommon for them to think the results are wrong because they find implicit bias revealed in areas that do not align with their consciously chosen values. It's very difficult to recognize that implicit biases are not from our conscious mind. The depth of systemic social conditioning is profound. Implicit bias comes from self-identity and perspectives, and it is influenced by deep experiences and messages we have received from the dominant culture and our gender, age, experience, authority, and learning styles and how we were taught, to name just a few sources.

REFLECTIVE PRACTICE

Use assessments and gather meaningful data about your unconscious bias. One widely used assessment is the **Implicit Association Test (IAT) Assessment from Project Implicit**, which asks a series of questions to help test takers discover areas where they may have implicit bias. Find the assessment at https://implicit.harvard.edu/implicit/takeatest.html.

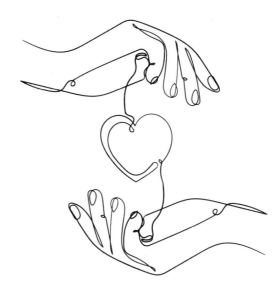

"We all want something to offer. This is how we belong. It's how we feel included. So if we want to include everyone, we have to help everyone develop their talents and use their gifts for the good of the community. That's what inclusion means—everyone is a contributor."

—Melinda Gates

Does your work or home environment intentionally create avenues for everyone to be a contributor, no matter how young or old, experienced or inexperienced? How do you help each person develop their talents and contribute to the community, organization, or family?

22

"Implicit biases . . . usually begin at a young age, and the biases do not necessarily align with personal identity. It's possible to unconsciously associate positive or negative traits with one's own race, gender, or another identity marker."

—Elena Aguilar

It's difficult to understand that we can have unconscious bias not only about others but also about ourselves. Internalized oppression happens when people internalize the ideology of inferiority; they see it reflected in institutions, they experience disrespect interpersonally from members of the dominant group, and they can eventually come to internalize the negative messages about themselves. This can happen for members of any marginalized group—women, people of color, elderly people, people who identify as LGBTQIAP+, nonliterate adults, people living with visible or invisible disabilities (temporary or permanent), people who are infertile, individuals who are dealing with low income, food insecurity, or homelessness, and others.

REFLECTIVE PRACTICE
Survey any areas where you may have internalized negative messages about yourself in any way, even if you "know better" intellectually. Clarify any internal disempowering perspectives or negative self-talk about yourself. It can manifest as a voice of self-judgment, or a pattern of minimizing your concerns or feelings of being marginalized or disrespected, or even as excuses for the disempowering behaviors of others. Write down the many different voices so you can see them clearly. This will help you catch them in action so you do not believe them.

Equity

In its broadest definition, equity is "the state, quality or ideal of being just, impartial, and fair," and it is synonymous with fairness and justice. It's imperative that we as individuals and leaders are dedicating our time and focused attention to examining and identifying ways in which our social circles, workplaces, and communities incorporate equity and inclusion, and that we promote social change in these areas.

"Not everything that is faced can be changed; but nothing can be changed until it is faced."

—James Baldwin

Even as issues of equity in our society are exposed and more and more people demand change, individuals remain at different levels of consciousness and awareness surrounding issues of equity, and they have differing personal experiences and access to opportunities. We don't all open up at the same pace, about the same issues, with the same level of passion. It's a great challenge in issues of equity to not fall into judging others who are not aligned with your journey or your pace of awakening. This is also true of personal awakening to any topic of life. For example, some are farther along in communicating or being emotionally intelligent and resilient. The first step is to wake up and face what's needed of us, personally and socially. Embodying humility, patience, and tolerance of diversity is always at the heart of transformational awakening. You are personally responsible for your own awakening, to face what you need to in order to change. Working in your sphere of influence with others you feel aligned with will help you influence society at large. Margaret Wheatley suggests that you not try to change the world but rather focus on your "island of sanity"* to bring forth change.

> **REFLECTIVE PRACTICE**
> In what specific areas have you been awakening, facing what you need to change? Do you notice you have some intolerance or impatience with others who are not doing the same in your particular area or at your pace? How would you describe your "island of sanity," or your sphere of influence where you can have an impact?

* Margaret J. Wheatley, *Who Do We Choose to Be? Facing Reality, Claiming Leadership, Restoring Sanity* (Oakland, CA: Berrett-Koehler, 2017), 17.

24

"If equality means giving everyone the same resources, equity means giving each student access to the resources they need to learn and thrive."

—Shane Safir

Equity and equality are frequently confused. Equality is about treating people the same (equally) regardless of individual needs. Equity is about ensuring justice and fairness by meeting an individual's or group's needs by considering differing starting points, including recognizing racial or social systemic inequities. Early in my career as a preschool teacher, I focused on equality, ensuring I treated all children the same. Certainly it was important that I not omit any services or attention to any child based on race, gender, disability, or other characteristics. Yet very quickly I began to recognize that children have different needs, for a variety of reasons. Some needed much more social-emotional caring attention than others. Some children had more difficulty separating from their parents; some needed more physical comfort, while others sought verbal support. Some were successful readers at age four, while others didn't really know how to turn pages and had no previous exposure to books or the alphabet. Treating these children equally would not be meeting anyone's needs. I learned to appreciate diverse personal, social, physical, and educational needs without unnecessarily labeling any child as difficult or "needy."

REFLECTIVE PRACTICE
To better differentiate equality and equity, take time to read resources or watch documentaries or TED Talks to further educate yourself. Many resources are provided on this Bias, Race, and Equity Resource List.

https://www.
redleafpress.org/
dre/11-24.pdf

25

"We must rise above the narrow confines of our individualistic concerns, with a broader concern for all humanity."

—Martin Luther King Jr.

Taking a view beyond their own ideas, needs, and desires allows leaders to truly represent the people they serve. Taking the stance of being a learner in the communities we serve helps us to not make assumptions about their needs, perspectives, and values. Do not assume we know what is best for the communities we work with. This can dramatically alter the direction we might travel and the decisions we might have to make. Developing protocols and systemic ways to gather collective input from the people and communities we serve is critical to not only revealing our own biases but also deepening our understanding of issues of equitable access to the services we provide.

REFLECTIVE PRACTICE
How are you intentionally informing yourself of the perspectives, needs, and voices of the people you serve? How will you know if it's truly representative of your community? What practices could you put in place both individually and with your team to ensure better representation?

26

"Diversity is a fact. Equity is a choice. Inclusion is an action. Belonging is an outcome."

—Attributed to Arthur Chan

Many values and behaviors in our lives and workplaces hold racism silently in place. The company Spark Decks has developed Spark Cards titled Practices for Dismantling Racism, a set of cards with practices for dismantling racism for individuals and groups to improve their skills and micro-practices in working together. These practices are organized into fourteen agreements, adapted from Tema Okun's *Dismantling Racism Workbook,* to combat the characteristics of dominant white culture that show up in our organizations. These are the agreements:

1. Dismantling Perfectionism
2. Dismantling "Only One Right Way"
3. Dismantling Either/Or Thinking
4. Dismantling Objectivity
5. Dismantling Worship of the Written Word
6. Dismantling a Sense of Urgency
7. Dismantling Quantity Over Quality
8. Dismantling "Progress is Bigger, More"
9. Dismantling Defensiveness
10. Dismantling Paternalism
11. Dismantling Power Hoarding
12. Dismantling Fear of Open Conflict
13. Dismantling the Right to Comfort
14. Dismantling Individualism*

> **REFLECTIVE PRACTICE**
> Examine these values and agreements and identify any that you personally could benefit from learning more about. Explore how these agreements and practices might merit further discussion in your workplace.

* Dismantling Racism Works (dRworks), *Dismantling Racism 2016 Workbook,* 2016, 28–35, https://resourcegeneration.org/wp-content/uploads/2018/01/2016-dRworks-workbook.pdf.

Power

Consider your beliefs about power and authority, including how a person acquires power, how they use it, and how it impacts social interactions, decision-making, policies, and procedures in our families, workplaces, and communities.

27

"Authority and power are two different things: power is the force by means of which you can oblige others to obey you. Authority is the right to direct and command, to be listened to or obeyed by others. Authority requests power. Power without authority is tyranny."

—Jacques Maritain

Many of us have never stopped to think about how authority and power differ. Positional power comes from one's position or role. Power can come from physical, emotional, or mental force, often leaning toward aggressive dominance. People in power tend to talk more, interrupt more, and guide the conversation by picking the topic. Authority can come from positional power or from one's role in society. But many people command authority when they have no traditional positional power. Think of people who are often quiet and don't say much, but when they do speak everyone listens. Authority is more about having influence and taking charge. It can come from having expertise, but when combined with passion, the sphere of influence is wider. Some influential authority comes from having mastery of the dance of human interactions, a talent for reading the room, cuing on subtle signs and body language, and displaying conversational mastery. Power often works against people or is a contrary or dominating energy. Influential authority works with and for people, engaging and including them. Some of us resist people in positional power and yet admire people with influential authority.

REFLECTIVE PRACTICE
As a leader, it's important to explore your own beliefs, values, and experiences of authority and power. Journal or have conversations exploring these questions: Where did you learn about what authority and power meant? Does one trigger you more than the other? Does one appeal to you more than the other? What are your values surrounding power and authority? How are your current thoughts, feelings, and behaviors aligned or conflicting with your values and what you believe?

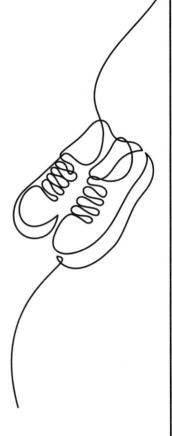

"Equality is giving everyone a shoe. Equity is giving everyone a shoe that fits. Justice is when we don't need to give everyone a shoe because they can get their own shoe . . . a shoe that fits."

—Attributed to Naheed Dosani

What gaps do you see in your organization in providing equity for all? If you are not sure, talk to a variety of people and ask their perspective. For example, choose people in multiple departments, salaried and hourly workers, employees with and without children, employees of different ages and generations, seasoned and new employees, and so on.

29

"Real power is basically the ability to change something if you want to change it. It's the ability to make change happen. Real power is unlimited—we don't need to fight over it because there is plenty to go around. And the great thing about real power is our ability to create it. Real power doesn't force us to take it away from others—it's something we create and build with others."

—Brené Brown

Understanding real power as the ability to make change happen as well as a creative endeavor done in collaboration with others can challenge many traditional Western cultural perspectives. This embraces the notion that power is unlimited and intrinsic, and therefore it eliminates the need to compete for power. If we are born into any dominant social identity, with inherent unearned power and privilege, how does this alternative notion of real power place a new sense of responsibility on us as individuals and leaders?

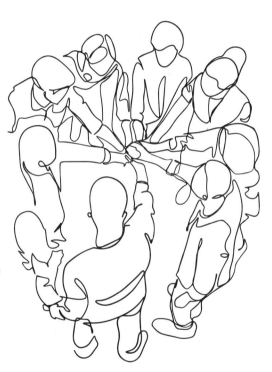

REFLECTIVE PRACTICE
In what areas of your life do you have power, and how did you come into that power? Name two areas in your life where you have privilege and unearned power. Can you name an example you have witnessed or experienced demonstrating collaborative creative power that did not compete or take power away from anyone else?

30

"Good leadership requires you surround yourself with people of diverse perspectives who can disagree with you without fear of retaliation."

—Doris Kearns Goodwin

Successful leaders ensure that they are not surrounded only by people who agree with them or who are too afraid to speak up with divergent viewpoints. Having an echo chamber can make for an easier, more comfortable, and less bumpy pathway, but a leader's comfort is not the measure of strong servant leadership. Leaders need to have a direct connection to the authentic pulse of the teams they work with and stakeholders they serve, and not just wait for someone to speak up. They are better served by an environment that fosters honest viewpoints and lets individuals feel comfortable sharing concerns, disagreement, and challenges to ideas, projects, and products.

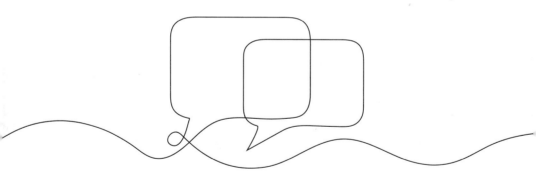

REFLECTIVE PRACTICE

What evidence do you have that people around you are not afraid to disagree with you and do not fear retaliation? How can you cultivate diverse avenues for honest and open communication and feedback?

31

"Preservation of one's own culture does not require contempt or disrespect for other cultures."

—Cesar Chavez

To maintain your own identity does not require any defense or contempt toward another person. Maintaining our sense of self and self-respect is an inside job. It comes from within, and it creates gracious space for others. Self-respect is not being self-absorbed or myopic—it actually opens up a world of possibilities and opportunities. The same is true for our culture, a foundational piece of who we are and the place from whence we launched ourselves. Building connection with others, individually or culturally, starts with appreciating and respecting our own roots and then extending the same respect to others, even when they are deeply different from us. Respect is a powerful commitment to make connection with others. Each person deserves respect, including yourself.

As a young woman, I was not very aware of how often I automatically dismissed my own feelings and physical needs. Due to early challenges in my childhood, I had learned that my needs were not likely to be met and I internalized a belief that my needs were not important. As I got older, I would often work very long hours at the expense of my health and well-being. I dismissed and ignored my own emotional needs, toughing it out or not expecting very much from other people. In turn, I was demanding and had harsh expectations for how much others should work. I minimized their feelings and was not particularly empathetic. Over the last decades of doing my own healing, I have become more aware of the lack of self-care and ultimately self-respect I had for myself and how this, in turn, often negatively influenced how I interacted with others. I was demanding and dominating and lacked empathy or even awareness of the needs of others. My current awareness, self-care practices, and interactions with others have greatly improved, and I have come a long way. And I continue to reflect and keep growing in these areas, getting better at getting better. It starts with self-respect and the experience of opening your heart and mind, increasing your capacity to give to others.

REFLECTIVE PRACTICE
Review any ways you feel like you have diminished another person or culture in defense of yourself or your culture. Explore the relationship between the amount of your own self-respect and your ability to respect others, even if you feel you have been harmed or misunderstood.

Chapter 12

COMMUNICATION AND RELATIONSHIPS

Being skillful in communication goes hand in hand with developing trusting relationships. There are many dimensions to communicating effectively; communication is a skill that can be deepened unendingly. It is worth honing these qualities that nurture and inspire thriving, trustful relationships, especially in the face of conflict.

The Art of Listening

Listening is perhaps the most important communication skill for fostering trust and understanding in relationships. Listening plays a powerful part in influencing and guiding others. Reflection helps you learn to listen to yourself.

"We are what we repeatedly do. Excellence, then, is not an act but a habit."

—Will Durant

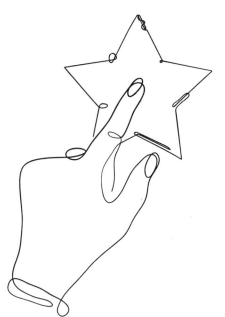

Reflection is a form of self-listening as well as a way of listening to others. The stronger our own practices of reflective self-listening, the more sensitive and fully present we will be with others. Reflective listening deepens our ability to get inside another person's frame of reference. Reflection lets us help others listen to themselves. When we listen empathetically, setting our agendas aside and being fully present, it offers a unique space for others to witness their own thinking, which in turn cultivates their own self-listening and reflection. Listening is a profound gift for others and for yourself—a gift of presence.

REFLECTIVE PRACTICE
Reflect on a theme you notice in your journey as an educator, coach, or leader. Why has this been significant for you? How do you listen within yourself, and which methods have been most valuable? Have you made this act a repeated habit? How has your own self-listening reflective practice helped you listen to and cultivate reflective practices in those you work with? Can you polish, expand, or make a habit of your self-listening practice to increase your excellence as an educator, coach, or leader?

2

"The art of conversation lies in listening."

—Widely attributed to Malcolm Forbes

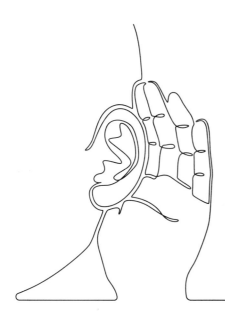

The art of listening springs from being genuinely curious about the other person—about what they are saying and about their perspective, experiences, and feelings. To not speak is not necessarily the same thing as listening. It has more to do with how you focus on what the other person is saying. Conversation is an exchange between people; it's not a monologue and it's not just waiting to make your own point. A conversation is a dance of receiving and giving. One cannot effectively give to others unless we are also able to receive. A balance is needed between sharing one's self and receiving the other person through listening, seeking to understand, and feeling the impact of what they say.

REFLECTIVE PRACTICE

Is your listening a strategic positioning to set up what you want to share? Listening receptively creates an opening within yourself and requires open-mindedness. Focus on your capacity to listen receptively today. Explore how you might deepen your listening.

> "Deep listening doesn't hear just the facts and chronology of events; it hears the pain, the wants, the requests of the story."

—Grace Churchill

Pausing is like the white space on a page. It creates space for listening. Pausing requires intentionality and awareness. It is the fine art of knowing when to bite your tongue. Pausing may be the most important and foundational human communication tool. Until one pauses, listening is not an option. The essence of the pause also matters. To just not speak is not the same as listening. To not speak while conjuring what you want to say in response is also not really listening. It's autobiographical listening, with your focus on yourself rather than the other person. Listening to understand rather than listening to respond is the heart of empathetic listening. It requires a mindset shift to want to understand more than to be understood. There is grace and compassion contained in empathetic listening, understanding the perspective and experience of the person with respect. To listen and be empathetic does not mean you have to agree with or condone their perspective. But you do need to really hear and listen deeply and let go, at least in the moment, of your own perspective and positioning. Deep listening can be vulnerable, and it can also expand our capacity to care and love.

REFLECTIVE PRACTICE
What stops you from genuinely pausing to listen? What gets in the way of listening empathetically? Watch for your patterns and habits and reflect on them to develop stronger and more conscious listening habits.

4

"Listen with curiosity. Speak with honesty. Act with integrity. The greatest problem with communication is we don't listen to understand. We listen to reply. When we listen with curiosity, we don't listen with the intent to reply. We listen for what's behind the words."

—Roy T. Bennett

As coaches, we often spend a lot of time asking questions, which can be helpful in promoting reflection. Yet we can also get caught up in unconscious loops of questioning without offering the necessary time for people to deeply think things through. This requires pausing and not speaking while they ponder, while also letting go of the agendas we have and the answers we think are correct. Instead we need to offer open-ended questions, questions we do not know the answer to, based in inquiry and curiosity. To understand another's perspective, the reasons they behave the way they do, or what they really want will not come from persuasion or asking leading questions. It will come from really wanting to understand and by listening to where they currently are. Only then can you address their desires, goals, and concerns, which will motivate them from within rather than trying to convince them from your outside viewpoint.

> **REFLECTIVE PRACTICE**
> Recall a time you wanted to persuade someone to do something or think the way you do. It could be to get a teenager to take the trash out or to have a staff person interrupt less in staff meetings. Did you approach them with telling, convincing, or listening? Did your approach create any lasting change? Contemplate how you might approach this or similar situations by asking authentically curious, open-ended questions and pausing to really listen. Seek to understand what is underneath the behavior or action, and you might open a valuable conversation that lets you partner with them to find solutions.

5

"One of the best ways to persuade others is with your ears—by listening."

—Attributed to Dean Rusk

Most people do not like to be told what to think or what to do. We like to make up our own minds. It often helps to talk things through with someone, but that requires someone who is willing to listen and who cares about what we think. We can give this respectful gift by really listening, seeking to understand. This means not listening through the lens of our own opinions or with a desire to convince. To really listen opens the possibility of sharing ideas and helping someone clarify things for themselves. Being present and listening is really quite a service and kindness.

REFLECTIVE PRACTICE
Listen to your own inner wisdom to know when to listen and when to talk today. At the end of the day, reflect on how successful you were in listening to yourself and to others. To listen to your inner wisdom and to authentically deepen your listening to others, will you need reminders? Consider small things you can do to remind yourself of this focus: perhaps place a sticky note in a prime spot, add it as the first item on your daily to-do list, or send yourself reminder notifications throughout the day.

6 "Connecting is deeper and more lasting than just communicating. When you are communicating, one person has to speak and the other has to hear. But when you are connecting, the intention of the speech and the speaker, and the intention of the listener and how empathetically he actually listens, actually matter."

—Peter Guber

Communicating to connect with another person takes more than just speaking and listening. It involves having an open mind and an open heart and having the conscious desire to cultivate connection. It's easier to communicate like this with someone we already feel a connection with. It's harder and necessitates more mindful awareness when we are communicating with someone with whom we don't have an established connection, someone with whom we have difficulty or conflict, or someone who holds a very different perspective than you.

REFLECTIVE PRACTICE
Over the next week, witness your communication and assess whether you are actually creating connection. How might you want to modify your style, your intentions, or your manner of communicating to be more successful at connecting? Then the following week, be mindful to invest in cultivating connection before having conversations.

7

"The word *listen* contains the same letters as the word *silent*."

—Attributed to Alfred Brendel

Contemplate why you might be tempted to not fully listen or why you might want to speak too much. Do you experience discomfort when there is silence? Do you think helping means you must give answers or advice? Have you undervalued the deep gift of listening and being present? Journal about what you are learning about the relationship between pausing, listening to understand, and cultivating the art of reflection and mindful practices in yourself and in those you support.

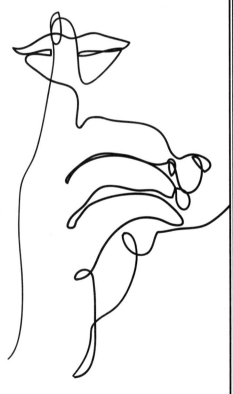

Questioning and Inquiry

The best questions are generated from wonder, not from knowing or thinking you have the answer. Create strong bridges in relationships through the manner and tone in which you ask questions, by using a variety of types of questions and being authentically curious with a desire to understand.

8

"I think, at a child's birth, if a mother could ask a fairy godmother to endow it with the most useful gift, that gift would be curiosity."

—Eleanor Roosevelt

Curiosity demonstrates an open mind, an attitude of not knowing and wondering. The demeanor of curiosity is the antidote to judgment and bias, and it leads to questioning and clarifying rather than making assumptions. Curiosity opens up joy, discovery, and learning. Even in the face of conflict and challenges, being curious offers the possibility for ending separation, creating connection, and deepening compassion.

REFLECTIVE PRACTICE
What are you authentically curious about? What about yourself are you curious about? Which relationships in your life might improve if you were more curious about them?

9

"The moment we ask a question, we begin to create change."

—Adage of Appreciative Inquiry

The act of questioning is leaning into wonder and the unknown. When we are too full of knowing or needing to know, we lack room to learn and grow. We have to empty out our minds to create space to be open-minded. We can think that we are open-minded when in fact we are blinded by our own thoughts, bias, or perspective, so our questions are actually justifying our known way and not really fostering curiosity and wonder. When we start asking questions, it is an act of humility. Just asking the question begins the journey of change. We have choice and control over our willingness to inquire, wonder, and ask questions. Through questions, we can change our perspective, open our minds, clarify, focus on what we want, and in time discover ways to make intentional changes. Lasting sustainable change comes from within.

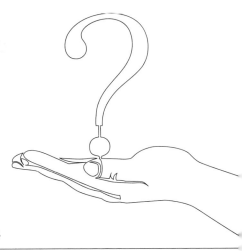

REFLECTIVE PRACTICE
Pick an issue, a situation, or a relationship where you feel locked into a perspective, have a very strong opinion, have triggered feelings, or feel stuck. Start to ask questions rather than making statements. Ask questions of yourself first—any question! Let yourself tiptoe or run into curiosity and explore what you don't know. Don't worry about answering the questions right now. Just list a bunch of questions and see what happens.

10

"Don't think about why you question, simply don't stop questioning. Don't worry about what you don't answer, and don't try to explain why you can't know. Curiosity is its own reason. Have holy curiosity."

—Albert Einstein

The art of inquiry is founded on curiosity and wonder. There really are no right questions. What is useful is asking questions to expand your wonder, your thinking, and your awareness. When practicing the art of inquiry, explore the power of questioning without driving toward an answer or right solution. People are often so focused on solutions, fixing and bridging gaps, that they get myopic, and this actually closes down curiosity and inquiry. If you think of a funnel, the open end is where curiosity, wonder, options, and possibilities exist. Curiosity needs space, and the art of inquiry is an act of expansion. Of course, it's necessary at times to find solutions and answers, but this is not the same as curiosity. The narrow end of the funnel is more about focusing in on choices, actions, and decisions. All too often, trying to focus in on answers happens prematurely, but settling on just one idea before considering all the options kills curiosity. Consider whether your questions are generated by wonder or fear. Let wonder widen your reflection and awareness. Questions can deepen your reflection without answering any of the questions. Questions can beget questions. Asking different types of questions can stretch your perspective and trigger new avenues of contemplation. You may be surprised to find how much movement can happen from just asking yourself questions with no goal of finding an answer. And this expansive wonder can really help when a choice, action, or solution is eventually needed.

REFLECTIVE PRACTICE
Practice "holy curiosity" questioning. Identify a topic, issue, or problem you want more clarity about, or choose something you just want to think more deeply about. Write the topic on the top of a paper. Then start to ask questions, listing one question after another on the paper. Write questions for a minimum of five minutes—and I encourage you to go for ten minutes or longer. Let yourself wonder and inquire with no pressure to find solutions. You will likely hit a wall, but do not stop. The most juicy questions usually come after you have pushed through the wall and moved beyond your typical questions. Consider asking Who, What, When, Where, Why, and What If questions. Ask clarifying questions. Question your assumptions, perspectives, and needs, your own questioning patterns, and what you think you want.

"The question we most commonly ask is the 'what' question—what subjects shall we teach? When the conversation goes a bit deeper, we ask the 'how' question—what methods and techniques are required to teach well? Occasionally, when it goes deeper still, we ask the 'why' question—for what purpose and to what ends do we teach? But seldom do we ask the 'who' question—who is the self that teaches?"

—Parker Palmer

This quote is just as relevant for coaches and leaders as it is for educators. Who is the self that teaches, coaches, or leads? This quote points to the importance of becoming self-aware and knowing thyself as essential to being effective in not just what we do, how we do it, or why we do it, but to critically clarify who we are in what we do. The very questions we ask ourselves or others come from our internal frame of reference or our perspectives. Consider where you ask questions from. Who is doing the questioning, and for what purpose? Expand your capacity and attitude of curiosity to master the art of inquiry. Expand your mindset so you can model it and facilitate others to do the same.

> **REFLECTIVE PRACTICE**
> In your role as educator, coach, leader, friend, or parent, ponder and witness what propels your curiosity, thoughts, feelings, behaviors, and interactions and where you ask your questions from. Who is doing the questioning and interacting, and for what purpose? Contemplate who you are in what you do.

Kindness and Humility

The qualities of kindness and compassion require humility and are the foundation for strong leadership. They are the source of real power and influence.

"Too often we underestimate the power of a touch, a smile, a kind word, a listening ear, an honest compliment, or the smallest act of caring, all of which have the potential to turn a life around."

—Leo Buscaglia

A study published in the *Journal of Experimental Psychology* in August 2022 shared findings that people who perform a random act of kindness tend to underestimate how much the recipient will appreciate it.* And the researchers believe that this miscalculation could hold many of us back from doing nice things for others more often. Even small gestures can help lower people's daily stress levels. Our simple acts of connection—a note, a text, buying someone tea, leaving a sticky note with a heart or word of encouragement on a computer screen, or paying for coffee for the person in line behind you—mean more than many of us realize. It also has an impact on the person's own giving in the future. Don't overthink it when a random act of kindness pops into your head, whether it's for a stranger or someone you know. It matters . . . do it!

> **REFLECTIVE PRACTICE**
> Create a habit of doing random acts of kindness. They can always be simple. Be creative. If you are a leader, be intentional about ways to touch your team with kind acts.

* A. Kumar and N. Epley, "A Little Good Goes an Unexpectedly Long Way: Underestimating the Positive Impact of Kindness on Recipients," *Journal of Experimental Psychology: General* 152, no. 1 (2023): 236–52, https://psycnet.apa.org/doiLanding?doi=10.1037%2Fxge0001271.

> "Kind words elicit trust. Kind thoughts create depth. Kind deeds bring love."
>
> —Unknown

As leaders, it is worth being mindful of how frequently we have kind thoughts, speak kind words, and act kindly. Consider building trust with those you serve through kindness. You need trust as the foundation to build successful teams.

REFLECTIVE PRACTICE
Do you model kindness? Name specific ways you do that. How can you cultivate a work culture that promotes kindness?

WEEKLY REFLECTIVE PRACTICE

> "Feeling compassion for ourselves in no way releases us from responsibility for our actions. Rather, it releases us from the self-hatred that prevents us from responding to our life with clarity and balance."
>
> —Tara Brach

Review your week and reflect on your level and frequency of compassion for others and for yourself. What's stopping you from increasing the frequency and deepening the impact of your compassion? What are a few small steps you could take to behave more compassionately, especially with yourself? Start by doing one of those things this week.

15

"For me, forgiveness and compassion are always linked: how do we hold people accountable for wrongdoing and yet at the same time remain in touch with their humanity enough to believe in their capacity to be transformed?"

—bell hooks

Those of us who work with or raise children know the importance of having compassion and offering positive guidance to cultivate learning, rather than using unkind punishments that only foster fear and break trust. These same approaches work equally well for adults—so why do we tend to be less compassionate and forgiving when adults make mistakes or fall short of a commitment? We can still communicate with a calm, caring, respectful tone and manner when holding people accountable. Harshness or frustration doesn't help. It's a good time to remember the Golden Rule of treating others as you would like to be treated. Remembering that humans, including ourselves, are less than perfect can shift our harsh expectations. Then we can find more respect, compassion, and forgiveness in the belief that people can learn from mistakes and that everyone has the capacity for transformation and growth.

REFLECTIVE PRACTICE
When someone you support or work with makes a mistake, what is your first reaction? Do you lean toward judgment, irritation, or an inner harshness? What would it take for you to develop more compassion and openheartedness as a response, even when you need to hold someone accountable? Develop new, kinder ways for how to do this. It might be by starting with inquiry and a desire to understand what happened that didn't go well, rather than blaming the person. It might be by sharing an example of when you made a mistake. It might be as simple as lowering your voice or shifting your perspective before interacting. How would you appreciate someone interacting with you when you didn't follow through or needed to be held accountable for something?

> "Humility involves having the capacity to take a more confrontational stance, having the capacity to retaliate if you wish, yet deliberately deciding not to do so."

—Dalai Lama [Tenzin Gyatso]

Making an intentional decision to step down in a confrontational situation requires self-awareness and self-regulation. It's a conscious decision to exert power or authority. Indeed, inspiring leaders often display humility rather than posturing from ego or position. Being humble has nothing to do with a lack of self-worth or feeling less than others. Another word for this is graciousness, when we extend a hand of connection rather than contributing to separation. It doesn't mean avoiding a conflict that needs resolution, but instead finding an openhearted and open-minded avenue to explore ways forward.

REFLECTIVE PRACTICE

What are your experiences of others displaying humility? What does it take for you to be humble? What gets in the way of this for you?

17

"Arrogance pretends it knows. Humility shows up to learn."

—Anonymous

Learning is an openhearted endeavor that requires not taking a defensive or arrogant position. Often people who are being coached or supported are resistant or defensive, for a variety of reasons. People almost certainly resist or defend themselves when coaches or leaders show any attitude or tone of being a know-it-all. If we as coaches and leaders have the humility to set aside being a content expert or thinking we have (or are supposed to have) answers, it sets a distinctly different basis for building a trusting relationship. If we can show up with humility to learn about the person we are supporting and display an attitude of discovery, being curious about their strength, hopes, and needs, it helps resistant or fearful coachees relax and build trust. It models for them that being vulnerable to learn not only is safe but can be an exciting prospect.

REFLECTIVE PRACTICE
Recall a time you had a coachee or someone you were supporting who was resistant or defensive. Consider how your entry into the relationship may have contributed to this response. Reflect on your stance as an authority or position as a content expert, and consider how having or giving answers could have set a tone such that they felt the need to protect themselves. Explore modifying your own mindset surrounding the role of a leader or coach as a facilitator of change, helping people to self-refect rather than being a content expert or someone with the answers. What might change? What could open up for you and those you support?

18

> "One of the toughest things for leaders to master is kindness. Kindness shares credit and offers enthusiastic praise for others' work. It's a balancing act between being genuinely kind and not looking weak."

—Travis Bradberry

The idea of leadership is tightly woven into our cultural, social, and personal identities. The values that embrace humility, kindness, and vulnerability as part of leadership often challenge more traditional ideas of leadership or values held by previous generations. In the last century, as more women have stepped into more leadership positions in all walks of life, the meaning of leadership has been evolving. In some circles and cultures, the idea that leaders do not have to evoke strength at all times, that they do not have to be at the top of an authority pyramid, that they can share power and be authentic, and that they don't need to have all the answers is a new direction.

REFLECTIVE PRACTICE
How have your own ideas of leadership changed during your life? What are some of your current beliefs about leadership?

Conflict

Navigating conflict is one of the most essential aspects of maintaining strong relationships as a transformational leader or change agent. The communication skills of listening and inquiry are important tools. Maintaining self-awareness and accountability for our triggered reactions in the face of conflict is a critical reason to invest in routine habits of self-reflection.

19 "The quality of our lives depends not on whether or not we have conflicts, but how we respond to them."

—Attributed to Thomas Crum

We learn a lot about how to handle conflict from our family of origin and our culture. Often how we handle conflict is a default setting within ourselves rather than a conscious, intentional response. Many of us did not receive strong, positive messages or modeling on how to deal with conflict. Often we just operate from our conditioning and then defend that position without really taking the time to examine our default conflict response. It takes courage and intent to be self-aware and, if necessary, learn different skills and modify your conditioned way of feeling and behaving. Honestly assessing how we deal with and resolve conflicts may be one of the most significant areas for anyone, especially leaders, to deliberately examine to enhance our communication and enrich our relationships. The success of all relationships, whether personal or professional, rests on how we respond to conflict. An inability to navigate conflict will undermine team-building and organizational goals.

REFLECTIVE PRACTICE

When you are upset or experiencing conflict with another person, identify the instinctive thing you want to do or what your default setting is:

- to stick your head in the ground like an ostrich
- to inflate like a puffer fish with spikes out
- to roar like a lion
- to posture like a bear
- to run like a rabbit
- to strut like a peacock

Reflect on what causes you to react this way. What is your underlying attitude, feeling, fear, or concern? Is this aligned with who you want to be? As you identify this and expand your awareness of your habitual default setting, identify a quality or create an image of how you would prefer to respond in the face of conflict. What is one small step to break or replace that habit with a positive new one?

"Because people aren't perfect and relationships are messy, we all need to learn how to resolve conflicts."

—Attributed to John Maxwell

When people feel stressed, they often have a fight, flight, or freeze response, and the same is true when they deal with conflict, since conflict is stressful. The typical conflict responses are violence, silence, or checking out. Violence consists of any verbal strategy that attempts to convince, control, or compel others to your point of view. It violates safety by trying to force meaning on the people you are engaged with. These behaviors are often controlling, labeling, and attacking and can include name-calling, dominating the conversation, yelling, or making threats. Others resort to more aggressive and dominating behaviors that push a point of view or stand their ground. Silence is any act to purposefully withhold information, feelings, or thoughts from the people you are engaged with. This can include avoiding conflict altogether to feel safe, acting as if everything is OK, or saying nothing even though you disagree or are disturbed. Checking out can happen when someone simply gets up and leaves the room. In other cases, the person disconnects from themselves and others, often feeling numb, emotionally shutting down, or getting confused. Any of these approaches undermine trust and relationships and diminish collaboration and team building. Become aware of your own tendencies in responding to stressful conflict situations. As a leader, also note others' tendency to respond with silence, violence, or checking out when they are stressed. Invest in professional development opportunities to offer training on conflict resolution. In addition, offer your folks opportunities to reflect individually and as a team about their habits of conflict response, considering what works and what doesn't.

REFLECTIVE PRACTICE
Do your own reflection about your own conflict responses; consider what is or was your style. Identify whether and how you have changed any of these ineffective habits in the past. Share this with your team. Decide how you might create a safe space to have a team conversation about this or facilitate a Community of Practice to jointly discuss options for handling conflict. Consider how to make team agreements concerning how to interact when conflict arises.

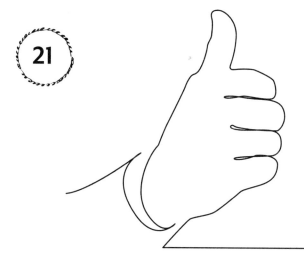

21

"Whenever you're in conflict with someone, there is one factor that can make the difference between damaging your relationship and deepening it. That factor is attitude."

—Unknown

What attitude can you hold that would actively contribute to deepening the relationship with someone you are in conflict with, so you do not act in ways that damage your relationship? When in conflict with someone, how can you hold an attitude, clarify a goal, or make a pledge to yourself that you will do your best to not defend yourself, go silent, act aggressively, or disengage?

"Conflict can destroy a team that hasn't spent time learning to deal with it."

22

—Thomas Isgar

A key skill of effective leaders is the capacity to proficiently address emotionally and politically risky issues. The foundational skills for building a functional and collaborative team are trust and the ability to handle and use conflict productively. People need to build trust by learning about and coming to understand each other. Trust is required in order to venture into the zone of conflict, which is scary and vulnerable. It's important that individuals gain self-awareness and consider which of their habitual ways of responding to conflict are not productive. Start by looking at the messages we grew up with from our family of origin or culture that set a tone for how to handle conflict. A strong team-building activity features facilitated conversations during which members share their own cultural or family of origin messages about handling conflict. Leaders need to do this work themselves and replace ineffectual habits with productive conflict skills. They also need to learn pathways by which they can facilitate others in doing their own reflective work, both individually and as a team. It is wise for leaders to speak in vulnerable discussions like this, revealing and sharing about themselves. Studies have shown the biggest predictor of success or failure of projects that involve cross-functional cooperation was whether people could hold five specific crucial conversations,* such as speaking up rather than going silent when someone thinks the scope of a project or schedule are unworkable or when a colleague is not fully contributing as agreed. It can be particularly awkward and difficult to know how to handle these situations when the leader fails to provide necessary leadership for having these conversations.

REFLECTIVE PRACTICE
Ponder (alone or in conversation with siblings or other close relatives) what your own cultural or family of origin messages were about conflict. What did you learn about dealing with conflict? Consider how you currently deal with conflict and what influence the early messages you received still have on you today or how you have changed, in ineffectual or productive ways.

* Kerry Patterson, Joseph Grenny, Ron McMillan, and Al Switzler, *Crucial Conversations: Tools for Talking When Stakes Are High*, 2nd ed. (New York: McGraw Hill, 2012), 12.

23

"Conflict is the beginning of consciousness."

—M. Ester Harding

It is inevitable that each of us will find ourselves in challenging but crucial conversations. The authors of the book *Crucial Conversations* define crucial conversations as "a discussion between two or more people where 1) stakes are high, 2) opinions vary, and 3) emotions run strong." They say people usually do one of three things: avoid them, face them and handle them poorly, or face them and handle them well.* We all would love to think we would face difficult discussions and handle them well, but when we have strong opinions and feelings, often our layers of generational conditioning override our rational, intelligent, and kind responses. Many people experience conflict as highly stressful, which releases the hormone cortisol in our bodies and overrides reason, so we revert to fight, flight, or freeze responses. Learning how to resolve conflicts starts with developing self-awareness to recognize that you are triggered, and then being able to read your own physical symptoms and identify what you are feeling in the moment. With this mindfulness, you are able to stay calm and make intentional choices in how you respond, not falling victim to your default gut instinct and stress-reactive brain response, but able to intercede using your prefrontal cortex, the part of the brain that uses reason to make decisions. To be watchful and make those conscious choices takes repeated mindfulness practices to expand self-awareness.

REFLECTIVE PRACTICE

It's valuable to do an honest self-assessment of how we actually respond when dealing with conflict rather than just assuming we handle stress well. Recall a past conflict or crucial conversation you tried to have. If possible, recall what physical symptoms you had that indicated you were distressed—flushed face, tight jaw, stomachache, spike in cortisol, feeling physically afraid. Name the feelings that were triggered—anger, fear, tears, numbness. List the actual behaviors of how you responded—did you withdraw emotionally or physically; avoid, repress, and say nothing; become more defensive, aggressive, or argumentative? Perhaps you got confused, had difficulty thinking, and behaved as if you were perplexed or baffled. This self-assessment is the first step toward recognizing your habitual responses. Then you can decide whether you want and are motivated to change how you respond. If so, continue to reflect about what you want and options for what next steps to take.

* Kerry Patterson, Joseph Grenny, Ron McMillan, and Al Switzler, *Crucial Conversations: Tools for Talking When Stakes Are High*, 2nd ed. (New York: McGraw Hill, 2012), 3–4.

24

"When patterns are broken, new worlds emerge."

—Tuli Kupferberg

In every relationship, it is natural that conflict will show up. Our attitudes about conflict will heavily influence how we respond. We all have patterns for dealing with conflict, many of which are not helpful and cause separation, such as defense, aggression, withdrawal, blame, or self-righteousness. When either of you behaves in a way that rips the connection, how you respond and approach the other person is where real opportunities lie. John Gottman of the Gottman Institute describes a repair attempt as "any statement or action—silly or otherwise—meant to defuse negativity and keep a conflict from escalating out of control."* Repair attempts are also bids for connection, so we can communicate more effectively. He offers a few examples of ways to attempt to repair rips in connection that can break patterns:

- "I see your point."
- "I really messed up; I can see my part in this."
- "I know this isn't your fault."
- "I want to say this more gently, but I don't know how to."
- "Let me try again."
- "Can we take a break?"**

REFLECTIVE PRACTICE

Identify the most common pattern you fall into when you are dealing with conflict. Are you honestly willing to explore ways to break your patterns so you don't continue causing separation with others? What habit or habits would you have to let go of? Can you consider using any of the repair-attempt bids above, or similar ones? What would a positive replacement behavior be?

* David Khalaf and Constantino Khalaf, "How to Make Repair Attempts So Your Partner Feels Loved," Gottman Institute, www.gottman.com/blog/make-repair-attempts-partner-feels-loved.

** Zach Brittle, "R Is for Repair," Gottman Institute, www.gottman.com/blog/r-is-for-repair.

Building Authentic Connections and Relationships

Humans are social beings, and the strength and depth of our relationships creates the container for our belonging, learning, creativity, and loving. Science shows that relationships matter from birth to death. Building healthy attachment and human connection not only is a protective factor for becoming more resilient and thriving but also helps us live longer and with more purpose and meaning.

25

"Connection is fundamentally a basic human need, like shelter, food, and water, meaning it's crucial to our well-being and productivity. Forming bonds with colleagues results in teams feeling more comfortable seeking help, providing feedback, and taking part in open discussion. This can play a role in boosting innovation, motivation, and psychological safety."

—Gemma Leigh Roberts

Transformational leaders and coaches are in a unique position to develop relationships that help ignite passions and support people to thoughtfully grow throughout their journey as professionals and as human beings. Leaders provide support for others to hone professional skills as well as broaden perspectives by modeling the value of reflective mindfulness, the vulnerability of taking risks, and the power of never giving up. Improving the efficacy of the individuals around you happens one step at a time, helping them become self-aware so they examine and understand the relationship between their behaviors and the underlying beliefs, attitudes, and thoughts that hold their actions in place. Then they can come to understand that they have the power to make changes. You can make a difference by inspiring people to have the stamina and resilience to continue to get better at getting better and become lifelong learners.

> **REFLECTIVE PRACTICE**
> What kind of difference do you want to make? Write or share about it to clarify your understanding. Then observe whether your behaviors and actions are aligned with your desire for change.

26

"When we judge, we are pushing
people away; we are creating a wall,
a barrier. When we forgive we are
destroying barriers, we come closer
to others."

—Jean Vanier

Judgments come from our values, beliefs, and thoughts. Unfortunately we often mistake our beliefs and perspectives as truth rather than recognizing them as our opinion or perception. When we lack self-awareness, we can easily believe every thought we have as if it were true. It takes self-awareness to assess which of our thoughts are empowering, productive, and connecting and which are disempowering and undermining of ourselves or others. Our thoughts and attitudes can be changed, and we need to frequently revisit them to see when it is necessary. We must choose between holding onto a position or an opinion or being right when it creates separation, or investing in connecting with others, which may take humility, letting go, and forgiveness.

REFLECTIVE PRACTICE
Keep your values in sight and reflect on whether these values cultivate connection or separation. Contemplate whether your actions are a demonstration of your values. Are your actions and behaviors demonstrations investing in maintaining and nurturing connection or are they defensive, taking a position, blaming, and protective?

27

"To handle yourself, use your head; to handle others, use your heart."

—Anonymous

Managing the influence our thoughts have on us and our behaviors is a key component of being responsible for ourselves in all of our relationships. Assuming or jumping to conclusions contributes to so much strife and separation. It helps to routinely ask ourselves what we are assuming or making things mean, especially about other people's behaviors, since we don't know others' intentions unless we ask them. We assign significance to circumstances, situations, policies, and people's actions based on our personal frame of reference, which may or may not be an accurate interpretation or summary. Most separation comes from the mind, the ego, and the attention we put on ourselves rather than on the care of others. What would it take to assume the good intent of others, assume an empowering interpretation rather than a judgmental one? It takes a conscious effort to be mindful of ourselves in order to really stay present for others.

REFLECTIVE PRACTICE
What ways do you have available to manage your mind so you can authentically use your heart when dealing with others so you assume the best? When you notice there is separation with another person, what helps you to stay open, honest, and caring without protecting, defending, or blaming?

"It is an absolute human certainty that no one can know his own beauty or perceive a sense of his own worth until it has been reflected back to him in the mirror of another loving, caring human being."

—John Joseph Powell

Review your week: Have you been gracious in being a positive mirror for people to see themselves and feel their worth through your perspective, sharing, interactions, and behaviors toward them? How can you expand your capacity and ability to improve your behaviors toward being a caring human being next week?

29

"It's relaxing to be in a room with a bunch of people who agree with you. The problem: If they don't disagree, they're likely not fully analyzing a decision or generating a rich discussion. What won't be relaxing is when the team underdelivers because people were afraid to raise an opposing viewpoint."

—Marie Kondo and Scott Sonenshein

Building trust creates an atmosphere and foundation for everyone to be honest. It takes trust for people to risk being open and sharing their viewpoints, especially when they differ from others. Trust is particularly necessary for someone to be able to speak up to a leader or authority figure, which inherently holds risk. Are you actively and intentionally cultivating a trust-based environment? Building trust comes from exposing oneself and being open and vulnerable. Leaders need to go first! Model sharing personal concerns and challenges you have now or have had to overcome. Foster a climate for healthy conflict, not tolerating conflict avoidance or aggressive behaviors in yourself or others. Model really listening and staying open when people share differing perspectives so they know that it is safe to speak up. Asking people what they really think, especially when you know it differs from your thoughts, will set the tone for inquiry, listening, hearing, and open-mindedness.

REFLECTIVE PRACTICE
As a leader, model being vulnerable and open. Share first in team meetings about mistakes you've made or concerns you have had to grapple with and discuss what you learned. Then invite others to do the same. When discussing projects or strategic planning, invite a variety of viewpoints and perspectives from others and let them speak first. Really listen and do not pass judgment or approval in the moment. Paraphrase what you heard and share how you understood their viewpoint. Don't assume you understand, but rather use a tentative tone and ask them to confirm that you got it as they intended it.

30

"It really boils down to this: that all life is interre-lated. We are all caught in an inescapable net-work of mutuality, tied into a single garment of destiny. Whatever affects one destiny, affects all indirectly."

—Martin Luther King Jr.

Organizations that build a culture where individuals are praised for successful results instead of collective teams or efforts are undermining the trust, collaboration, and commitment it takes for any individual to succeed. Acknowledging individual successes is not bad, but it is important to always highlight the fabric that supports success. Empowering leaders demonstrate and reveal the importance of how individual actions create collective effects and how each individual's efforts affect others. Clearly acknowledge the intersecting threads that connect the group. Get in the habit of speaking about how the strength of the group is like a fishnet, created by a network that distributes the weight and load. Speak about the lines connecting the many knots and explain how the net holds power and functions even if one knot or line is broken. The strength is in the collective.

REFLECTIVE PRACTICE
Think of your life and the people in your life using the metaphor of a fishnet. Who are the people (in the past and currently) in your network, and how have they contributed to your journey and your success? How can you use this metaphor to share your story and your insights so you contribute to building stronger connections with those you live and work with? Find ways to acknowledge the people in your network.

"When you succeed, don't forget the responsibility of making somebody else succeed."

—Attributed to Antonia Novello

Relationships matter more than outcomes or tasks. Someone invested in your success by cultivating you and your relationship, not just by rewarding your actions. It's the only way any of us truly succeed. The best way to be grateful to them is to pay this support forward, which is an investment toward all the success in all our futures. But be specific about really investing in someone else's success, through relationship, attention, and care. Be generous with yourself.

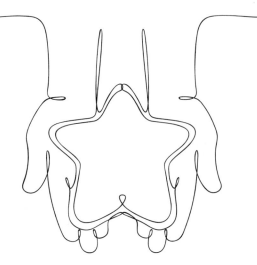

REFLECTIVE PRACTICE
Think of the people in your network: How can you lift them up, encourage them, open doors, and invest in them with no strings attached, for them to succeed in ways they might not even imagine as possible? Perhaps you want to focus on someone specific or practice how to do this with everyone you are in relationship with as an act of servant leadership.

Summary

Getting to know ourselves is a layered expedition that happens over time. As we deepen our knowledge and understanding of ourselves, having a foundation of awareness provides insight and wisdom to guide our choices, so we design the life we want and become who we want to be. Reflection is the tool we use to expand our awareness of ourselves and others and make meaning about our life and experiences in order to purposefully attain our aspirations.

My hope is that this book has offered you the opportunity to learn about the art of reflecting and strengthened your desire for and proficiency in embedding routine reflective practices in your life that will serve you in your journey. I have presented several topics for you to focus on—content areas that are

important to nurture your own growth and to deepen your ability to support others to learn, enhance, and transform their own personal and professional journeys. These themes are by no means an exhaustive list of topics, yet hopefully they have provided a reflective guideline to begin, reinforce, and sustain your daily reflections. Thank you for your time, contemplation, and practice!

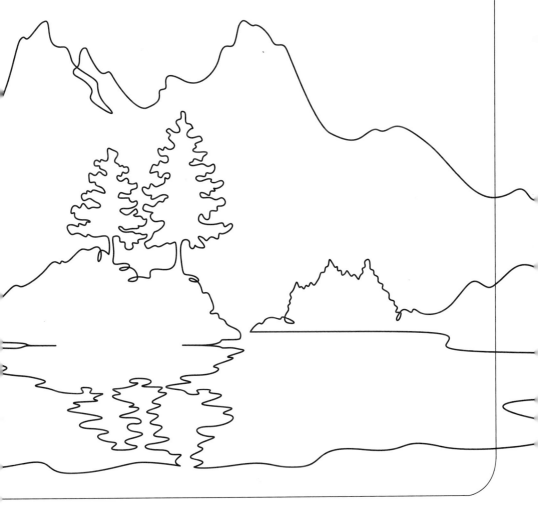